P9-ELU-839

SEXUAL ABUSE
AND
EATING DISORDERS

Edited by

Mark F. Schwartz, Sc.D.
and
Leigh Cohn, M.A.T.

BRUNNER/MAZEL
A member of the Taylor & Francis Group

Library of Congress Cataloging-in-Publication Data

Sexual abuse and eating disorders / edited by
  Mark F. Schwartz and Leigh Cohn.
      p.   cm.
    Includes bibliographical references and index.
    ISBN 0-87630-794-2 (hardcover)
    1. Eating disorders. 2. Adult child sexual abuse victims.
  I. Schwartz, Mark F. II. Cohn, Leigh.
    [DNLM: 1. Eating Disorders—etiology. 2. Child Abuse, Sexual-
  -psychology. 3. Eating Disorders—therapy. 4. Eating Disorders-
  -psychology. 5. Memory. WM 175 S518 1996]
  RC552.E18S49 1996
  616.85′26071—dc20
  DNLM/DLC
  for Library of Congress   95-26500
                                                                CIP

Copyright © 1996 by Brunner/Mazel, Inc.

All rights reserved. No part of this book may be reproduced by
any process whatsoever without the written permission of the copyright owner.

Chapters 1–7, 9, 12–15 originally appeared in *Eating Disorders: The Journal of Treatment
and Prevention* and are reprinted here with permission.

For information and ordering, contact:
BRUNNER/MAZEL
A member of the Taylor & Francis Group
1900 Frost Road, Suite 101
Bristol, PA 19007
1-800-821-8312

Manufactured in the United States of America

2 3 4 5 6 7 8 9 0 BRBR 0 9 8 7

Contents

Contributors

Eileen T. Bills, Ph.D., is the pseudonym of a psychotherapist who specializes in eating disorders.

Mary Chewning-Korpach, Ph.D., is with the Youth Forensic Services Commission of British Columbia, Canada.

Michael T. Coe, M.A., is a doctoral candidate in clinical psychology at the California School of Professional Psychology, San Diego.

Leigh Cohn, M.A.T., is Executive Editor of *Eating Disorders: The Journal of Treatment and Prevention.*

Carolyn Costin, M.A., M.F.C.C., is the Director of the Eating Disorder Center of California. She also serves as director of the eating disorder program for Charter Hospital of Thousand Oaks and as the clinical consultant for the Radar Institute, both in California.

Constance J. Dalenberg, Ph.D., is Associate Professor of Psychology at the California School of Professional Psychology, San Diego.

Lori D. Galperin, L.C.S.W., is Clinical Co-Director, Masters & Johnson Sexual Trauma, Sexual Compulsivity and Dissociative Disorder Programs in St. Louis.

Paula Gay, Ph.D., is Clinical Director of the Sexual Trauma Eating Disorders Program of the River Oaks Hospital in New Orleans.

Ann Kearney-Cooke, Ph.D., is a psychologist in private practice in Cincinnati, Ohio.

Philip S. Mehler, M.D., is Assistant Professor of Medicine, University of Colorado Health Sciences Center, and Attending Physician, Denver General Hospital.

Katherine J. Miller, Ph.D., is with the Counseling Psychology Program at Temple University in Philadelphia.

Roy J. O'Shaughnessy, M.D., FRCPC, is with the Youth Forensic Services Commission of British Columbia, Canada. He is also with the Division of Forensic Psychiatry, Department of Psychiatry, at the University of British Columbia.

Niva Piran, Ph.D., is Associate Professor in the Department of Applied Psychology, Ontario Institute for Studies in Education, in Toronto, Canada.

Cathy S. Reto, M.A., R.N., is a doctoral candidate in clinical psychology at the California School of Professional Psychology, San Diego.

Marcia Rorty, Ph.D., is a Postdoctoral Fellow at the Neuropsychiatric Institute, Department of Psychiatry and Biobehavioral Sciences at the University of California, Los Angeles.

Mark F. Schwartz, Sc.D., is Director, Masters & Johnson Institute, and Masters & Johnson Sexual Trauma, Sexual Compulsivity and Dissociative Disorder Programs in St. Louis, New Orleans, and Kansas City.

Peter M. Sheridan, M.A., is a doctoral candidate in clinical psychology at York University in Toronto, Canada.

Larry Stephens, is a counseling student at Amber College in Dallas, Texas.

Lana Stermac, Ph.D., is Associate Professor in the Department of Applied Psychology, Ontario Institute for Studies in Education in Toronto, Canada.

Ruth H. Striegel-Moore, Ph.D., is Assistant Professor of Psychology at Wesleyan University in Middletown, Connecticut.

Walter Vandereycken, M.D., Ph.D., is Professor of Psychiatry at the Catholic University of Leuven, Belgium.

Johan Vanderlinden, Ph.D., is Clinical Psychologist at the University Center St. Jozef in Kortenberg, Belgium.

Edward J. Weiner, M.D., is in private practice as a Board Certified Internal Medicine physician. He is also a Marriage and Family Therapist and Addictionist as well as an Eating Disorders Specialist.

Kenneth L. Weiner, M.D., is Medical Director of the Eating Treatment Center, Bethesda PsycHealth System, and Assistant Clinical Professor of Psychiatry at the University of Colorado Health Sciences Center.

Susan C. Wooley, Ph.D., is Professor of Psychology and Co-Director, Eating Disorders Center, at the University of Cincinnati College of Medicine in Cincinnati, Ohio.

Joel Yager, M.D., is Professor of Psychiatry at the University of New Mexico in Albuquerque.

Kathryn J. Zerbe, M.D., is Vice President for Education and Research and a staff psychoanalyst and staff psychiatrist at the Menninger Clinic in Topeka, Kansas.

Preface

Many of the chapters in this book first appeared in a special edition of *Eating Disorders: The Journal of Treatment and Prevention*, of which I am executive editor. Mark Schwartz served as guest editor for that issue. In response to the interest generated by the issue, we were asked by our publisher to put together a book—an invitation we accepted gladly, adding several important new chapters to the collection along the way.

We have chosen to open this complicated discussion with a powerful autobiographical chapter, by Eileen T. Bills, which vividly describes how repeated sexual assaults led the author to develop anorexia nervosa and bulimia. This compelling piece puts a human face on a complex subject. The chapters that follow in Part I, "Prevalence and Prediction," provide access to the broader context, with studies that investigate the prevalence of sexual abuse among individuals with eating disorders and examine how a history of sexual violence can serve as a predictor of subsequent problems with food. The final contribution in Part I, by Lana Stermac, Niva Piran, and Peter M. Sheridan, looks at social and cultural factors of concern and offers insight into future directions for prevention programs.

Part II, "Clinical Perspectives and Treatment Strategies," begins with a clear and useful review of trauma-based theory, dissociation, and abreactive and ego-states therapy by Mark Schwartz and Paula Gay. Treating body image disturbance, a crucial concern for sexually traumatized eating disorder patients, is considered in a chapter by Carolyn Costin. Drs. Mehler and Weiner describe applicable medical presentations, and Kathryn Zerbe offers a significant theoretical and practical discussion on the emerging sexual self of the patient with an eating disorder. Part II closes with a thorough presentation of effective treatment techniques by Ann Kearney-Cooke and Ruth H. Striegel-Moore.

Controversies are discussed in Part III, "Dialogue," using a point–counterpoint structure. Mary Chewning-Korpach starts off by addressing the process of revictimization. Susan Wooley responds to this and other concerns in an important dissection of cultural issues. Mark

Schwartz and Lori Galperin also respond to the subject of victimization in their chapter, "Reenactment and Trauma." In turn, Mary Chewning-Korpach and Roy J. O'Shaughnessy offer a final argument. This discussion is especially valuable in demonstrating that the topic of sexual trauma and eating disorders can and should be approached from a variety of points of view. We attempt to provide the most up-to-date thinking on this subject, keeping in mind that research and analysis are ongoing.

Finally, we could not end this book without examining the much-debated topic of false memory, or delayed memory, syndrome in an Epilogue that places into context the backlash that has polarized the mental health field and threatens every therapist reading this book. With the stakes so high for everyone involved, we felt it essential to add our own voices.

Mark and I would like to thank all of the authors who contributed to this book in addition to Maria P. P. Root, who wrote an editorial in the original journal and helped to solicit some of the articles; Arnold Andersen, John Foreyt, and Margo Maine, senior editors of the journal; Susan Kent Cakars, managing editor of the journal; Natalie Gilman and Mark Tracten at Brunner/Mazel; and our families.

Leigh Cohn

Introduction:
Eating Disorders and
Sexual Trauma

Mark F. Schwartz

Leigh Cohn

It has been suggested by Judith Herman (1992) that children exposed to inescapable stress throughout childhood will be at risk for compulsivity and reenactment of trauma by self-abuse syndromes. It is likely that interfamilial sexual abuse is often part of a syndrome that includes chronic abuse and neglect on a daily basis. It is an important advancement to consider childhood sexual abuse and inescapable stress as syndromes capable of resulting in posttraumatic stress, dissociative symptoms, and susceptibility to compulsive reenactments (frequently including eating disorder symptomatology) and revictimizations developmentally. Additionally, because sexual abuse is such an extreme example of a boundary violation, as well as a component of the disruption of attachment and bonding, it is likely that some clients will exhibit symptoms of self-injury to the body; one form of such injury is eating disorder.

The fundamental question is: Why has it taken so long to recognize the association if, as has been reported by one major center (the Rader Institute, W. Rader, 1993), 80% of their sample of eating-disordered patients have a history of sexual abuse? And why is there still controversy as to the interrelations? The reason is that the connections are not simple and predictable. Certainly some eating-disordered clients were not sexually or physically abused or neglected, and many sexually abused clients do not have eating disorders. Eating disorders are determined by a multitude of factors, and there are many syndromes associated with eating disorders, some of which are directly and indirectly influenced by sexual trauma.

There also may be more surreptitious reasons for the "not knowing." Traumatized clients often discover forgotten details of their childhood and they say, "I always knew that." Sexual trauma is often a syndrome of "knowing and not knowing" simultaneously. The resistance to knowing is characteristic of our clients, even though rehabilitation ultimately requires retrieval, reconstruction, and integration of memory that has been previously fragmented, distorted, dissociated, or repressed. Resistance to knowing is also characteristic of professionals and society in general. Certainly Freud's repudiation of his recognition of sexual abuse as an etiologic factor in hysteria is one classical example. Sexual abuse was estimated in the 1960s in a major textbook in psychiatry (Freedman & Kaplan, 1967) to be 1 in 1,000, but by the 1980s numerous publications found an incidence of 1 in 3 females and 1 in 7 males. In major U.S. cities, as many as 2,000 to 3,000 new cases of incest per year were being validated throughout the past decade. The National Committee to Prevent Child Abuse reported that in 1993, 2.9 million children were reported to protective services for child abuse, neglect, or both, and 16% of these were for sexual abuse. If 2 million cases were substantiated as an incidence figure each year, the prevalence of early trauma would be 60–90 million (of the 225 million total population), and the prevalence of adult survivors of severe abuse and neglect would be 11 million. Why then has there been such resistance to knowing and believing? Perhaps recognition of the high incidence of child abuse shatters individuals' conceptual systems of the world. Janoff-Bulman (1985) writes, "Whether we like it or not, each human being forms a theory of reality that brings order into what otherwise would be a chaotic world of experience. We need a theory to make sense of the world." The postulates of these frameworks for a manageable reality include the belief in personal invulnerability and a perception of the world as meaningful and comprehensible. In order to maintain their illusions, clinicians may need to sometimes not know or not see. The absence in the literature of recognition of the interconnections among sexual trauma, dissociation, and eating disorder has been partially due to a blind spot in clinicians' and researchers' ability to know and see.

Recently there has been controversy as to whether memories of childhood abuse are accurate. Memories are never factual, but they are actively construed and then reassimilated over time, subject to childhood misattributions (i.e., "I caused it"), developmental idiosyncracies (i.e., "I thought I was being killed" or "I wanted to be special"), and consolidation of memory and memory retrieval distortions. However, this does not mean that the person was not abused. On the contrary, the developmental distortions often make abuse more injurious because of the child's developmental limitations in information processing and resultant interpretation and attribution. It is the intensification, reconstruction, and prolonged or irrational elaboration of memories and emotions that lead to posttraumatic stress disorder (PTSD) (Horowitz & Reidbord, 1993). The controversy regarding memory processing in trauma resolution is only another manifestation of the backlash of professionals' need to not know.

Another critical question is why early trauma would influence eating behavior. There are many probable interrelations that make eating disorder symptoms logical target symptoms for abused children. One fundamental reason is that eating is often associated with family meals, nurturing, and proof that parents care for children. Thus, feeding and then abusing the child are incongruent, confusing, and difficult to assimilate and integrate. Likewise, the family meal in destructive families is often conflictual at best; at worst, it is a ritual of terror—in which the autocratic father exerts violent control over a young child for eating behavior and the destructive family dynamics are played out. Sustenance therefore becomes associated with fear.

Sexual abuse and other forms of physical boundary violation with children would also be likely to be manifest in eating disorder symptoms. Dissociation often prevents memory of the actual event, particularly for young children, and they are instead left with behavioral or somatic reenactments as clues to their abuse. When children have been unable to control what has gone into the body, they tend to react by overcontrolling those elements that are within their power. Throwing up compulsively and taking laxatives to purge the self of unwanted substances constitutes a logical symbolic message.

When sexual abuse has occurred, the body and sex organs become the enemy in the context of the distorted survival strategy of children who must maintain the belief that adults are good (safe) and therefore they (the body) must be bad and deserve to be punished. Their feminine or masculine body becomes a source of shame. For the woman, eating influences body size, interferes with "feminine" development, and quite literally can decrease the probability that a man will "abuse" her or that she will have to deal with her "bad" sexual urges or incapacity to say "no." For other women, the body becomes the only reason a man would approach since they feel internally damaged. Making the body attractive (i.e., thin) becomes an obsession, the only way to escape being alone.

When internal schemas for safety are disrupted, food may also serve as a transitional object—parents and living objects are too scary. Also, fasting and eating can be utilized to create mood alteration and thereby can be numbing when the individual is terrified or alerting when s/he is too numb. For these reasons and many more (see Chapter 7 by Schwartz & Gay), eating disorders are likely symptoms for early trauma.

What is clear from this discussion is that eating disorder specialists also need to be skilled in working with trauma and dissociative disorder, and trauma and dissociative disorder specialists need to be skilled in eating disorders. The following chapters to bridge the gap in the research, theory, technique, and politics around this subject.

REFERENCES

Freedman, A., & Kaplan, H. (1967). *Textbook of psychiatry*. Baltimore: Williams & Wilkins.

Herman, J. (1992). *Trauma and recovery: The aftermath of violence—from domestic abuse to political terror*. New York: Basic Books.

Horowitz, M., & Reidbord, S. (1993). Memory, emotion and response to trauma. In S. Christianson (Ed.), *Handbook of emotion and memory*. Stockholm: Lawrence Erlbaum.

Janoff-Bulman, R. (1985). The aftermath of victimization—Rebuilding shattered assumptions. In C. Figley (Ed.), *Trauma and its wake, Volume 1* (pp. 15–35). New York: Brunner/Mazel.

National Committee to Prevent Child Abuse. (1994). *Current trends in child abuse reporting and fatalities: The results of the 1993 annual fifty state survey*. Chicago: NCPCA Publications.

Rader, W. (1993). Personal communication.

Prologue:

From Sexual Abuse to Empowerment*

EILEEN T. BILLS

INTRODUCTION BY LEIGH COHN**

Eileen T. Bills is the pseudonym of a psychotherapist who has specialized in eating disorders for more than a decade. Initially, Eileen wrote to Lindsey Hall, my wife and frequent coauthor, and me to thank us for the inspiration she received from a booklet we wrote on bulimia in 1980. We were so moved by her letter that we reprinted part of it in a book we wrote some six years later. Shortly after, another note came from Eileen, who had seen her letter excerpted, and she and Lindsey continued corresponding.

We learned about Eileen's interest in the topic of sexual abuse when she sent us a copy of her dissertation, "Eating Disorders and Their Correlates in Earlier Episodes of Incest," which led Lindsey to ask her to write a chapter for her book, *Full Lives*. Although Eileen had never attempted to write about her own experiences and Lindsey was not aware of the full extent of the abuse Eileen had endured, we all sensed that there would be power in her story. Upon reading the initial draft, Lindsey noticed a curious thing. After the first few pages, the narrative slipped from the first to the third person as Eileen began describing specific incidents of

---

*Reprinted by permission from *Full Lives: Women Who Have Freed Themselves from Food and Weight Obsession*, by Lindsey Hall. Copyright © 1993 Gürze Books.
**Leigh Cohn's introduction has been added for the publication of this book.

sexual abuse in more detail. Apparently, it was still difficult for her to face what had happened to her as a child—even after having gone through recovery from anorexia nervosa and bulimia, receiving a doctorate in counseling psychology, and working in the field for years.

Mark Schwartz and I decided to reproduce Eileen's chapter in *Full Lives* here because it offers a crucial point of view for professionals interested in gaining a complete understanding of this subject. Case studies show the severity of sexual trauma but with a detached voice, even if compassionate and insightful. Eileen, however, vividly describes the horror and pain of childhood sexual abuse and how it directly resulted in anorexia nervosa and bulimia. She writes with passion and intelligence in conveying her struggle and recovery.

Eileen's story is useful because it makes such a clear connection between trauma and eating disorders. Moreover, it reminds clinicians that theories, figures, research, and methodology are based on real people who have been deeply hurt. While it is relevant to address the social and sexual pressures on women, it is more meaningful to discuss these issues within the context of an actual woman's life. By sharing such intimate details of her experience, Eileen brings the subject matter of this book out of the head and into the heart.

I therefore put forward the thesis that at the bottom of every case of hysteria there are one or more occurrences of premature sexual experiences, occurrences which belong in the earliest years of childhood.—Freud, 1905

At that time, anorexia nervosa was considered a hysterical neurosis.—Lasegue, 1873; Janet, 1903

THE TRAVESTY

My mother was very unhappy when I was a little girl. She cried all the time and fought wretchedly with my father. Sometimes the fighting got so bad that the neighbors called the police.

My father was usually a passive participant in these fights. While my mother was screaming hysterically, he would just walk away. This would upset my mother even more and she would go after him. Finally, his control would give way and he would spew out some vicious remark and shove my mother back. Eventually, one or the other would decide that it was time to get away. Frequently, my father would make motions to leave but my mother would get in the car and take off first. Then there was a struggle as to who would take the car. My mom usually won and would not return for days. I remember one time my father getting into the car, but my mother would not let him leave her and got in too. They drove away and left me alone. The next morning my father had stitches in his head, the car was smashed, and he showed me his blood-drenched shirt, saying, "See what your mother did to me!"

I was very afraid when they fought, but stayed close, believing that my presence prevented them from hurting each other too badly. Most of the time, they didn't even notice me pleading with them to stop, nor were they careful about what they said or did in front of me. Going to sleep at night was awful when my parents were fighting. Our house felt empty and cold, and I felt alone and unsafe.

My father owned and operated a motel on the beach, and our house was connected to the motel. We had no neighbors, only transient guests. I was very lonely. We went to a cafeteria about once a week for dinner. When I was finished eating, I walked around the cafeteria and said "Hi" to all the people there.

One time I met an old man who asked me to sit by him in his booth. He was very tall and slim, had a greyish-white, straggly beard, extraordinarily long fingernails, and wore a tattered, black suit that hung long on his elderly body. He had a leather coin purse and when he took money out of it, his hands shook. He had a distinctive odor, too. It wasn't really foul but it nauseated me. Each time we went to the cafeteria, he was there and I began feeling obligated to visit with him every time.

I don't remember if it started on my first visit or a later one, but as I sat by him, he would put his hand up my dress, pull the crotch of my panties aside, and stroke my genitals. I would sit there and pretend that nothing was happening. Inside I wanted to get up and leave or ask him not to do that, but I didn't want to hurt his feelings, so I just sat there 'till he stopped. Then I rejoined my family and said nothing. As young as I was (maybe six or seven), I already knew how "nasty" it was having that part of my body touched, and I was too ashamed to tell. I do remember though that my mother always insisted that I wear dresses even though I asked her many times if I could wear pants—especially the nights we went to the cafeteria.

I also made friends with the motel guests. It was easy because my dad would frequently ask me to take someone a lightbulb or towels. One day, a man moved into #17. I think he was in his 30s. He always wore black-laced shoes, black pants, a white shirt and greased his black hair back with Brylcreme. He was one of our semipermanent tenants as he had a kitchen, and my dad didn't rent out kitchens with the rooms unless the person was going to stay for a while.

It was in the kitchen that this man started doing things to me like the old man had done. He would ask me to sit on his lap. It's funny the memories that get triggered when I think about this stuff. I remember the chair—it was yellow, and where it was in the kitchen—against the wall that had the window. He would reach around my body and put his hand into my underpants and rub me. I don't remember my age but I can recall that I didn't have pubic hair. I was probably around eight or nine. A weird thing happened as he was touching me. My faced got all flushed, a wave of heat came over my body, my genitals became very warm and then there was a good feeling. The guilt that I felt afterwards was tremendous. As in the earlier encounter with the old man, I would pretend that nothing was happening and would leave soon afterward, walking down the corridor and the steps to my house, saying nothing to anyone.

One day the man in #17 did something that frightened me, after which I never went back. Maybe he moved soon after. He had bought a package of hot dogs. I was sitting on the chair opposite the window. He took the hot dogs out of the refrigerator and with an uncooked spaghetti noodle, he poked a hole in the tip of one end of the hot dog. I became afraid. Almost immediately, I realized that he was finding a way to introduce me to his penis. I remember thinking that I had asked for this as I had kept coming back to visit with him and had let him touch me. Then he took the hot dog and put it in his mouth and made his lips move up and down on it. He said that it could be sucked on, and if it was blown just the right way, it would whistle. Then he handed it to me and told me to try it.

I tried to blow, but it wouldn't whistle. Then he dropped his pants and a huge erect penis was exposed. It was ugly and there was dark hair all around. He took my head and bent it toward his penis. I knew what I was supposed to do, even though recalling this event, I cannot tell you how I knew about this, young as I was. He held onto my head very tightly and I opened my mouth and he moved my head back and forth on his penis. He made it go too deep and I choked. Then he picked me up and carried me to the bed and took down my panties and tried to insert his penis into me. It hurt, but I was too afraid to make a sound because I didn't want my father to know that such a nasty thing was happening to me—especially since I felt that I had asked for it. At some point he stopped pushing but had me face him again and had me orally stimulate him until his penis grew larger and then a horrible tasting, sticky stuff came out while his penis pulsated. When he removed it, I closed my jaw with considerable difficulty and as it closed, it cracked. For days my sore jaw was a sick reminder of this incident.

Around this same time, my mother's younger brother, Tony, came to live with us. He was 16 or 17 and had gotten into drugs. His parents couldn't handle him anymore and thought that helping out at the motel might straighten him out.

Saturday nights, when my parents went out, was Uncle Tony's "free for all." He had complete reign over the house and approximately six hours alone with me. To this day, I wonder why my parents left me alone with him. Even if they didn't know about how he took advantage of me sexually, they knew about the drugs and they must have been aware of how badly he treated me when they were around. I guess that my mom was too involved with her own life to see what was happening to me. My dad, in his typical style, chose to be oblivious.

One night, when my parents were out, Uncle Tony called me in his room. He was lying on his bed, his pants were off, and his penis was erect. He asked me to hold his penis and to move it up and down. He showed me just how he wanted me to do it. I don't remember if he came or not, or how it ended that night, but that was the beginning of the sexual encounters with my uncle on Saturday nights that I came to dread.

In the beginning, it wasn't really threatening. He would ask me to masturbate him and then he would touch me and it would feel good. But then, Uncle Tony started getting more and more into drugs and alcohol.

Reds were his favorite. He would become very hostile and aggressive when he was high. He would tell me that if I'd do it he would be nice to me the rest of the evening, or he wouldn't beat me up. I remember so often that I'd believe him and do what he wanted, and he'd beat me up anyway. I can remember saying, "But you promised. . . . "

To get me to do what he wanted, he would threaten to break one of my toys that he knew that I really liked. Another trick he used was to stand by the breaker switch and tell me that he would blow up the house by pulling the switches down if I didn't comply. (It didn't even occur to me that by doing that, he would have blown himself up too.) He even threatened to tell my parents what we did. There was so much shame surrounding what was happening that I didn't even see my own innocence. I felt all alone and unprotected in those days, too ashamed to tell, and not certain that I would be believed, anyway.

All these incidents happened to me before I was 12.

THE EFFECTS

From the earliest grades, I had trouble sleeping. I was exhausted most of the time. Sometimes it was because I had been left alone in the house and I was afraid that I would be attacked by someone. I slept with a hairbrush for protection. I didn't choose anything more lethal because I figured the intruder would take a knife, or other weapon I chose, and use it on me. Nights that I wasn't left alone, my mind was filled with distressing thoughts, making sleep nearly impossible.

There was absolutely no similarity between my world and that of the children with whom I went to the private school. I was sure that everyone knew that I was an outcast—a product of a chaotic, drug-infested, violent environment. My emotional development was uneven, my social development warped. Paradoxically, I was both a very young, emotionally insecure, frightened child, and a streetwise individual who had had adult sexual experiences.

I felt dirty, unlikable, and different from everyone else. I had no friends. I believed that my "badness" was transparent and I think I gave off vibes to keep other kids away from me. I had too many secrets to maintain. I also isolated myself on one of the green school benches because of pain in my genital area. This experience was too distressing and consumed all my attention. That was grammar school. I don't remember learning. I don't remember playing. I don't remember being happy.

Puberty brought the issues surrounding my abuse to full force. I didn't want to grow up and be a sexual human being. There was too much terror associated with that idea. A developing body, sexuality, guilt, shame, powerlessness, and being out of control were all one and the same thing and I wanted none of it.

Once I started to develop physically, though, I seemed to attract boys and adult men who would fondle me, have me touch them, or want sex from me. My self-esteem was so low that I didn't know how to say "No," didn't think I had the right, thought that *that* was what my body was for, and felt that somehow I must have asked for it. My insecurities made it obvious that I was too afraid to tell. Someone was bound to be mad at me, and I couldn't bear the rejection—it would have been all my fault. I might hurt somebody's feelings if I didn't allow them to do what they wanted with me.

Puberty was just too painful an experience to allow to proceed. (In retrospect, I am amazed at how powerful the psyche is. I stopped menstruating even before any weight loss!) I was emotionally still eight years old. There was no hope of integrating the sexual aspects of my maturing body into me as a whole person, because I wasn't one.

Repeatedly, over the years, I had lost control of my body and my will—vital connections to my emerging sense of self. Nor was I immune to the social emphasis placed on a woman's body. Thinness was equated with self-worth, success, and social acceptance. At the time, the prepubescent, boyish look was in, i.e., straight hips, no fat—a total disregard for the normal female shape. In search of an identity, I was extremely vulnerable to this value system. So, when puberty and adolescence struck (the critical development period of identity formation), I went looking for a sense of myself through my body and through control over it. After all, my body was the earliest identity I had. I went back to find it. The alternative, I believe, was to go crazy.

THE PERFECT SOLUTION

One day I was walking home from school experimenting with a more deliberate walking style, and I felt a calmness inside. I had figured out a way to regain my innocence. It involved being deliberate in everything I did and thought. In a way, it was a great solution for where I was emotionally at the time—in search of an identity. This new plan necessitated that I stop and examine what I wanted in every situation in which I found myself.

It became a problem when I needed extreme control in all situations. No, I wasn't going to allow anyone to "feel me up" anymore. I didn't want that. But I was also going to dress very carefully, fold my collar just so, and walk with my heel touching first, my knees very rigid, and my posture erect. I was going to run between the two piers on the beach every day and do my series of floor exercises. I could only eat once a day, and only after postponing it (mainly with exercise) as long as I could. In fact, eating was not allowed unless I had completed my exercise rituals and organized certain of my belongings in special ways. I carefully selected and measured portions of the same (''healthy'') food day after day, chewing each bite a certain number of times and putting my fork and knife down between bites.

I changed my writing style by printing very neatly and extremely small. I also changed my tempo of speech and I chose when and to whom I spoke. I started withdrawing from people and feelings because I felt that I could maintain my path better without these interferences. I became extremely controlled in all areas of my life, especially those areas related to eating and exercising. With this new lifestyle, I started losing weight and defying puberty.

As the pounds came off, I began to feel cleaner inside. I still didn't have any friends, but my obsession with my body shape, weight loss, and exercise camouflaged my need for companionship. Instead of feeling like an outcast and undeserving of friends, my obsession allowed me to feel like I was rejecting them, instead. I didn't need them and, in fact, I was better than they were because I was becoming pure inside from not eating.

I can see clearly today the choice I made back then. My body, my femininity, and my sexuality became the enemy because, if it hadn't been for these, those vile sexual acts wouldn't have occurred. I wouldn't have been prey to others who used my body—used me—to gratify their own selfish needs. The experience of guilt because my body had become sexually aroused by such ''unacceptable'' acts was tremendous. I truly believed that I was ''making up for my sins,'' and becoming pure, by feeling the gnawing tightness in my stomach from not eating or from making special additions to my exercise routine.

I never learned to trust. I had shameful secrets inside of me that I would never dare tell anyone. So, no one could ever know the ''real me.'' Relationships remained shallow and unfulfilling. I never felt connected to anyone. I didn't love or care for myself. I didn't even know myself. How could I get to know, love, and care for someone else, let alone ever believe they felt anything nice toward me?

The issues surrounding my weight and the food I consumed, vomited, or denied myself continued to be my companion, my identity, the tools

I used to disguise my pain, and the measures of my worth and lovability. However, while my eating disorder had helped me cope with the issues that surfaced during and in the early aftermath of the sexual abuse, it now caused me more feelings of self-loathing and shame. My capacity for relationships and for intimacy further deteriorated, fueling the eating disorder into adulthood. For this reason, resolving the issues affecting my capacity for relationships and for intimacy was at the core of recovery.

THE FIRST STEPS TOWARD HEALING

The sequence of events from early adolescence until I first went for help is basically an eating disorder blur. I developed a bona fide case of anorexia nervosa, was obsessed in that arena for a good two years, added bulimic behavior to my regimen, and alternated between the two for about 10 years.

Although what brought me into therapy was a bad relationship, I really went because I threw up food, on purpose, and I was not able to stop on my own. After eight months, my therapist had earned my trust and I was strong enough to tell her about this behavior. She wanted me to explore deeper, but I just couldn't relate to the idea that there were issues underlying my need for an eating disorder.

Once I let my secret out, I was ecstatic to learn that I wasn't the only one in the world to do this. There were even books written on the subject. I would plant myself in the psychology section of our school library and go through book after book, journal after journal, day after day.

During this implosion period I began my first attempt at quitting cold turkey, which actually worked for a couple of months. I'd dream about it though, that I had eaten something forbidden, but I was unable to find privacy to throw it up. I'd wake up relieved that it had only been a dream, but also overwhelmed by the power of this disorder. Eventually, I couldn't take abstaining any longer. I needed to feel that relief from throwing up.

Once I blew cold turkey, it became harder to believe that I could just quit. I kept having to devise more complicated ways to prevent the behavior. I'd come up with things that were more important to me than throwing up, like a favorite T-shirt, my harmonica, an album. One time it was $100. What was sad was that I didn't consider me an important-enough person to fight for. I used so many ''tricks'' on myself.

Still, I was able to make progress. I gave myself stars for each day I went without vomiting. I learned to look at progress in cumulative increments. I built up memories and experiences of my ability to keep food inside under various circumstances and conditions. If I could resist throwing up during a "nearly impossible" time, I had that memory to carry with me the next time an extremely difficult situation arose. I also drew upon my recollections of the "afterglow" when I succeeded and the pain and sadness when I didn't.

When I moved to another state after five years of therapy, I was better, but not completely well. I had learned that it was possible for me to eat and keep the food inside, and I did feel better about myself. I was occasionally able to feel what came to be labeled as "connected" although it never seemed to last. Much of the time I experienced my body as being "shattered"—not completely lost, but the parts were disconnected from my heart and mind. I also remained ferociously angry with my mother but didn't understand why. I began putting it all together one night in a group I had joined in my new town.

THE UNDERSTANDING

It was the last five minutes. The topic must have been families or something. As I recalled mine, a feeling of intense hatred and disgust for Uncle Tony welled up inside of me. I said how much I hated him, unable to stop repeating it. I became wild and then suddenly sullen. Sinking from my seat onto the floor, I collapsed like a rag doll. I felt beaten, exhausted, with no will left. I was experiencing for the first time the emotions I had kept buried for 20 years.

I had been a member of this personal growth group for one and a half years, but I was too ashamed to tell these seemingly normal people that I was working on an eating disorder. Until that night, I had no feelings related to the sexual abuse that I had experienced as a child, and had convinced myself that this latter experience was irrelevant to my present state of unhappiness and not worth bringing up. Besides, I had plenty of issues to work on! I had low self-esteem, was uncomfortable around people, and couldn't break down and cry about anything. I was lonely, depressed, and came across as helpless. In fact, my appearance and demeanor were frequently described as childlike.

But that night, I felt hatred as I had never felt it before. A woman in the group asked if Uncle Tony had sexually abused me. I nodded. Group ended. As I walked to my car, emotions flooded over me. I felt terrified, naked from exposure, and afraid of what was to come. Driving home I couldn't get the images and memories out of my mind.

Over the next several weeks, it became nearly impossible for me to sleep. Self-hatred and shame had been reawakened. Intrusive thoughts and memories of the past offered me no relief. I decided to try individual therapy again, this time with a male therapist, the group leader.

Sleep continued to be scant during those first few weeks of intensive therapy. I was afraid of something, afraid to let go, lose control, and dream. I was exhausted, running on empty anxiety, thinking about the past—things I had not thought about in a long time. Rather than anger at my abusers, though, I was feeling ashamed and embarrassed. What did those people in the group think of me? I felt so dirty. I wanted to hide and never show my face again.

The night before my third individual session, I did not sleep at all. I drove to my psychologist's office as though in a trance. His approach seemed different this time. There was more questioning, more prying. With a will weak from sleep deprivation and defenses in a fog, a window finally opened. The hesitancy that had previously accompanied my speech was gone. This time images poured into my mind and the words flowed without scrutiny.

I told about the pain I had felt when Uncle Tony would punch me in the breasts. "It made him laugh," I said. I told how he would hold me down, with his knees upon on my wrists, letting spit drool from his mouth into my eye. "He peed on me, too," I shuddered.

Then I told about Saturday nights being left alone with him. An image came into my mind as vivid as if it were happening right then. I was about eight years old. It was Saturday night. I was standing in the alley behind my house. My parents were all dressed up—my father in a suit and my mother wearing her mink coat. I watched their car back out of the garage and drive away. My voice rose, becoming frantic as I begged my mom not to leave me alone with him. "I would beg her!" I repeated, becoming hysterical. And in a torrent of tears I exclaimed, "She didn't care!"

I was shocked at the intensity of my rage. I believed that if indeed I was not sleeping because I was afraid to face something, it must have been some sadistic, sexual experience that I had not, as yet, recalled. However, *the rage that I was so afraid to face was directed toward my mother for failing to protect me all those years.* I hadn't told and she hadn't seen. That night I slept 17 hours!

As the months went on and memories surfaced, I came in touch with live emotions from the past. I not only came to understand the choice I made at age 14 to diet, but I felt it. I was able to sense myself back then and feel my reasoning with clarity. Somewhere deep down inside of me, I raged at my vulnerability, my femaleness, my powerlessness, and at the vultures to whom I had been exposed. I had tried many times to vomit up that rage. For me, dieting and weight loss became an obsession because I had been repeatedly sexually abused, and there was no one available to protect me. Indeed, these obsessions were my salvation.

This was one of the first things I was helped to acknowledge—that the choice I made was not only reasonable, but it very likely saved me. However, it took more than working through the past and understanding my choices to put the eating disorder behind me for the last time.

The early work I did—going through the struggles of keeping food inside of me despite the anxiety, daring to gain a pound, whittling away at my forbidden list, learning to exercise reasonably and not compulsively, failing and having the courage to start again, substituting adaptive for maladaptive behaviors, learning to trust my body and myself—was critical to overcoming the disordered eating pattern. However, what I believe made it stick for good was that I finally believed that the little girl in the school yard wasn't at all bad or unlikable. She was really very loveable. She did what she did to *survive*.

In order to come to this realization of my unconditional worth, I had to dredge up the past and reawaken the emotions and thoughts of the child. Next, with an adult mind, I had to challenge those feelings, beliefs, and thoughts. Then I understood the travesty and its effects. With this understanding came love and acceptance of myself, which enabled me to finally risk intimacy and thereby accomplish the final stage of my recovery.

INTIMACY, RELATING, AND RECOVERY: THE FINAL STAGE

As an adolescent, I avoided relationships and intimacy because I didn't want anyone to get close enough to me to hate me as much as I did. As a young adult, I had sex because I thought it was expected. There was no relating, feeling close, or feeling love. I just felt used and trapped. I didn't know that I had the right to say "No," and feared I would lose whatever companionship I had if I did. Rejection, I believed, was worse than 30 minutes or so of feeling exploited.

As I came to find out later, I followed a pattern found in many other individuals with abuse histories who get involved with another abuser and repeat the past in hopes of making it go better this time, or who believe they are getting what they deserve. Thankfully, I got help and eventually became strong enough to sustain the uncertainty of being alone and starting anew.

As I came to like myself better, I was able to risk having others get to know me. I began to gain control of how much intimacy I got, and I stopped agreeing to sex when I didn't want it. This made me feel empowered. As I began to assert myself more, the intrusive memories of my abuse experiences were no longer being triggered, and they went away. This meant that I no longer needed the obsessions with food and weight to block out negative thoughts and emotions, and I stopped needing to starve to prove my worth and power, resulting in even greater gains in self-esteem and personal integrity. I began to feel free and strong enough to relate to others as me. Being able to connect with others was filling the void I had inside, and the empty craving for thinness became less and less intense. I felt more in charge of me, and therefore needed less and less to be in charge of food.

Inside, I began to feel and enjoy my femininity. My sexuality became fun, exciting, and something I got pleasure and satisfaction from sharing. Perhaps the most significant change in light of my abuse experiences is that I came to feel proud rather than exploited when my sexuality was appreciated and enjoyed. My partner was my lover and friend, not an extension or reminder of all my former abusers. I was finally feeling loveable inside and out.

A RETROSPECTIVE LOOK AND TODAY

Where did I begin? I got desperate—so miserable I wanted to die. Then I let someone earn my trust and I asked for help. I explored myself and how I got to be me. I wrote and read a lot. I learned to think for myself and challenged my beliefs. I tried new behaviors, and new ways of relating. And I kept on working.

I tried several therapists until I found one who felt right to me (this in itself was a sign of "wellness"). I worked through my experiences of sexual abuse—I remembered, I cried, I grieved. I understood my choices and I found no present relevancy for these. Toward the end, I concentrated on relationships, intimacy, and finally on learning to "parent" myself.

Recovery for me was like climbing a sand dune. The effort was continuous and tremendous, the progress tediously slow, and the slips were numerous. But there came a time when I saw that I never slipped as far back as where I had started. Eventually the slips got fewer and their duration shorter until, one day, I realized that I was really free—free from my eating disorder and from my past experiences of sexual abuse. I am left with me and that is finally a secure and comforting experience.

It's morning. I wake up to a crying baby. I bring her to my bed and nurse her under the covers. I feel her warm body against mine. We fall back to sleep. I feel a gentle kiss as my husband leaves for work. Some time later, I feel a soft tapping on my arm. My four-year-old wants us to get up 'cause she's hungry and wants some Honey Nut Cheerios. I ask for another minute or five, but she's persistent. We all get up and the day begins. At 7:45 the school bus comes for my seven-year-old. A seemingly ordinary scene, but miraculous to me.

REFERENCES

Freud, S. (1905). A fragment of analysis of a case of hysteria (Dora). In J. Strachey (Ed. and Trans.), *The standard edition of the complete psychological works of Sigmund Freud* (Vol. 7, pp. 3–122). London: Hogarth Press.

Janet, P. (1903). *Les obsession et la psychasthenie.* Paris: Felix Alcan.

Lasegue, E.C. (1873). De l'anorexie hysterique. *Archives of General Medicine, 2,* 385.

PART I

Prevalence and Prevention

1

Is Sexual Abuse a Risk Factor for Developing an Eating Disorder?

JOHAN VANDERLINDEN

WALTER VANDEREYCKEN

Some critical comments are made with regard to the possible relationship between a history of sexual abuse and the development of an eating disorder. In a case of sexual abuse, many factors and variables interacting with one another may play a role in the development of psychiatric sequelae, including eating disorders. The fact that a linear causal link does not exist does not mean that sexual abuse is not a risk factor for eating disorders.

In recent years, more and more reports have appeared about serious traumatic experiences—especially physical and sexual abuse—in anorexia nervosa (AN) and bulimia nervosa (BN) patients (Finn et al., 1986; Goldfarb, 1987; Hall et al., 1989; McFarlane et al., 1988; Oppenheimer et al., 1985; Root & Fallon, 1988; Schechter et al., 1987; Sloan & Leichner, 1986; Torem, 1986; Vanderlinden & Vandereycken, 1993; Waller, 1991; Wooley & Kearney-Cooke, 1986). Traumatic experiences are more frequently reported by bulimics than by restricting anorexics. Systematic inquiry into the occurrence of sexual traumata in eating disorder patients resulted in alarming prevalence figures. Oppenheimer et al. (1985) reported sexual abuse during childhood and/or adolescence in 70% of 78 eating disorder patients. Kearney-Cooke (1988) found 58% with a history of sexual trauma of 75 bulimic patients. Root and Fallon (1988) reported that in a group of 172 eating disorder patients, 65% had been physically abused, 23% raped, 28% sexually abused in childhood, and 23% maltreated in actual relationships. Hall et al. (1989) found 40% sexually abused women in a group of 158 eating disorder patients.

One recent report stands in contrast with these findings. In a systematic study of 112 consecutive referrals of normal-weight bulimic women, Lacey (1990) found that only eight patients (7%) mentioned a history of sexual abuse involving physical contact. Four of these (3.6%) described incest, but only in two cases (1.8%) did the incest occur during childhood. Sexual abuse occurred in those "multi-impulsive" bulimics who also abuse alcohol or drugs. Interestingly, Lacey also mentioned that an additional 18 patients reported "incestuous fantasies." But on the basis of what kind of considerations and/or methods did the author make this distinction between reality and fantasy, especially since this information was only gained at the initial assessment interview? In cases of serious childhood sexual abuse, there might exist amnesia for the abuse; consequently, the patient will not report it in a first interview. According to the author, however, it is unlikely that actual cases of sexual abuse were missed, since most patients subsequently entered psychotherapy with female therapists and no further cases came to light. But the fact that patients enter psychotherapy does not guarantee that they will disclose sexual abuse. Especially in psychoanalytically oriented psychotherapy, the likelihood that stories about sexual abuse will be interpreted as fantasy or the result of transferential issues cannot be denied. Finally, we are wondering what type of bulimic patients were studied. Except for the DSM-III-R diagnosis, no other information on the patient sample (demographic status and other important clinical characteristics) is presented. In sum, the low prevalence of reported sexual abuse in Lacey's study may be biased by: 1) the data collection method; 2) the selection of a specific patient sample; and 3) the psychodynamic orientation of the therapists. However, notwithstanding these critical annotations, Lacey's (1990) conclusion that his therapeutic work confirms his impression that incest and child sexual abuse mostly occurred in multi-impulsive bulimics is consistent, to a great extent, with our own findings (Vanderlinden & Vandereycken, 1993). In our studies on traumatic experiences in eating disorders (Vanderlinden, 1993), we found the highest prevalence of sexual abuse in patients showing both a complex eating pathology (bulimia, vomiting, laxative abuse) and a remarkable comorbidity (depression, alcohol abuse, kleptomania, promiscuity, automutilation), including severe dissociative symptoms (identity confusion, derealization, depersonalization, amnesia).

But a recent paper by Pope and Hudson (1992), reviewing the literature on sexual abuse in BN, questions even more the possible link between sexual abuse and BN. The authors stress that neither controlled nor uncontrolled studies of BN found higher rates of sexual abuse (varying from 7% to 69%) than in studies of the general population (varying from 27% to 67%) that used comparable methods. The differences in sexual abuse rates were partly due to the definition of sexual abuse employed in the various studies. Pope and Hudson conclude that current evidence does not support the hypothesis that childhood sexual abuse is a risk factor for BN. One has to remark, however, that the reported prevalence rates of sexual abuse in the general population of the United States are quite high and even higher than those found in European studies of psychiatric patient samples! The lowest sexual abuse rate reported in the general population of the United States is 27% (Finkelhor et al., 1990). How can these differences be explained? Are sociocultural factors involved in the prevalence of sexual abuse or in the likelihood of reporting it? Overall, these differences demonstrate very clearly the urgent need for both researchers and clinicians to agree on a clear definition of what should be considered sexual abuse and how it can be detected and/or assessed in a reliable way.

Besides this general remark, we believe that Pope and Hudson have used the wrong argument to defend their point of view. If child sexual abuse does not occur more frequently in eating disorder populations than in the general population, why should this mean that it is not a risk factor for BN? Following the authors' reasoning, one must conclude that sexual abuse is no longer a risk for any of the different psychiatric categories or problems, except for multiple personality disorders. Only in the latter have higher rates of sexual trauma been reported: more than 80% (Putnam, 1989; Ross, 1989). But the relationship between childhood abuse and different forms of psychiatric morbidity has been documented in a number of important studies in recent years (Boon & Draijer, 1993; Briere & Zaidi, 1989; Brown & Anderson, 1991; Bryer et al., 1987; Chu & Dill, 1986; de Wilde et al., 1992; Ensink, 1992; Herman et al., 1989; Margo & McLees, 1991; Morrison, 1989; Mullen et al., 1988; Ogata et al., 1990; Pribor & Dinwiddle, 1992; Ross et al., 1988; Stone et al., 1988; Swett et al., 1990; Wolfe et al., 1989; Zanarini et al., 1989).

In our view, Pope and Hudson (1992) may only conclude that a linear causal link does not exist between sexual abuse in childhood and eating disorders in adults. In the case of sexual abuse, many factors and variables interacting with one another may play a role in the development of psychiatric sequelae: 1) the functioning of the subject prior to the trauma (e.g., age and vulnerability of the child at the time when the abuse occurred); 2) family variables and dynamics; 3) the nature, severity and extent of traumatization (e.g., sexual abuse versus physical abuse alone, or a combination of sexual and physical abuse); 4) the initial response to the trauma (coping resources of the child, parental reactions to the trauma); and 5) longer-term reactions (later triggering events, personality development). Taking these factors into consideration, we believe there is no reasonable argument to question our conviction that sexual and/or physical abuse in childhood place adults at special risk for developing psychological crises and even psychiatric disorders, including anorexia nervosa and bulimia nervosa.

REFERENCES

Boon, S., & Draijer, N. (1993). *Multiple personality disorder in the Netherlands. A study on reliability and validity of the diagnosis.* Amsterdam/Lisse: Swetz & Zeitlinger.

Briere, J., & Zaidi, L. Y. (1989). Sexual abuse histories and sequelae in female psychiatric emergency room patients. *American Journal of Psychiatry, 146,* 1602–1606.

Brown, G. R., & Anderson, B. (1991). Psychiatric morbidity in adult inpatients with childhood histories of sexual abuse and physical abuse. *American Journal of Psychiatry, 148,* 55–61.

Bryer, J. B., Nelson, B. A., Miller, J. B., & Kroll, P. A. (1987). Childhood sexual and physical abuse as factors in adult psychiatric illness. *American Journal of Psychiatry, 144,* 1426–1430.

Chu, J. A., & Dill, D. L. (1990). Dissociative symptoms in relation to childhood physical and sexual abuse. *American Journal of Psychiatry, 147,* 887–892.

De Wilde, E. J., Kienhorst, I. C. W. M., Diekstra, R. F. W., & Wolters, W. H. G. (1992). The relationship between adolescent suicidal behavior and life events in childhood and adolescence. *American Journal of Psychiatry, 149,* 45–51.

Ensink, B. (1992). *Confusing realities: A study on child sexual abuse and psychiatric symptoms.* Amsterdam: VU University Press.

Finkelhor, D., Hotaling, G., Lewis, I. A., & Smith, C. (1990). Sexual abuse in a national survey of adult men and women: Prevalence, characteristics, and risk factors. *Child Abuse and Neglect, 14,* 19–28.

Finn, S., Hartman, M., Leon, G., & Lawson, L. (1986). Eating disorders and sexual abuse: Lack of confirmation for a clinical hypothesis. *International Journal of Eating Disorders, 5,* 1051–1060.

Goldfarb, L. (1987). Sexual abuse antecedent to anorexia nervosa, bulimia and compulsive overeating: Three case reports. *International Journal of Eating Disorders, 6,* 675–680.

Hall, R. C. W., Tice, L., Beresford, T. P., Wooley, B., & Hall, A. K. (1989). Sexual abuse in patients with anorexia nervosa and bulimia. *Psychosomatics, 30,* 79–88.

Herman, J. L., Perry, C. J., & van der Kolk, B. (1989). Childhood trauma in borderline personality disorder. *American Journal of Psychiatry, 146,* 490–495.

Kearney-Cooke, A. (1988). Group treatment of sexual abuse among women with eating disorders. *Women and Therapy, 7*, 5–22.

Lacey, J. H. (1990). Incest, incestuous fantasy and indecency: A clinical catchment area study of normal weight bulimic women. *British Journal of Psychiatry, 157*, 399–403.

Margo, G. M., & McLees, E. M. (1991). Further evidence for the significance of a childhood abuse history in psychiatric inpatients. *Comprehensive Psychiatry, 32*, 362–366.

McFarlane, A. C., McFarlane, C., & Gilchrist, P. N. (1988). Post-traumatic bulimia and anorexia nervosa. *International Journal of Eating Disorders, 7*, 705–708.

Morrison, J. (1989). Childhood sexual histories of women with somatization disorder. *American Journal of Psychiatry, 146*, 239–241.

Mullen, P. E., Romans-Clarkson, S. E., & Walton, V. A. (1988). Impact of sexual and physical abuse on women's mental health. *Lancet, 1*, 841–845.

Ogata, S. N., Silk, K. R., Goodrich, S., Lohr, N. E., Westen, D., & Hill, E. M. (1990). Childhood sexual and physical abuse in adult patients with borderline personality disorder. *American Journal of Psychiatry, 147*, 1008–1013.

Oppenheimer, R., Howells, K., Palmer, L., & Chaloner, D. (1985). Adverse sexual experiences in childhood and clinical eating disorders: A preliminary description. *Journal of Psychiatric Research, 19*, 157–161.

Pope, H. G., & Hudson, K. I. (1992). Is childhood sexual abuse a risk factor for bulimia nervosa? *American Journal of Psychiatry, 149*, 455–463.

Pribor, E. F., & Dinwiddle, S. H. (1992). Psychiatric correlates of incest in childhood. *American Journal of Psychiatry, 149*, 52–56.

Putnam, F. W. (1989). *Diagnosis and treatment of multiple personality disorder.* New York: Guilford Press.

Root, M. P., & Fallon, P. (1988). The incidence of victimization experiences in a bulimic sample. *Journal of Interpersonal Violence, 3*, 161–173.

Ross, C. A. (1989). *Multiple personality disorder: Diagnosis, features and treatment.* New York: Wiley.

Ross, C. A., Norton, G. R., & Anderson, G. (1988). The dissociative experiences scale: A replication study. *Dissociation, 1*, 21–22.

Schechter, I. D., Schwartz, H. P., & Greenfield, D. G. (1987). Sexual assault and anorexia nervosa. *International Journal of Eating Disorders, 6*, 313–316.

Sloan, G., & Leichner, P. (1986). Is there a relationship between sexual abuse or incest and eating disorders? *Canadian Journal of Psychiatry, 31*, 656–660.

Stone, M., Unwin, A., & Beacham, B. (1988). Incest in female borderlines: Its frequency and impact. *International Journal of Family Psychiatry, 9*, 277–293.

Swett, C., Surrey, J., & Cohen, C. (1990). Sexual abuse histories and psychiatric symptoms among male psychiatric outpatients. *American Journal of Psychiatry, 147*, 632–636.

Torem, M. S. (1986). Dissociative states presenting as an eating disorder. *American Journal of Clinical Hypnosis, 29*, 137–142.

Vanderlinden, J. (1993). *Dissociative experiences, trauma and hypnosis: Research findings and clinical applications in eating disorders.* Delft, The Netherlands: Eburon.

Vanderlinden, J., & Vandereycken, W. (1993). Dissociative experiences and trauma in eating disorders. *International Journal of Eating Disorders, 13*, 187–194.

Waller, G. (1991). Sexual abuse as a factor in eating disorders. *British Journal of Psychiatry, 159*, 664–671.

Wolfe, V. V., Gentile, C., & Wolfe, D. A. (1989). The impact of sexual abuse on children: A PTSD formulation. *Behavior Therapy, 20*, 215–228.

Wooley, S., & Kearney-Cooke, A. (1986). Intensive treatment of bulimia and body-image disturbance. In K. D. Brownell & J. P. Foreyt (Eds.), *Handbook of eating disorders:*

Physiology, psychology and treatment of obesity, anorexia and bulimia (pp. 476–502). New York: Basic Books.

Zanarini, M. C., Gunderson, J. G., Marino, M. F., Schwarz, E. O., & Frankenburg, F. R. (1989). Childhood experiences of borderline patients. *Comprehensive Psychiatry, 30*, 18–25.

2

Speculations on the Role of Childhood Abuse in the Development of Eating Disorders Among Women

MARCIA RORTY

JOEL YAGER*

Although many have suggested that child sexual and perhaps physical abuse may predispose young women to the development of eating disorders, others assert that little empirical evidence exists to support such assertions. Nonetheless, clinicians agree that for some women, the experience of abusive events in childhood may be conceptually important in understanding the complex genesis of their eating disorder and therefore in facilitating treatment. We propose that child abuse may be related to the subsequent development of eating disorders, particularly bulimic disorders, according to the following

*The authors gratefully acknowledge the editorial comments of Kimberly Monda, M.A., on an early draft of this manuscript. This paper was presented in part at the Eighth Annual Meeting of the International Society for Traumatic Stress Studies, Los Angeles, October 22–25, 1992.

preliminary model. The model includes the elements of: 1)
child abuse, including its developmental effects on self- and
body-concepts; 2) vulnerable temperaments; 3) predisposition
to comorbid conditions, particularly affective and alcohol/sub-
stance use disorders; 4) deficits in affect regulation; and 5)
family and/or peer environments emphasizing weight, appear-
ance, and dieting.

Several authors have drawn attention to possible associations between a history of sexual and, to a lesser extent, physical abuse, and eating disorders in women (e.g., Goldfarb, 1987; Sloan & Leichner, 1986) and have hypothesized causal links between a traumatic history and the subsequent development of eating pathology. Such links, if they exist, would be of great theoretical and practical interest. However, in a careful review of the existing literature on childhood sexual abuse in the histories of bulimia nervosa patients versus women without eating disorders, Pope and Hudson (1992) concluded that there is no empirical basis for the assertion that a history of child sexual abuse constitutes a risk factor for the emergence of this eating disorder. Far less attention has been paid to other forms of child abuse, such as physical abuse.

Empirical research cannot—and need not—answer questions of individual meaning. Clinical accounts, as well as our own work with eating-disordered women, have demonstrated that many women experience and interpret their eating disorder as an intricately connected direct or indirect response to the trauma of childhood abuse (Goldfarb, 1987; Hall et al., 1989; Sloan & Leichner, 1986; Tice et al., 1989). Anorexia nervosa has been portrayed as a means of avoiding sexual contacts and feelings and as a method of disgusting and repelling the perpetrator (Hall et al., 1989; Sloan & Leichner, 1986; Tice et al., 1989). Bulimic women have described their disorder as an indirect expression of overwhelming anger at the perpetrator, inflicted upon the woman herself as a form of punishment; a coping strategy aimed at quelling guilt, self-hatred, powerlessness, and posttraumatic symptoms related to severe boundary violations; and as a way to make oneself feel sexually unappealing (Hall et al., 1989; Root, 1991; Root & Fallon, 1989; Tice et al., 1989). Finally, it has been suggested that compulsive overeating represents a way to feel "armored" against assaults and express the self-loathing and anxiety associated with abuse (Hall et al., 1989; Tice et al., 1989). For many women, their eating disorder represents a powerful metaphor for or symbolic reliving of abusive experiences (e.g., Root & Fallon, 1989; Tice et al., 1989; van der Kolk, 1989).

Clearly, child abuse is neither a necessary nor sufficient precursor for the development of eating disorders (Pope & Hudson, 1992) or other psychopathology. However, because of the importance of an abuse history in many eating-disordered women's lives, it is useful to speculate as to how abuse, in conjunction with other factors, may increase a woman's vulnerability to developing significant eating pathology. We therefore propose a preliminary model, grounded in a stress-vulnerability context, to help account for the emergence of eating disorders among *some* women who have been abused in childhood. Figure 2-1 displays the components of this model.

Childhood abuse of all kinds—sexual, physical and psychological, both subtle and dramatic—represents a form of boundary violation in which the separateness and integrity of the child's physical and/or psychological self are treated with gross disregard. Child sexual abuse has been defined as "(a) forced or coerced sexual behavior imposed on a child, and (b) sexual activity between a child and a much older person, whether or not obvious coercion is involved (a common definition of 'much older' is 5 or more years)" (Browne & Finkelhor, 1986, p. 66). Child physical abuse is generally considered to consist of physical assault with physical injury (e.g., Surrey et al., 1990). Psychological abuse has been put in operational terms to include subjecting a child to frequent yelling, insults, criticism, guilt-inspiring statements, ridicule, embarrassment in front of others, and attempts to make the child feel like a bad person (Briere & Runtz, 1988, 1990).

We have also observed in our clinical work and in research interviews that subtler forms of maltreatment on the abuse continuum, such as excessive parental intrusiveness and inappropriately sexualized relationships with parents, constitute personal invasions or exploitation that may have extremely deleterious effects. Common manifestations of intrusiveness include failing to respect closed doors, listening to telephone conversations, going through trash, opening mail, or reading diaries. Inappropriately sexualized relationships with father figures, which Herman (1981) refers to as "seductive relationships," also fall on the abuse continuum. Such relationships, according to Herman, involve clear sexual motivation on the father's part, but do not include physical contact or demands for secrecy, as in cases of incest. For instance, a father might talk about his own sexual exploits and question his daughter about sexual encounters, leave pornographic materials for the daughter to find, expose himself, or observe his daughter during personal activities.

Abusive experiences, of which child sexual and physical abuse are the main forms studied, constitute major stressors and predisposing factors

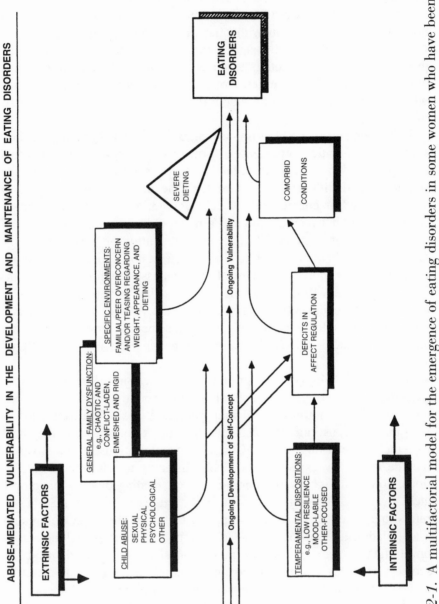

FIGURE 2-1. A multifactorial model for the emergence of eating disorders in some women who have been abused in childhood

for the development of psychopathology, including eating pathology. Other psychopathological outcomes frequently described in the literature include depression (Bagley & Ramsay, 1986; Briere & Runtz, 1988; Burnam et al., 1988; Sedney & Brooks, 1984), alcohol and drug use disorders (Briere, 1988; Brown & Anderson, 1991; Burnam et al., 1988), anxiety (Bagley & Ramsay, 1986; Briere & Runtz, 1988; Burnam et al., 1988; Sedney & Brooks, 1984), suicidality and self-abusive behavior (Briere, 1988; Briere & Runtz, 1986, 1988; Brown & Anderson, 1991; Sedney & Brooks, 1984), sexual problems (Briere, 1988; Briere & Runtz, 1990; Tsai et al., 1979), and low self-esteem, including low physical self-esteem (Alexander & Lupfer, 1987; Bagley & Ramsay, 1986; Briere & Runtz, 1990). The possible impact of frank and subtle abuse and intrusiveness are consistent with Goodsitt's (1983) description of the internal experience of the eating-disordered woman, who struggles desperately for boundaries and control:

> The body of the patient with an eating disorder is required to remain absolutely under self-control and not be subject to external influence . . . the control derives from a terrible sense that one's body, as an aspect of the self-organization, is out of control, easily influenced, invaded, exploited, and overwhelmed by external forces, be it peers, parents, or food. (p. 55)

It is also important to consider the interactive effects of abuse and native temperament on ongoing psychological development. Temperamentally, young women with eating disorders have been characterized as overcompliant with the wishes of others at the expense of their own needs, socially insecure, self-denigrating, harm-avoidant, and mood-labile, leaving them with little flexibility and resilience with which to cope with life stressors. There is some evidence to suggest that these features are not outcomes of the disease process, but rather reflect core traits that may be risk factors for the onset of an eating disorder (Casper, 1990; Johnson & Connors, 1987; Strober, 1980). Finkelhor (1987) outlined "traumagenic" developmental sequelae of child sexual abuse, including traumatic sexualization, or "the conditions in sexual abuse under which a child's sexuality is shaped in developmentally inappropriate . . . ways" (p. 355); stigmatization, in which the child learns that she is somehow "spoiled" by the experience; betrayal, which involves the realization by the child that she is being harmed or not protected by a person or persons on whom she depends for nurturance and protection; and powerlessness, which occurs because the child is repeatedly helpless in the face of the abuse and consequently comes to lose any sense of efficacy to influence outcomes in the world. Although the first two dynamics would seem to be particular to sexual abuse, betrayal and powerlessness have been highlighted in cases of physical abuse as well (Krugman, 1987). Further traumagenic factors specific to these and other forms of abuse might include the child's increasingly internalized beliefs that she is worthless and unloveable, has no right to physical or psychological boundaries, and/or is somehow responsible for or deserving of poor treatment. Child abuse has been associated with decrements in self-esteem and self-concept among abused girls (e.g., Tong et al., 1987) and women reporting retrospectively on their abusive childhoods (Alexander & Lupfer, 1987; Bagley & McDonald, 1984; Bagley & Ramsay, 1986; Brier & Runtz, 1990). Low self-concept, including decreased physical self-concept (Alexander & Lupfer, 1987), would then certainly be related to vulnerability to a variety of later difficulties, particularly if other stressors occurred to further aggravate these developmental deficits.

Additionally, particularly if abuse occurs early and within the family, the girl not only is traumatized by specific discrete abuse events (e.g., the physical pain of being hit), but perhaps more important, she may come to internalize and identify with the abuser/object and the nonprotector/object (i.e., the parent who may know of or suspect abuse but fail to protect the child from abuse) or come to identify herself with the role of victim (Haaken & Schlaps, 1991; Krugman, 1987; Rieker & Carmen, 1986). According to Krugman (1987):

> Having witnessed or experienced violence at home, the child has only maladaptive alternatives in the effort of mastering the terrifying feelings: identification with the aggressor and the denial of vulnerability, or identification as a victim desperately in need of protection but too vulnerable to be intimate. In the latter case, rage is split off, dissociated, and turned against a self regarded as bad, inadequate, or worthless. (p. 137)

Along these lines, it may be important to consider the existence of specific developmental windows or critical periods during which equivalent abuse may have disparate effects (van der Kolk, 1987). For example, sexual abuse at adolescence may cause the victim to associate her maturing body with vulnerability to (or responsibility for) sexual assault, whereas effects at an earlier age may be very different.

It may therefore be particularly important to distinguish between early abuse, especially intrafamilial or extrafamilial abuse that occurs repeatedly with knowledge or suspicion on the part of parent figures, and later abuse, especially abuse that is extrafamilial and limited in severity, duration, or frequency. Whereas the former is likely to be incorporated into the woman's object-relational world and sense of self as degraded and worthless, the latter may be able to be assimilated by the victim/survivor as a traumatic event that happened *to* her but was not *about* her as a person, particularly when adequate personality integration and sense of self have developed (Haaken & Schlaps, 1991). Women who have internalized abuse as part of their basic sense of self will be especially apt to manifest psychological difficulties.

Next, a predisposition by family history to comorbid psychopathology, particularly affective disorders and alcohol and substance use disorders, may compound the abused woman's vulnerability to an eating disorder. Unusually high rates of mood disorders and alcohol and substance use disorders have been reported among the first-degree relatives of patients with restricting anorexia nervosa and bulimia nervosa (Bulik, 1987; Gwirtsman et al., 1983; Halmi et al., 1991; Hudson et al., 1983; Hudson et al., 1987; Piran et al., 1985), suggesting a biological connection among the disorders. A woman's preexisting affective, alcohol use, and/or substance use disorders may also predispose her to the later onset of an eating disorder as part of a pattern of impulse control deficits. However, although such links are certainly plausible, familial mechanisms of transmission and direction of causality—or the existence of a common factor underlying all conditions—remain unclear (Mitchell, 1990).

Deficits in affect regulation, which may arise from a combination of constitutional insufficiencies and early experience, constitute an additional risk factor for eating disorders among women abused in childhood. There is substantial evidence that trauma, including abuse, may lead to permanent physiological deficits in the capacity to cope with difficulty (van der Kolk, 1987, 1989). Temperament, which is thought to have a strong genetic component (Thomas & Chess, 1977), then will interact with the effects of environmental deficiencies or trauma (Strober, 1991). Though the method is highly self-destructive, several experts have speculated that eating disorders represent an effort to cope with overwhelming affective states and to aid in self-regulation in a group for whom self-regulation is deficient or virtually absent (Casper, 1983; Goodsitt, 1983; Johnson & Connors, 1987). Comorbid conditions such as alcohol and substance abuse may serve similar regulating functions; other conditions, such as depressive disorders, anxiety disorders, and borderline personality disorder, may reflect these deficits. Goodsitt (1983) described the difficulties of the eating disorder patient:

Be it food, impulses, moods, behavior, or relationships, these patients either swing wildly from one extreme to the other, or they find one end of the spectrum and remain frozen there. They are deficient in self-esteem and tension-regulation. They rely on external cues such as obsessively counting calories to determine how much to eat. When they are unable to do this, they vomit to control their food intake. Internal psychic mechanisms of self-regulation are not reliable. (pp. 53–54)

Along similar lines, Casper (1983) summarized the dilemma of the anorexia nervosa patient:

Food has lost its primary function of nourishment and is usurped for the regulation of feelings and intrapsychic tension states with a thin body bearing testimony to superb self-control and equanimity. (p. 390)

For the bulimia nervosa patient, on the other hand, "food is comforting and simultaneously overwhelming" (p. 391), initially providing tension reduction during a binge but then "experienced physically as distending and emotionally as an oppressive presence" (p. 391), leading to purging behavior.

Empirical work has supported these notions. For example, difficulty handling emotions, most commonly feelings of depression, anxiety, loneliness, boredom, and anger, have been found to be related to onset and relapse in bulimia nervosa (Johnson et al., 1982; Mitchell et al., 1985). Moreover, recent studies have supported the proposition that impulse dyscontrol is more common among abused than nonabused eating disorder patients (Bulik et al., 1989; Lacey, 1990, 1991). It would seem logical that those eating-disordered individuals with traumatic histories would have particular difficulty coping with strong, especially negative affect, and would be especially likely to use the disturbed eating behavior as a means of coping with posttraumatic disturbance, such as flashbacks and autonomic hyperarousal (Root, 1989, 1991). Indeed, Wonderlich and colleagues (1992) found that the reaction to abuse of female incest victims with a history of eating disorder versus those with no eating disorder history could be distinguished by greater abuse-related vulnerability and isolation, detachment, intrusive behavior and emotion, and emotional control and numbing, supporting the notion that eating disorders may be one means of aiding in the regulation of intense abuse-related affect.

Finally, specific environmental factors may render predisposed young women especially vulnerable to the development of eating disorders, as opposed to—or in addition to—the many other abuse-related psychopathological outcomes previously described. The family's role in the etiology and maintenance of eating disorders has been well described (e.g.,

Strober & Humphrey, 1987); hence, we will focus on additional influences we believe to be important. Specifically, we argue that familial and peer group concerns with appearances and dieting, the experience or subjective appraisal of overweight during adolescence, and appearance-related teasing by family or peers may be potent risk factors.

The endurance of appearance-related teasing, perception of oneself as unattractive, perception of oneself as overweight (with or without actual overweight), maternal body image and depression, and mother–daughter competition via dieting during childhood and adolescence have been found to be associated with bulimic symptoms and associated difficulties, including depression, low self-esteem, poor body esteem, and dissatisfaction with appearance among female adolescents and adults (Attie & Brooks-Gunn, 1989; Brown et al., 1989; Fabian & Thompson, 1989; Rierdan et al., 1988; Toro et al., 1989; Wooley & Kearney-Cooke, 1986).

Traditional and conflicted sex-role attitudes may also play a role in the complex interweaving of environmental variables that may increase vulnerability to eating disturbance. Rost, Neuhaus, and Florin (1982) compared sex-role attitudes and behaviors among women with bulimia and women without bulimic symptoms. They found that bulimic women were characterized by more traditional attitudes and behaviors and a passive orientation toward one's sex role, as well as a greater disparity between attitudes and actions (with attitudes considerably more liberal than behaviors). Nonbulimic women presented more consistent attitudes and behaviors. Young women's role confusion engendered by a large disparity between parental roles and traits, with mothers tending to do stereotypical female work, either at home or in the workplace, and fathers engaging in stereotypical male professions, has also been implicated in the etiology of bulimia nervosa (Wooley & Kearney-Cooke, 1986). Finally, an excessive desire to please men and to attain a stereotypical feminine image have been posited as related to bulimia (Boskind-Lodahl, 1976). Growing up in a society preoccupied with women's pursuit of thinness as a vehicle toward attaining success and personal efficacy (Garner et al., 1980), young women from such environments may be especially prone to initiating a diet, leading to the physical and psychological experience of deprivation, and in turn promoting a disturbed relationship to food (Mitchell, 1990). The transition from "normal" female dieting to severe dieting and associated behaviors, well-described as initiating both restrictor anorexia nervosa and bulimic disorders (e.g., Mitchell, 1990; Polivy & Herman, 1985), may be more likely among women with the difficulties and deficits enumerated.

CONCLUSION

In an effort to provide a preliminary model, we propose that both the immediate trauma and the negative developmental consequences of childhood abuse provide setting conditions for numerous forms of psychopathology, including eating disturbance. This process occurs through a variety of mechanisms that decrease the woman's ability to manage strong affect, increase her vulnerability to PTSD-type disturbance, and negatively affect her self-esteem. Temperamental vulnerabilities and familial expression of affective and substance use disorders constitute added predisposing factors. If a woman's disturbed eating behaviors then increase her ability to regulate dysphoria and anxiety, albeit in a highly destructive manner, an eating disorder may be more likely to develop from "normal" female dieting and concern with the attainment of a culturally endorsed body shape. Finally, exposure to "eating-disorder-genic" environments conducive to concern with body weight and shape and sex-role confusion, particularly in the home, would tend to increase the likelihood of the development of food- and body-related concerns specifically.

Clinical work with eating-disordered women abused in childhood presents a number of challenges. Such patients are likely to elicit strong countertransference reactions, ranging from deep empathy with the woman to identification with the aggressor (Wooley, 1991). Comorbid conditions frequently require intervention and special attention. A variety of symptom constellations in the impulse-control domain, representing efforts to regulate intense affect, may emerge and shift in the process of therapy (Root, 1989). However, especially for psychologically minded individuals, in-depth therapeutic examination of their eating behavior as reenactment or an effort to master the trauma of childhood abuse through repetition may help permit these women to relinquish their troubling behaviors. If the therapist can tolerate the intensity of the affect generated during the healing process, including such combinations as simultaneous deep dependence and overwhelming rage in relation to the therapist, participation in the woman's recovery process may bring great rewards.

REFERENCES

Alexander, P. C., & Lupfer, S. L. (1987). Family characteristics and long-term consequences associated with sexual abuse. *Archives of Sexual Behavior, 16,* 235–245.

Attie, I., & Brooks-Gunn, J. (1989). Development of eating problems in adolescent girls: A longitudinal study. *Developmental Psychology, 25,* 70–79.

Bagley, C., & McDonald, M. (1984). Adult mental health sequels of child sexual abuse, physical abuse and neglect in maternally separated children. *Canadian Journal of Community Mental Health, 3,* 15–26.

Bagley, C., & Ramsay, R. (1986). Sexual abuse in childhood: Psychosocial outcomes and implications for social work practice. *Journal of Social Work and Human Sexuality, 4,* 33–47.

Boskind-Lodahl, M. (1976). Cinderella's stepsisters: A feminist perspective on anorexia nervosa and bulimia. *Women, Culture, and Society, 2,* 342–356.

Briere, J. (1988). The long-term clinical correlates of childhood sexual victimization. *Annals of the New York Academy of Sciences, 528,* 327–334.

Briere, J., & Runtz, M. (1986). Suicidal thoughts and behaviours in former sexual abuse victims. *Canadian Journal of Behavioural Sciences, 18,* 413–423.

Briere, J., & Runtz, M. (1988). Multivariate correlates of childhood psychological and physical maltreatment among university women. *Child Abuse and Neglect, 12,* 331–341.

Briere, J., & Runtz, M. (1990). Differential adult symptomatology associated with three types of child abuse histories. *Child Abuse and Neglect, 14,* 357–364.

Brown, G. R., & Anderson, B. (1991). Psychiatric morbidity in adult inpatients with childhood histories of sexual and physical abuse. *American Journal of Psychiatry, 148,* 55–61.

Brown, T. A., Cash, T. F., & Lewis, R. J. (1989). Body-image disturbances in adolescent female binge-purgers. *Journal of Child Psychology and Psychiatry, 30,* 605–613.

Browne, A., & Finkelhor, D. (1986). The impact of child sexual abuse: A review of the research. *Psychological Bulletin, 99,* 66–77.

Bulik, C. M. (1987). Drug and alcohol abuse by bulimic women and their families. *American Journal of Psychiatry, 144,* 1604–1606.

Bulik, C. M., Sullivan, P. F., & Rorty, M. (1989). Childhood sexual abuse in women with bulimia. *Journal of Clinical Psychiatry, 50,* 460–464.

Burnam, M. A., Stein, J. A., Golding, J. M., Siegel, J. M., Sorenson, S. B., Forsythe, A. B., & Telles, C. A. (1988). Sexual assault and mental disorders in a community population. *Journal of Consulting and Clinical Psychology, 56,* 843–850.

Casper, R. C. (1983). Some provisional ideas concerning the psychologic structure in anorexia nervosa and bulimia. In P. L. Darby, P. E. Garfinkel, D. M. Garner, & D. V. Coscina (Eds.), *Anorexia nervosa: Recent developments in research* (pp. 387–392). New York: Alan R. Liss.

Casper, R. C. (1990). Personality features of women with good outcome from restricting anorexia nervosa. *Psychosomatic Medicine, 52,* 156–170.

Fabian, L. J., & Thompson, J. K. (1989). Body image and eating disturbance in young females. *International Journal of Eating Disorders, 8,* 63–74.

Finkelhor, D. (1987). The trauma of child sexual abuse: Two models. *Journal of Interpersonal Violence, 2,* 348–366.

Garner, D. M., Garfinkel, P. E., Schwartz, D., & Thompson, M. (1980). Cultural expectations of thinness in women. *Psychological Reports, 47,* 483–491.

Goldfarb, L. A. (1987). Sexual abuse antecedent to anorexia nervosa, bulimia, and compulsive overeating: Three case reports. *International Journal of Eating Disorders, 6,* 675–680.

Goodsitt, A. (1983). Self-regulatory disturbances in eating disorders. *International Journal of Eating Disorders, 2,* 51–60.

Gwirtsman, H. E., Roy-Byrne, P., Yager, J., & Gerner, R. H. (1983). Neuroendocrine abnormalities in bulimia. *American Journal of Psychiatry, 140,* 559–563.

Haaken, J., & Schlaps, A. (1991). Incest resolution therapy and the objectification of sexual abuse. *Psychotherapy, 28,* 39–47.

Hall, R. C. W., Tice, L., Beresford, T. P., Wooley, B., & Hall, A. K. (1989). Sexual abuse in patients with anorexia nervosa and bulimia. *Psychosomatics, 30,* 73–79.

Halmi, K. A., Eckert, E., Marchi, P., Sampugnaro, V., Apple, R., & Cohen, J. (1991). Comorbidity of psychiatric diagnoses in anorexia nervosa. *Archives of General Psychiatry, 48*, 712–718.

Herman, J. (1981). *Father-daughter incest.* Cambridge, MA: Harvard University Press.

Hudson, J. I., Pope, H. G., Jonas, J. M., & Yurgelun-Todd, D. (1983). Family history study of anorexia nervosa and bulimia. *British Journal of Psychiatry, 142*, 133–138.

Hudson, J. I., Pope, H. G., Jonas, J. M., Yurgelun-Todd, D., & Frankenburg, F. R. (1987). A controlled family history study of bulimia. *Psychological Medicine, 17*, 883–890.

Johnson, C., & Connors, M. E. (1987). *The etiology and treatment of bulimia nervosa.* New York: Basic Books.

Johnson, C. L., Stuckey, M. K., Lewis, L. D., & Schwartz, D. M. (1982). Bulimia: A descriptive survey of 316 cases. *International Journal of Eating Disorders, 2*, 3–16.

Krugman, S. (1987). Trauma in the family: Perspectives on the intergenerational transmission of violence. In B. A. van der Kolk (Ed.), *Psychological trauma* (pp. 127–151). Washington, DC: American Psychiatric Press.

Lacey, J. H. (1990). Incest, incestuous fantasy, and indecency: A clinical catchment area study of normal-weight bulimic women. *British Journal of Psychiatry, 157*, 399–403.

Lacey, J. H. (1991). Childhood sex abuse and incest in a bulimic population. *BASH Magazine, 10*, 77–80.

Mitchell, J. E. (1990). *Bulimia nervosa.* Minneapolis: University of Minnesota Press.

Mitchell, J. E., Davis, L., & Goff, G. (1985). The process of relapse in patients with bulimia. *International Journal of Eating Disorders, 4*, 457–463.

Piran, N., Kennedy, S., Garfinkel, P. E., & Owens, M. (1985). Affective disturbance in eating disorders. *Journal of Nervous and Mental Disease, 173*, 395–400.

Polivy, J., & Herman, C. P. (1985). Dieting and bingeing: A causal analysis. *American Psychologist, 40*, 193–201.

Pope, H. G., & Hudson, J. I. (1992). Is childhood sexual abuse a risk factor for bulimia nervosa? *American Journal of Psychiatry, 149*, 455–463.

Rieker, P. P., & Carmen, E. H. (1986). The victim-to-patient process: The disconfirmation and transformation of abuse. *American Journal of Orthopsychiatry, 56*, 360–370.

Rierdan, J., Koff, E., & Stubbs, M. L. (1988). Gender, depression, and body image in early adolescence. *Journal of Early Adolescence, 8*, 109–117.

Root, M. P. P. (1989). Treatment failures: The role of sexual victimization in women's addictive behavior. *American Journal of Orthopsychiatry, 59*, 542–549.

Root, M. P. P. (1991). Persistent, disordered eating as a gender-specific, post-traumatic stress response to sexual assault. *Psychotherapy, 28*, 96–102.

Root, M. P. P., & Fallon, P. (1989). Treating the victimized bulimic. *Journal of Interpersonal Violence, 4*, 90–100.

Rost, W., Neuhaus, M., & Florin, I. (1982). Bulimia nervosa: Sex role attitude, sex role behavior, and sex role related locus of control in bulimarexic women. *Journal of Psychosomatic Research, 26*, 403–408.

Sedney, M. A., & Brooks, B. (1984). Factors associated with a history of childhood sexual experiences in a nonclinical female population. *Journal of the American Academy of Child Psychiatry, 23*, 215–218.

Sloan, G., & Leichner, P. (1986). Is there a relationship between sexual abuse or incest and eating disorders? *Canadian Journal of Psychiatry, 31*, 656–660.

Strober, M. (1980). Personality and symptomatological features in young, nonchronic, anorexia nervosa patients. *Journal of Psychosomatic Research, 24*, 353–359.

Strober, M. (1991). Disorders of the self in anorexia nervosa: An organismic-developmental paradigm. In C. Johnson (Ed.), *Psychodynamic treatment of anorexia nervosa and bulimia* (pp. 354–373). New York: Guilford Press.

Strober, M., & Humphrey, L. L. (1987). Familial contributions to the etiology and course of anorexia nervosa and bulimia. *Journal of Consulting and Clinical Psychology, 55*, 654–659.

Surrey, J., Swett, C., Michaels, A., & Levin, S. (1990). Reported history of physical and sexual abuse and severity of symptomatology in women psychiatric outpatients. *American Journal of Orthopsychiatry, 60*, 412–417.

Thomas, A., & Chess, S. (1977). *Temperament and development.* New York: Brunner/ Mazel.

Tice, L., Hall, R. C. W., Beresford, T. P., Quinones, J., & Hall, A. K. (1989). Sexual abuse in patients with eating disorders. *Psychiatric Medicine, 7*, 257–267.

Tong, L., Oates, K., & McDowell, M. (1987). Personality development following sexual abuse. *Child Abuse and Neglect, 11*, 371–383.

Toro, J., Castro, J., Garcia, M., Perez, P., & Cuesta, L. (1989). Eating attitudes, sociodemographic factors and body shape evaluation in adolescence. *British Journal of Medical Psychology, 62*, 61–70.

Tsai, M., Feldman-Summers, S., & Edgar, M. (197). Childhood molestation: Variables related to differential impacts on psychosexual functioning in adult women. *Journal of Abnormal Psychology, 88*, 407–417.

van der Kolk, B. A. (1989). The compulsion to repeat the trauma. *Psychiatric Clinics of North America, 12*, 389–411.

van der Kolk, B. A. (1987). The separation cry and the trauma response: Developmental issues in the psychobiology of attachment and separation. In B. A. van der Kolk (Ed.), *Psychological trauma* (pp. 31–62). Washington, DC: American Psychiatric Press.

Wonderlich, S., Donaldson, M. A., Staton, D., Carson, D., Gertz, L., & Johnson, M. (1992, April). Eating disturbance and incest. Paper presented at the fifth International Conference on Eating Disorders, New York.

Wooley, S. C. (1991). Uses of countertransference in the treatment of eating disorders: A gender perspective. In C. Johnson (Ed.), *Psychodynamic treatment of anorexia nervosa and bulimia* (pp. 245–294). New York: Guilford Press.

Wooley, S. C., & Kearney-Cooke, A. (1986). Intensive treatment of bulimia and body image disturbance. In K. D. Brownell & J. P. Foreyt (Eds.), *Physiology, psychology and treatment of eating disorders* (pp. 476–502). New York: Basic Books.

3

Prevalence and Process of Disclosure of Childhood Sexual Abuse Among Eating-Disordered Women*

KATHERINE J. MILLER**

This study examined childhood sexual abuse (CSA) prevalence and the process of disclosure among 100 eating-disordered women in residential treatment. A question on the intake questionnaire asked about sexual abuse, and subjects were interviewed about childhood sexual experiences after four or more weeks of treatment using inverted funnel questioning. Thirty percent reported sexual abuse on the intake questionnaire, while 61% reported CSA at the interview. Data gathered on abuse variables were used to make comparisons with community studies. Only 45.8% of the 131 perpetrators had been disclosed within a year of occurrence, two-thirds of these to

*This study is based on dissertation research conducted while at Temple University. Data were collected in 1989 at The Renfrew Center in Philadelphia, and the cooperation and support of the Renfrew staff and residents are gratefully acknowledged.

**The author thanks Maria Root for her encouragement to publish this research, and Portia Hunt, David Gleaves, Max Molinaro, Jacquelyn Zavodnick, Rachel Ginzberg, and Andrea Haupt for their help in preparing the manuscript. Mary Ann Heverly provided statistical consultation.

family or peers/acquaintances before residential treatment. Methodological and clinical implications are discussed.

The prevalence of childhood sexual abuse (CSA) and long-term sequelae within eating-disordered populations are topics that have been under increasing empirical investigation in the last eight years (Conners & Morse, 1993; Pope & Hudson, 1992). Researchers have used widely varying definitions of sexual abuse and methodologies, which makes findings difficult to compare. Only two studies have compared CSA prevalence in DSM-III-R eating-disordered samples with community populations, an issue which pertains to the question of what, if any, are the connections between CSA and eating disorder pathology. Stuart, Laraia, Ballenger, and Lydiard (1990) found that 50% of the bulimia nervosa group reported CSA, while 28% of normal controls did, a large but statistically insignificant difference. Steiger and Zanko (1990) reported a 30% prevalence rate for anorexia and bulimia nervosa patients, and 33% for normal controls; bulimics with no history of anorexia reported a 46% rate of CSA, while restricting anorectics reported 6%.

CSA prevalence has been reported to be between 6% (Siegel et al., 1987) and 62% (Wyatt, 1985) in US community studies. In eating-disordered populations, CSA rates have reportedly ranged from 20% (Ross et al., 1989) to 69% (Abramson & Lucido, 1991; Folsom et al., 1993). These studies vary in definition of CSA and methodology, and also include different diagnoses, treatment settings, and length of treatment. Few studies report data on abuse variables such as age of victim, frequency of abuse, sexual acts, or relationship, sex, and age of the perpetrator.

The extreme variation in CSA prevalence rates may reflect, in part, nondisclosure based on psychological reactions to the abuse itself. That is, many victims of CSA evidence dissociative symptoms in which memories, images, feelings, and/or sensations are removed from conscious awareness; this has been demonstrated in nonclinical (Briere & Runtz, 1988b), clinical (Briere & Conte, 1993; Briere & Runtz, 1988a; Chu & Dill, 1990; Herman & Schatzow, 1987; Ross et al., 1989), and eating-disordered samples (Vanderlinden et al., 1993). Herman and Schatzow (1987) and Briere and Conte (1993) found evidence that worse abuse (e.g., earlier, longer, more physical injury) produces more amnesia, and others have found that worse abuse is less often disclosed (Farrell, 1988; Hall et al., 1989). Some CSA victims have full-blown posttraumatic stress disorder (PTSD) at some point in their lives (Rowan & Foy, 1993), which, according to DSM-III-R criteria (APA, 1987), is characterized by alternating numbing/amnestic and reexperiencing phases. What this means for researchers is that asking about CSA during an amnestic phase would yield a false negative.

Other survivors who do remember the abuse may avoid talking about it because of shame and guilt, fear of "going crazy" or losing control, fear of stigmatization, and mistrust of authority figures (Courtois, 1988). Many of them have experienced adverse reactions from those to whom they have disclosed, such as disbelief, humiliation, or abandonment (Herman & Hirschman, 1977; Waller, 1991). Others handle the feelings about the abuse by minimizing its severity, since it has terrifying effects on basic assumptions about themselves and the world (Janoff-Bulman, 1992). Victims tend to blame themselves and see themselves as unworthy, as well as seeing the world as a less safe and meaningful place.

In a national survey, Finkelhor, Hotaling, Lewis, and Smith (1990) found that only 33% of CSA events had ever been disclosed to anyone. Regarding women with eating disorders, Abramson and Lucido (1991) found that none of the bulimics in their study had previously disclosed their sexual abuse, while all of the nonclinical controls had. Stuart et al. (1990) found that 78% of the bulimic group who had been raped or sexually molested had disclosed the abuse, compared with 100% of the controls and 66% of those with major depressive disorder. Hall et al. (1989) found that most sexual abuse had not been disclosed to previous caregivers, with the exception of rape; the least likely type of abuse to be disclosed was incest with penetration. These studies give conflicting evidence about disclosure in nonclinical groups and eating-disordered groups.

Methodological Issues

Other differences among prevalence rates rest on the definition of CSA, with the more inclusive definitions gaining higher rates. In addition, some studies are vague about the definition of CSA. The ages defining childhood, the range of sexual behaviors included, intrafamilial and/or extrafamilial perpetrators, requirement of the use of force, and peer abuse are all areas of variation. Wyatt and Peters (1986a) demonstrated the importance of definition by reanalyzing Wyatt's 1985 data by Russell's (1983) narrower definition; Wyatt's rate changed from 62% to 42%, making it very close to Russell's finding of 38%.

The framing of questions in CSA prevalence studies is especially critical given the sensitive nature of the topic and the propensity of survivors to forget the events, classify them as nonabusive, or take the blame for them. Funnel-type questions (Kahn & Cannell, 1957) such as "Have you ever been sexually abused?'' require subjects to recall their experiences, categorize them as abusive, and then evaluate if they apply to the questioner's intent. ''Yes'' answers are followed by detailed questions. Inverted funnel questioning reverses this order and asks many specific and overlapping questions that define what the researcher is asking about. By asking about different behaviors, categories of perpetrators, and time periods, the researcher can facilitate the recovery and identification of abuse memories (Wyatt & Peters, 1986b). Russell (1983) and Wyatt (1985) have found the highest CSA rates among community studies using interviews with inverted funnel questioning as well as trained interviewers, matched to subjects by race and sex.

It is clear that direct questioning about CSA elicits many more reports than chart review or expecting clients to initiate the disclosure (Briere & Zaidi, 1989; Stinson & Hendrick, 1992). In earlier studies it appeared that interviews elicited more reports than questionnaires (Wyatt & Peters, 1986b), although this was confounded by the fact that most questionnaires used funnel questioning. Waller (1991) and Stinson and Hendrick (1992) found no differences in CSA prevalence rates between administering a questionnaire in written or verbal form at intake. Dill, Chu, Grob, and Eisen (1991) compared brief questioning about abuse at intake interviews to subsequent responses to comprehensive questionnaires; they found the sexual abuse rate rose from 35% to 52%. It appears therefore that thoroughness of the questioning is more critical than format. Several researchers have noted that some clients are willing to disclose CSA only after developing a therapeutic relationship (e.g., Hall et al., 1989; Palmer et al., 1990; Waller, 1991).

The secrecy surrounding CSA makes it difficult to corroborate, but 74% of Herman and Schatzow's (1987) group of incest survivors were able to obtain outside confirmation of their CSA. In addition, 9% did not ask directly but had family members indicate they had also been sexually abused; 11% did not try to obtain corroboration, and only 6% tried and could not obtain it. Coons and Milstein (1986) found 17 of 20 reports of CSA by patients with multiple personality disorder to be corroborated by a family member or emergency room reports. Nigg et al. (1991) interviewed informants for 11 borderline subjects who had reported CSA, and the report was confirmed by 7 (64%).

Abuse Variables

Recent reviews of CSA sequelae in adulthood have suggested that use of force, abuse by a father or stepfather, penetration, and greater number of perpetrators are most harmful; there are contradictory findings on duration, frequency, and age of abuse (Beitchman et al., 1992; Browne & Finkelhor, 1986). Severity of abuse has been found to be associated with personality disorder and anorexia, bulimic subtype (McClelland et al., 1991; Waller, 1993). Two studies have found severity of eating disorder symptomatology to correlate with higher numbers of CSA events (Abramson & Lucido, 1991; Williams et al., 1992).

In summary, the literature demonstrates widely varying CSA rates in both community and eating-disordered populations. Subjects are unable or unwilling to disclose CSA because of responses to the CSA such as amnesia, shame, minimization, and fears about others' responses to disclosure. Higher CSA rates are found with broader definitions of CSA, inverted funnel questioning, and a greater level of trust in the investigator. Many studies lack a clear definition of CSA and fail to report abuse variables. Few have examined the process of disclosure.

This study of eating-disordered women in residential treatment was designed to remove barriers to disclosure as much as possible in examining CSA prevalence. The methodology was modeled after Russell's (1983) and Wyatt's (1985) community studies, which have reported the highest prevalence rates. Details on abuse variables are reported to facilitate comparisons with other studies and to provide a clearer picture of the range of experiences suffered by this population. Finally, this study examines the process of disclosure to learn more about when, under what conditions, to whom, and with what results survivors disclosed.

A modification of Wyatt's (1985) definition of CSA was used to facilitate comparisons, since it was the broadest and would allow examination of subcategories of the data. Childhood sexual abuse was defined in this study as interactions in which a child under age 18 is being used for the sexual stimulation of the perpetrator or another person, where the perpetrator is an adult or five or more years older than the victim. Consensual peer interactions, when the peer is not more than five years older, are not considered abuse. Any sexual acts which are done against the person's will are considered abuse.

Noncontact abuse includes being exposed to exhibitionism, verbal sexual abuse, voyeurism, and solicitations or sexual advances not acted on. Russell's (1983) definitions of levels of sexually abusive acts were used for the contact abuse. Level 1, *very serious sexual abuse,* includes completed and attempted vaginal, oral, and anal intercourse; cunnilingus, and analingus. Level 2, *serious sexual abuse,* is completed and attempted genital fondling, simulated intercourse, and digital penetration. *Least serious abuse,* Level 3, includes completed and attempted acts of intentional sexual touching of buttocks, thigh, leg or other body part, clothed breasts or genitals, and unwanted kissing. All three categories include forced and unforced acts.

The use of force, physical coercion used to gain someone's participation in sexual activities, includes engaging in sexual activities with someone while the person is unable to consent, as, for example, when asleep or incapacitated because of drugs or alcohol.

METHOD

Subjects

The sample consisted of the first 100 clients at a residential treatment center for eating-disordered women who were aged 18 and older and who consented to participate in the study after four or more weeks of treatment. Of the 127 potential subjects 17 left the program before their fifth week and so were unavailable. Of the 110 eligible there was a 91% participation rate; three were judged by their primary clinicians to be too fragile for the interview, three residents did not want to participate, three missed their appointments and could not be rescheduled, and one began the interview but became too upset when discussing her family to continue.

Using DSM-III-R criteria (APA, 1987), 89 subjects had bulimia nervosa and 11 anorexia nervosa (seven restricting, four bulimic subtype). Subjects came from all sections of the United States, ranged from 18 to 40 years of age (X = 24.06); all were Caucasian; 81% were single and 19% married; 89% had at least some college education, and most came from middle- to upper-class socioeconomic status. Prior outpatient therapy averaged 1.68 years (SD = 2.55), ranging from 0 to 10 years, and only seven subjects had had no prior therapy. Twenty-seven had been hospitalized between one and 10 times for their eating disorders, and eight had been psychiatric inpatients for other reasons.

The average age at onset of the eating disorder was 16.27 years (SD = 4.11, range 10–35 years) with a mean duration of 7.79 years (SD = 4.07). Weight at entry into the program, compared with the Metropolitan (1983) tables for lowest mortality, was 107.25% for bulimics (n = 89) and 85% for anorectics. The average fluctuation between lowest and highest adult weights was 39.55 pounds (SD = 21.82).

For descriptive purposes, diagnostic groups were contrasted using one-way ANOVAs; the only statistically significant differences were current weight, lowest adult weight (but not highest adult weight or difference between highest and lowest), and average age of onset (bulimics = 15.73 years; restricting anorectics = 20.0 years; bulimic anorectics = 21.0 years).

Instruments

Background and Trauma History Interview Schedule. The questions asked in the semistructured interview moved from nonthreatening material to the sexual abuse questions. Sections were demographic data, family relationships, traumatic stressors and symptoms, eating disorder history and symptoms, drug and alcohol use, and childhood sexual experiences and adult sexual abuse. The last section was modified from the published questions from Russell's (1983) and Wyatt's (1985) studies; it contained 18 specific, general, and overlapping questions consistent with the inverted funnel method. Examples are, "During childhood and adolescence (before age 18), did anyone ever expose themselves (their sexual organs) to you?" "Did a relative, family friend or stranger ever touch or fondle your body, including your breasts or genitals, or attempt to arouse you sexually?" "During childhood and adolescence, did anyone ever feel you, grab you, or kiss you in a way you felt was sexually threatening or inappropriate, even if some of it was pleasurable to you?" When an instance of childhood sexual abuse was reported, a series of specific questions was asked regarding age at abuse; age, sex, and relationship of the perpetrator; sexual acts; age and receiver of disclosure; outcome of disclosure; initial and long-term effects of the abuse; and if and when the incident had been discussed in therapy.

Chart Information. The intake questionnaire, modified from Johnson's (1985) Diagnostic Survey for Eating Disorders, yielded age and marital status, and the answer to the question "Have you ever been sexually abused?" Residents were asked to check "No"; "Yes, 1–2 times"; "Yes, 3–5 times"; or "Yes, more than 5 times."

Procedures

Each client was contacted in week four of her stay in residential treatment, with the permission of her primary clinician, to explain the nature of the study and invite her participation. The interview was described as including questions about her background, eating disorder, and childhood sexual experiences. If she agreed, an interview was scheduled when the consent form was signed and the Background and Trauma History Questionnaire administered, followed by debriefing of her feelings about the experience. The subjects were assured the interviews were confidential, including from the staff.

RESULTS

Prevalence

Results regarding abuse variables are presented in Table 3-1. Sixty-one percent of the 100 subjects were sexually abused before age 18 by noncontact or contact abuse; 58% suffered contact abuse, and 3% noncontact abuse only. The age range of onset of abuse was 2–17 years, with an average of 10.75 years. Eighteen percent of the CSA victims were sexually abused once, with a median occurrence of three times (adding frequencies for all perpetrators for each subject).

Fifty percent of the subjects reported sexual abuse with the use of force. The *most serious level* of abuse (Level 1) was reported by 31% of the 100 subjects; for 23% it involved intercourse. Most abuse was by adults, and most were familiar people; one-fourth of the sample reported CSA by one or more family members, and almost half by acquaintances.

There were 131 perpetrators; 112 (85.5%) used contact abuse, 27 (19.1%) intercourse, and 83 (63.4%) force. Average age of the perpetrators was 27.4 years (SD = 16.4), ranging from 8 to 74 years. In terms of age level, 68.7% were adults, 22.9% adolescents, and 8.4% children. Six perpetrators (4.6%) were female—sister, cousin, grandmother, and three girlfriends—and 125 (95.4%) were male; 24.4% of perpetrators were family members, 61.1% acquaintances, and 14.5% strangers.

The reported age of onset of the eating disorder was *after* the earliest reported CSA for 85.3% of the abused subjects.

Disclosure

On the intake questionnaire, 65 subjects reported that they had never been sexually abused, 30 reported some sexual abuse, and 5 did not answer the question. Two of the affirmative responses related to sexual abuse in adulthood, according to the reports in the research interviews. Thus 33% of the subjects reported CSA in the research interview which they did not disclose on the intake questionnaire. Of the 30 who did report sexual abuse, 10 reported a lower frequency at intake than in the later research interview.

Only 60 (45.8%) of the perpetrators had been disclosed within a year of occurrence. The CSA by 104 of the 131 perpetrators (79.4%) had been disclosed to one or more persons prior to the research interview. Eighty-eight (67%) of the perpetrators had been reported to family and/or friends, and sometimes authorities or therapists in addition, before residential treatment, and 16 perpetrators (12.2%) were disclosed for the first time

TABLE 3-1
Abuse Variables for Percentages of Sample and CSA Group

Variables	% of Sample (N = 100)	% of Victims (N = 61)
Relationship of perpetrator		
Father, stepfather	5.0	8.2
Sibling, stepsibling	14.0	23.0
Extended family	13.0	21.3
Acquaintance	47.0	77.0
Stranger	19.0	31.1
Use of force	50.0	82.0
Number of perpetrators		
1	21.0	34.4
2	21.0	34.4
3–5	18.0	29.5
6–9	1.0	1.6
Severest level of sexual acts		
Level 1	31.0	50.8
Level 2	15.0	24.6
Level 3	12.0	19.7
Noncontact abuse	3.0	4.9
Frequency of CSA		
Once	11.0	18.0
Twice	12.0	19.7
3–9 times	18.0	29.5
10–99 times	12.0	19.7
100 or more times	8.0	13.1
Total duration of all CSA		
less than 0.1 year	26.0	42.6
0.1–1.0 year	13.0	21.3
1.1–2.9 years	9.0	14.8
3.0–18.0 years	12.0	19.7
Sex of perpetrators		
Male	59.0	96.7
Female	6.0	9.8
Perpetrator age level		
Adult	51.0	83.6
Adolescent	18.0	29.5
Child	11.0	18.0

during residential treatment. The sexual abuse by 27 of the 131 perpetrators, or 20.6%, had never been disclosed to anyone before the research interview.

Authorities or former therapists were never sole recipients of disclosure, whereas 9.2% of the perpetrators were disclosed only to a family member and 15.3% only to a peer or friend.

TABLE 3-2
Recipients of Disclosure About 104 Perpetrators by Level of Abuse

Recipient	Percentages of Perpetrators				
	1[a]	2	3	Noncontact	Total
Family	28.6	37.9	48.0	80.0	43.3
Peer/friend	42.9	37.9	48.0	33.3	41.3
Authority	8.6	0.0	4.0	40.0	9.6
Former therapist	31.4	37.9	28.0	6.7	28.8
Current therapist	77.1	69.0	56.0	6.7	59.6

[a]Level 1 = most serious, 2 = serious, 3 = least serious.

There were major differences in the recipients of disclosure according to the severity of sexual behaviors experienced (see Table 3-2). For family members there was an inverse relationship between disclosure and severity of abuse, while for former and current therapists greater severity correlated with a greater likelihood of disclosure. Peers/friends received the largest number of disclosures of Level 1 abuse prior to residential treatment, and equal numbers of disclosures to family members for Levels 2 and 3. Noncontact abuse was reported to family and authorities far more than any contact abuse.

The 104 disclosed CSA events were compared with the 27 events not disclosed prior to the research interview on abuse variables using chi-squares, and there were no significant differences on age of abuse, duration, frequency, severity of sexual acts, or perpetrator age, sex, or relationship. Because of small cell sizes there may have been insufficient power to detect a relationship, particularly in three instances. All CSA that lasted three or more years had been disclosed to at least one person previously. The nondisclosed group of events had more acquaintances as perpetrators (81.5% vs. 55.8%) and more Level 3 abuse (48.1% vs. 24.0%) than the disclosed group.

Subjects were asked about the responses to and outcomes of each disclosure, and about their feelings about the responses and outcomes. Based on these reports, each disclosure was categorized by the researcher as receiving a positive/neutral, negative, or mixed response in the subject's eyes. Disclosures to most confidants received positive or neutral reactions, but this was true for only about half of family recipients (see Table 3-3).

The known consequences of disclosure for the perpetrators were few. Nine were reported to the police—six exhibitionists and three rapists; three were prosecuted and two penalized. Eight disclosures to other authority figures resulted in effectively stopping the abuse, with only one perpetrator being penalized.

TABLE 3-3
Subjects' Evaluations of Responses to CSA Disclosure

Recipient	Positive or Neutral	Negative	Mixed
Family	24	10	11
Peer/acquaintance	37	4	2
Authority	8	0	2
Former therapist	29	1	0
Current therapist	62	0	0

DISCUSSION

The 61% prevalence rate of CSA in this eating-disordered population appeared about the same as Russell's (1983) and Wyatt's (1985) community studies. Since slightly different CSA definitions were used, however, the data from this study were reanalyzed following Wyatt's example (Wyatt & Peters, 1986a). To conform to Russell's (1983) "narrow definition" of CSA, all noncontact CSA and all extrafamilial sexual experiences between ages 14 and 17 except rape and attempted rape were deleted. Z-tests were performed to determine whether the proportions of each category in this sample differed significantly from the proportions reported by Russell and Wyatt. This sample then reported significantly more total CSA and more extrafamilial CSA than both Russell's and Wyatt's samples (see Table 3-4).

Second, the data were altered according to Wyatt's (1985) original criteria by omitting the six cases where the partner was five or more years older but participation was voluntary. The total CSA rate was comparable,

TABLE 3-4
CSA Prevalences Using Russell's "Narrow Definition":
Percentages of Subjects in Three Studies

Category of CSA	Russell (N=930)	Wyatt (N=248)	Miller (N=100)
Intrafamilial	16	21	23
Extrafamilial	31	29	45[a]*
Intrafamilial and extrafamilial	9	8	13
Intrafamilial and/or extrafamilial	38	42	55[b]*

[a]comparison with Russell, $z = 3.03$; with Wyatt, $z = 3.53$
[b]comparison with Russell, $z = 3.50$; with Wyatt, $z = 2.63$
*$p<.01$

TABLE 3-5
CSA Prevalences Using Wyatt's Definition of CSA

Category of CSA	Wyatt (N=248)	Miller (N=100)	z-value
Contact abuse			
Intrafamilial	21%	24%	0.74
Extrafamilial	32%	51%	4.07*
Intrafamilial and extrafamilial	8%	16%	2.95*
Intrafamilial and/or extrafamilial	45%	58%	2.61*
Noncontact abuse only	17%	3%	3.73*
Contact and/or noncontact abuse	62%	61%	0.21

*$p<.01$

but Wyatt's sample had significantly more noncontact abuse only, while this sample had significantly more contact abuse in all but the intrafamilial only category (see Table 3-5).

This eating-disordered sample, then, reported significantly more contact CSA than Russell's (1983) and Wyatt's (1985) community samples using the same definitions, with extrafamilial contact abuse accounting for the difference. One might expect a population in intensive treatment to disclose more of their abuse experiences even if the actual prevalences were equal because of the intensive search to understand their lives, at least in an environment that accepted them. It is unclear, however, why this would occur only with the extrafamilial CSA. It could be that its actual occurrence is higher in eating disorder groups; Beckman and Burns (1990) found significantly more forced extrafamilial CSA before age 12 among bulimic subjects than in normal controls. Another possibility is that incest is underreported in community and/or eating disorder groups more than extrafamilial CSA.

The percentages of each level of abuse were tabulated for the five categories of relationship of the perpetrator, and the cells were compared with Russell's (1983) data, using her definition of CSA. Using z-tests to compare proportions, significantly more siblings or stepsiblings in this study used Level 1 sexual acts ($z = 1.95$, $p<.05$), Level 2 acts ($z = 2.66$, $p<.01$), and Level 3 acts ($z = 3.71$, $p<.001$), and more strangers perpetrated Level 3 acts ($z = 6.88$, $p<.001$) than in Russell's study. Significantly more acquaintances in Russell's study used Level 2 sexual acts ($z = -2.16$, $p<.05$) and more strangers used Level 1 acts ($z = -1.92$, $p<.05$) than in this study.

The percentages of perpetrators by relationship to victim (five categories) were compared with Wyatt's figures using her criteria. There were no significant differences between father/stepfather or extended family frequencies, but this study found significantly more CSA by siblings/stepsiblings ($z = 4.81$, $p<.001$) and acquaintances ($z = 6.37$, $p<.001$), while Wyatt found more CSA by strangers ($z = -7.16$, $p<.01$).

The finding of higher sibling/stepsibling CSA in this sample is one that needs further exploration, in that it could be related to family variables such as mutual neglect and lack of support (Humphrey, 1988).

The use of force reported in this study was 50% for the entire sample, or 82% of the abuse survivors. This is a much higher rate than Wyatt's 25% or Russell's 41% and could indicate that CSA experiences of eating-disordered women are more violent than those of other groups. However, it could also be that this method of questioning, which asked about subjects' attempts to get away from the abuser or stop the abuse, elicited more information about their subjective experiences and/or enabled them to recognize that physical coercion was a factor in the experience.

The range of forms and degrees of violence within the criteria of force suggest that future studies would do well to define levels of force. While fear and shame over helplessness were concomitants of being overpowered in any way, some types of force were more frightening or degrading than others.

The pattern of disclosure in this study showed that less than half of the perpetrators were reported to anyone within one year of the occurrence of sexual abuse, and two-thirds had been disclosed to family or peers and friends. Most felt ashamed or guilty. Typical reasons given for not disclosing were that others would not understand, believe, and/or do anything about the abuse. These fears were strongly felt in relation to parents, and the worst abuse was reported more to peers/acquaintances than to parents. Furthermore, almost half of disclosures to parents did result in some negative experience for the victim, ranging from lack of empathy to humiliation or lack of protection, while only 10 perpetrators are known to have suffered any negative consequences for their actions. Nevertheless, the majority of disclosures received positive or neutral responses. While these disclosure experiences are not unique to eating-disordered women, they do indicate the clinical importance of inquiring about prior disclosures—why one did or did not disclose, results, and perceptions and feelings about others' responses.

The finding that 60% of the CSA—12% for the first time—was disclosed in the residential treatment setting supports Josephson and Fong-Beyette's (1987) findings that reasons for disclosure include direct questioning by counselors, encouragement by others, and the belief that disclosure would help them feel better.

On the other hand, some subjects had not told even their current therapists about certain CSA experiences because they compared their abuse to even worse experiences shared by others in group therapy and feared they would either appear foolish by seeming to overdramatize, or become a focal point of therapeutic work to the same degree as someone else when they felt it was not needed or wanted. Clients needed to know that they could choose when to work on this issue, although it was hard to distinguish this distrust from the fear of experiencing feelings associated with sexual abuse. Several felt relieved after divulging their secrets in the interview and decided to incorporate them into their therapy sessions. Researcher confidentiality was essential.

The most commonly reported reasons for not disclosing CSA prior to the research interview were embarrassment/shame and fear of the listeners' reactions (14 subjects). Others said the events were "not important" or blamed themselves. Six cases were boyfriends at age 16 or 17 who were more than five years older, and sex was voluntary; this speaks to an overly broad element in the definition of CSA, which is not useful.

The findings of this study can best be generalized to women with similar demographic and clinical characteristics. The subjects were mainly middle- to upper-SES, well-educated, white, an average of 24 years old, bulimic, and had had prior therapy. The treatment setting was more intensive than outpatient, but one that screened out those with the severest psychiatric and medical problems.

The limitations of this study include all of the problems of a retrospective study, such as failure to recall or report CSA, or even giving false reports, although many reports had been validated by family or friends during the treatment.

The results of this study portray very serious sexual abuse experiences among an eating-disordered population. Comparisons with community studies by Russell (1983) and Wyatt (1985) suggest the possibility that there is more extrafamilial contact CSA and more sibling/stepsibling abuse among eating-disordered women. The examination of disclosure demonstrates the clinical importance of asking directly about CSA, preferably in an inverted funnel style, understanding that clients may have to overcome distrust born of experience to discuss it.

REFERENCES

Abramson, E. E., & Lucido, G. M. (1991). Childhood sexual experience and bulimia. *Addictive Behaviors, 16,* 529–532.

American Psychiatric Association (1987). *Diagnostic and statistical manual of mental disorders* (3rd ed., rev.). Washington, DC: APA.

Beckman, K. A., & Burns, G. L. (1990). Relation of sexual abuse and bulimia in college women. *International Journal of Eating Disorders, 9,* 487–492.

Beitchman, J. H., Zucker, K. J., Hood, J. E., DaCosta, G. A., Akman, D., & Cassavia, E. (1992). A review of the long-term effects of child sexual abuse. *Child Abuse & Neglect, 16,* 101–118.

Briere, J., & Conte, J. (1993). Self-reported amnesia for abuse in adults molested as children. *Journal of Traumatic Stress, 6,* 21–31.

Briere, J., & Runtz, M. (1988a). Post sexual abuse trauma: Data and implications for clinical practice. *Journal of Interpersonal Violence, 2,* 367–369.

Briere, J., & Runtz, M. (1988b). Symptomatology associated with childhood sexual victimization in a nonclinical adult sample. *Child Abuse & Neglect, 12,* 51–59.

Briere, J., & Zaidi, L. Y. (1989). Sexual abuse histories and sequelae in female psychiatric emergency room patients. *American Journal of Psychiatry, 146,* 1602–1606.

Browne, A., & Finkelhor, D. (1986). Impact of child sexual abuse: A review of the research. *Psychological Bulletin, 99,* 66–77.

Chu, J. A., & Dill, D. L. (1990). Dissociative symptoms in relation to childhood physical and sexual abuse. *American Journal of Psychiatry, 147,* 887–892.

Conners, M. E., & Morse, W. (1993). Sexual abuse and eating disorders: A review. *International Journal of Eating Disorders, 13,* 1–11.

Coons, P. M., & Milstein, V. (1986). Psychosexual disturbances in multiple personality: Characteristics, etiology, and treatment. *Journal of Clinical Psychiatry, 47,* 106–110.

Courtois, C. A. (1988). *Healing the incest wound: Adult survivors in therapy.* New York: Norton.

Dill, D. L., Chu, J. A., Grob, M. C., & Eisen, S. V. (1991). The reliability of abuse history reports: A comparison of two inquiry formats. *Comprehensive Psychiatry, 32,* 166–169.

Farrell, L. T. (1988). Factors that affect a victim's self-disclosure in father-daughter incest. *Child Welfare, 67,* 462–468.

Finkelhor, D., Hotaling, G., Lewis, I. A., & Smith, C. (1990). Sexual abuse in a national survey of adult men and women: Prevalence, characteristics, and risk factors. *Child Abuse & Neglect, 14,* 19–28.

Folsom, V., Krahn, D., Nairn, K., Gold, L., Demitrack, M. A., & Silk, K. R. (1993). The impact of sexual and physical abuse on eating disordered and psychiatric symptoms: A comparison of eating disordered and psychiatric inpatients. *International Journal of Eating Disorders, 13,* 249–257.

Hall, R. C. W., Tice, L., Beresford, T. P., Wooley, B., & Hall, A. K. (1989). Sexual abuse in patients with anorexia nervosa and bulimia. *Psychosomatics, 30,* 73–79.

Herman, J. L., & Hirschman, L. (1977). Father-daughter incest. *Signs: Journal of Women in Culture and Society, 2,* 735–756.

Herman, J. L., & Schatzow, E. (1987). Recovery and verification of memories of childhood sexual trauma. *Journal of Orthopsychiatry, 56,* 137–141.

Humphrey, L. L. (1988). Relationships within subtypes of anorexic, bulimic, and normal families. *Journal of the American Academy of Child & Adolescent Psychiatry, 27,* 544–551.

Janoff-Bulman, R. (1992). *Shattered assumptions: Towards a new psychology of trauma.* New York: Free Press.

Johnson, C. (1985). Initial consultation for patients with bulimia and anorexia nervosa. In D. M. Garner & P. E. Garfinkel (Eds.), *Handbook of psychotherapy for anorexia nervosa and bulimia* (pp. 19–51). New York: Guilford Press.

Josephson, G. S., & Fong-Beyette, M. L. (1987). Factors assisting female clients' disclosure of incest during counseling. *Journal of Counseling & Development, 65,* 475–478.

Kahn, R. L., & Cannell, C. F. (1957). *The dynamics of interviewing: Theory, technique and cases.* New York: Wiley.

McClelland, L., Mynors-Wallis, L., Fahy, T., & Treasure, J. (1991). Sexual abuse, disordered personality and eating disorders. *British Journal of Psychiatry, 158* (Suppl. 10), 63–68.

Metropolitan Life Foundation (1983). 1983 Metropolitan height and weight tables. *Statistical Bulletin, 64,* 2–9.

Nigg, J. T., Silk, K. R., Westen, D., Lohr, N. E., Gold, L. J., Goodrich, S., & Ogata, S. (1991). Object representation in the early memories of sexually abused borderline patients. *American Journal of Psychiatry, 148,* 864–869.

Palmer, R. L., Oppenheimer, R., Dignon, A., Chaloner, D. A., & Howells, K. (1990). Childhood sexual experiences with adults reported by women with eating disorders: An extended series. *British Journal of Psychiatry, 156,* 699–703.

Pope, H. G., Jr., & Hudson, J. I. (1992). Is childhood sexual abuse a risk factor for bulimia nervosa? *American Journal of Psychiatry, 149,* 455–463.

Ross, C. A., Heber, S., Norton, G. R., & Anderson, G. (1989). Differences between multiple personality disorder and other diagnostic groups on structured interview. *Journal of Nervous & Mental Disease, 177,* 487–491.

Rowan, A. B., & Foy, D. W. (1993). Post-traumatic stress disorder in child sexual abuse survivors: A literature review. *Journal of Traumatic Stress, 6,* 3–20.

Russell, D. E. H. (1983). The incidence and prevalence of intrafamilial and extrafamilial sexual abuse of female children. *Child Abuse & Neglect, 7,* 133–146.

Siegel, J. M., Sorenson, S. B., Golding, J. M., Burnam, M. A., & Stein, J. A. (1987). The prevalence of childhood sexual assault: The Los Angeles Epidemiologic Catchment Area project. *American Journal of Epidemiology, 126,* 1141–1153.

Steiger, H., & Zanko, M. (1990). Sexual traumata among eating-disordered, psychiatric, and normal female groups. *Journal of Interpersonal Violence, 5,* 74–86.

Stinson, M. H., & Hendrick, S. S. (1992). Reported child sexual abuse in university counseling center clients. *Journal of Counseling Psychology, 39,* 370–374.

Stuart, G. W., Laraia, M. T., Ballenger, J. C., & Lydiard, R. B. (1990). Early family experiences of women with bulimia and depression. *Archives of Psychiatric Nursing, 4,* 43–52.

Vanderlinden, J., Vandereycken, W., van Dyck, R., & Vertommen, H. (1993). Dissociative experiences and trauma in eating disorders. *International Journal of Eating Disorders, 13,* 187–193.

Waller, G. (1991). Sexual abuse as a factor in eating disorders. *British Journal of Psychiatry, 159,* 664–671.

Waller, G. (1993). Association of sexual abuse and borderline personality disorder in eating disordered women. *International Journal of Eating Disorders, 13,* 259–263.

Williams, H. J., Wagner, H. L., & Calam, R. M. (1992). Eating attitudes in survivors of unwanted sexual experiences. *British Journal of Clinical Psychology, 31,* 203–206.

Wyatt, G. E. (1985). The sexual abuse of Afro-American and white-American women in childhood. *Child Abuse & Neglect, 9,* 507–519.

Wyatt, G. E., & Peters, S. D. (1986a). Issues in the definition of child sexual abuse in prevalence research. *Child Abuse & Neglect, 10,* 231–240.

Wyatt, G. E., & Peters, S. D. (1986b). Methodological considerations in research on the prevalence of child sexual abuse. *Child Abuse & Neglect, 10,* 241–251.

4

Dissociation and Physical Abuse as Predictors of Bulimic Symptomatology and Impulse Dysregulation

CATHY S. RETO

CONSTANCE J. DALENBERG

MICHAEL T. COE

The current study examined the relationship among physical abuse, dissociation, bulimic symptomatology, and impulse dysregulation. Subjects were 126 female and 57 male undergraduate and graduate psychology students. Child physical abuse, as measured by the Violence History Questionnaire, was reported by 32% of the sample. The results of this study provide support for the role of violence history in predicting the presence and severity of bulimic symptomatology and impulse dysregulation. Additionally, violence effects were gender specific, yielding higher correlations to bulimia in men and impulsivity in women. Dissociation, though predictive of bulimia for women, did not clearly function as a mediator of violence history.

The reconceptualization of dissociation from an isolated defense mechanism to a dispositional style of escaping and avoiding overwhelming thoughts and emotions has significant clinical and theoretical implications for a variety of disorders. In addition to a host of disorders delineated by dissociation (APA, 1987), the contribution of dissociation to other diagnoses such as posttraumatic stress disorder, substance abuse, and eating disorders is emerging in a growing body of literature.

Several authors have provided theoretical and anecdotal accounts of a dissociative mechanism at work in individuals presenting with eating disorders. Clinical descriptions of bulimia frequently include feelings of depersonalization, derealization, disturbances of self, psychomotor numbing, and amnesia (McCallum et al., 1992; Root, 1991; Sands, 1991; Torem, 1986, 1992). Empirical evidence of increased hypnotizability (Groth-Marnat & Schumaker, 1990; Pettinati et al., 1985) as well as a wide array of cognitive and perceptual distortions is well documented (Powers et al., 1987). Comparatively, it appears that eating disorder subjects evidence significantly more dissociative phenomena than normal controls (Demitrack et al., 1990). Overall, dissociative experiences are reported more frequently in bulimics than anorectics (Pettinati et al., 1985; Sanders, 1986; Vanderlinden et al., 1993). A contiguous relationship between episodes of bingeing, purging, active dietary restriction, and dissociated experiences has recently been suggested (McCallum et al., 1992).

Recently, several authors have linked the overdevelopment of a dissociative response to those clients presenting with histories of childhood abuse (Briere, 1989; Chu & Dill, 1990). Likewise, a number of eating-disordered women report histories of victimization (Oppenheimer et al., 1985; Root & Fallon, 1988). It is conceivable that the dissociative symptoms seen within the eating disorders have their genesis in earlier traumatic experiences. Currently, the vehicle of trauma most frequently discussed in relation to eating disorders is that of childhood sexual abuse (CSA). Vanderlinden et al. (1993) have shown significantly higher levels of dissociative experiences in eating-disordered subjects with histories of sexual abuse and suggest that trauma-induced dissociation plays a role in the development of bulimia.

Presently, the empirical findings linking sexual abuse and eating disorders are equivocal and do not adequately support a hypothesized causal relationship. Aggregate studies indicate prevalence rates of 7% to 66% for CSA in eating-disordered populations (Abramson & Lucido, 1991; Connors & Morse, 1993; Lacey, 1990; Oppenheimer et al., 1985; Pope & Hudson, 1992), with most estimates of abuse within this population higher than the normative findings for women. Although compelling, these findings have been attributed to the high base rates of both disordered eating and CSA in clinical populations (Finn et al., 1986) as well as other methodological difficulties (Pope & Hudson, 1992).

Controlled studies attempting to establish a direct relationship yield conflicting results. Smolak, Levine, and Sullins (1990) found that abused undergraduates had higher scores on the Eating Disorders Inventory (EDI: Garner et al., 1983) than nonabused undergraduates, while others have found no relationship between sexual abuse and disordered eating in clinical samples (Bulick et al., 1989; Finn et al., 1986). Disparities across sample populations, diagnostic groups, and definitions of both eating disorders and CSA make direct comparisons between studies problematic.

These findings, however, do not serve to nullify the possibility of a connection, but simply suggest that abuse is neither necessary nor sufficient for the occurrence of an eating disorder. Further empirical attempts to elucidate this complex relationship require variables salient to both abuse and eating disorders to be partialled out and analyzed with respect to their mediating or moderating effects.

Although overall correlations of CSA and bulimia do not appear meaningful, significant relationships that do emerge appear to stem from sexual abuse experiences entailing physical force. In their examination of sexual abuse and bulimia, Calam and Slade (1988) report that experiences of forced sexual abuse yielded the only significant correlations to the total Eating Attitudes Test (EAT: Garner & Garfinkle, 1979; Garner et al., 1982) and the EAT Dieting and Bulimia subscales. In their attempt to establish a connection between CSA and bulimia, Beckman and Burns (1990) found the only CSA experience significantly differentiating bulimics from nonbulimics was forced sex with a nonrelative after age 12. Waller (1992) reports that bulimic subjects who experienced forced CSA showed significantly higher frequencies of bingeing than the unforced abuse or nonabused groups, and suggests that force may serve as an index of severity. Abramson and Lucido (1991) report that a fearful and/or shocking response to the CSA event was not only significantly correlated to the Bulimia Test (BULIT: Smith & Thelan, 1984) but was found to be the most significant predictor of BULIT scores, accounting for 44% of the variance.

To date, the focus within the eating disorder/abuse literature has been on CSA. However, the significance of physical force and threat as well as fear and shock suggests that physical child abuse and/or violent sexual abuse may be more powerful predictors of bulimia than sexual abuse in general. In the first study to delineate victimization by type, Root and

Fallon (1988) report that 29.1% of their abused bulimic sample report histories of physical abuse and 28.5% report sexual abuse. Bailey and Gibbons (1989) found that child physical abuse (CPA), *not* CSA, was significantly correlated to both the presence and severity of bulimia. Odds ratios of 10.4 for physical abuse versus 1.4 for molestation demonstrate the strength of this relationship. Correspondingly, in an examination of both sexually and physically abused subjects, McCallum et al. (1992) found that those subjects experiencing physical abuse, *not* sexual abuse, tended to report higher levels of dissociative experiences.

Bailey and Gibbons's (1989) work is particularly sophisticated in its analysis of bulimia, which was treated as both a categorical and a continuous variable. However, in keeping with several studies using categorical data, physical abuse was analyzed by a single item ("Were you ever physically abused as a child?"). Root and Fallon's (1988) assessment, while based on a questionnaire (BREDS: Root & Fallon, 1983) and a more extensive clinical interview, still yielded a yes/no victimization outcome. In this research, a continuous measure of violence history, Dalenberg's (1982) Violence History Questionnaire (VHQ), was utilized.

Clearly the analysis of a meaningful relationship between childhood abuse and bulimia calls for greater methodological sophistication. Mediational models of abuse and eating disorders have not been tested sufficiently in the current literature. As such, the current study represents a preliminary exploration of connections among dissociation, physical abuse, and bulimic symptomatology as well as a test of a provisional mediation model.

The present study represents a subset of a larger investigation of the factor structure and predictive utility of the Bernstein and Putnam (1986) Dissociative Experiences Scale (DES). The DES, the VHQ, and the Drive for Thinness, Bulimia, and Impulse Regulation subscales of the EDI were used to explore the following hypotheses:

1. Disciplinary actions including physical violence experienced in childhood were predicted to lead to greater use of dissociation, which in turn should predict greater eating disorder symptomatology. A two-stage forced hierarchical regression analysis was used to test this model. Evidence for dissociation mediating the relationship between violence history and bulimic symptoms would accrue if either DES measure significantly predicted eating symptoms while the relationship between violence history and eating symptoms became nonsignificant. On the other hand, evidence for independent, additive effects for dissociation and violence history would accrue if both the VHQ and DES retained significant regression weights in the second step. The use of the final forced simultaneous regression to test for the effects of dissociation and violence follows

the recommendations of Briere's (1988) excellent methodological review on child abuse research.

2. The roles of violence history and dissociation in predicting Drive for Thinness were hypothesized to be additive, rather than following the mediational model described above. Violence history, but not dissociation, was expected to predict problems with impulse control.

METHOD

Subjects

Subjects were 100 community college psychology students and 83 first-year graduate students from three community colleges and two graduate institutions in Southern California. Of these, 114 were participants in a normative survey for a revised dissociation measure, during which they completed measures for the study reported here; 69 subjects completed the measures at the beginning of a related experimental study.

Participants were 57 males and 126 females, ranging in age from 17 to 59, with a mean age of 29.5. Ethnic background reported by subjects was 169 Caucasian and 14 Hispanic. Forty-five subjects were married, 62 "in a committed relationship," 32 dating, and 43 "not currently involved."

Relationship status had no significant effect on any criterion measure. Undergraduate students reported greater drive for thinness ($F(1,181) = 5.30, p < .03$) and more impulse regulation problems than graduate students ($F(1,181) = 7.58, p < .01$). Ethnic background affected several variables, so 14 subjects from distinct ethnic groups were excluded (since insufficient sample size would not allow an analysis of differences). Hispanics endorsed infrequently scored dissociative items at a higher rate than Caucasians ($F(1,181) = 4.69, p < .04$). When variance due to subject source and race were statistically removed, there were no significant differences according to situation (normative survey versus experimental setting) or age. Gender differences are reported in detail below.

Part of the strength of this study rests in its continuous measurement of physical violence history. However, for purposes of comparison, it could be noted that 38 females (30% of the female sample) and 20 males (35% of the male sample) reported types of violence defined as "nonordinary" by Gelles and Straus (1988).

Measures

Dissociation was assessed with a revised 41-item version of the Dissociative Experiences Scale (DES: Bernstein & Putnam, 1986), which is currently in development by the authors. For the present study, only the first 28 items were used, corresponding to the original 28-item measure. Subjects rated these original items on a modified six-point scale ranging from "never" to "more than once a week." A subscale was empirically derived for this study by selecting DES items with heavily skewed distributions that were very rarely endorsed in the sample; items 3–5, 8, and 11 were thus combined to form an extreme dissociative experience subscale to help differentiate normal from extreme dissociation.

Eating disorder symptoms were measured using three subscales from the EDI (Garner et al., 1983): Drive for Thinness, Bulimia, and Impulse Regulation. Drive for Thinness is reported to be the best general predictor of disordered eating; Bulimia was chosen to aid in specifying results for bulimic symptoms; Impulse Regulation, with items relating to cognitive, affective, behavioral, and relationship instability, was chosen for its likely relationship to violence and dissociation.

Childhood physical abuse was assessed with the Violence History Questionnaire (VHQ: Dalenberg, 1982), a 12-item scale of family violence and discipline techniques experienced in childhood. This instrument has been demonstrated to have acceptable test-retest reliability (r's > .82, p < .001) over a three-month period. In tests of discriminant validity, the scale identified 22% of a college freshmen sample (n = 1,260) and 100% of a court-referred physically abused sample (n = 42) as abused (Dalenberg, 1982). The VHQ includes subscales for Violence (total of all endorsed violence items) and Nonordinary Violence (items which are endorsed with low frequency in the population and which are predictive of multiple and extreme forms of family violence). The total score reflects the total amount of disciplinary actions (violent or nonviolent) experienced by the subject as a child.

Procedures

Subjects in the normative survey read a brief nonspecific description of the purposes of the study, then filled out a demographic questionnaire, the revised DES, a five-item attachment-style questionnaire, the EDI subscales, and the VHQ. Packets were administered in classroom settings, followed by a short debriefing and discussion of issues relating the study to class material.

Subjects in the experimental study read a similar brief introduction to the study, then filled out the questionnaires in the same order, after which a series of other tasks were completed. These subjects were tested individually, and were individually debriefed following the entire experimental procedure.

TABLE 4-1
Means or Frequency of Demographics and Key Variables

	Females n=126		Males n=57	
Age	30.8	(10.5)	26.6	(7.9)
Race				
Caucasian	118		51	
Hispanic	8		6	
Bulimia	1.20	(2.35)	.67	(1.57)
Impulse Regulation	2.02	(3.75)	2.19	(2.88)
Drive for Thinness	4.55	(5.78)	1.56	(3.01)
Violence History	19.68	(12.26)	20.53	(11.64)
DES Total	30.05	(12.23)	31.74	(12.93)
DES Extremes	1.13	(1.64)	1.23	(1.70)

Note. Means are reported prior to residualizing on race and subject source. Standard deviations are in parentheses.

RESULTS

Gender differences on both eating disorder measures and violence history instruments are frequently reported in the literature (Briere, 1989). Bulimia in particular is reported to be more common in female samples (Halmi et al., 1981). Thus, regression analyses were separately conducted for men and women (see Table 4-1 for means and standard deviations on key variables).

All main analyses were performed after residualizing data based on subject source and race to remove variance associated with these factors. In the first step, the VHQ was entered predicting bulimia scores, in order to test for a relationship between violence history and bulimic symptoms. In the second step, DES total and DES extreme scores were added to the model. After residualization, the VHQ predicted the Bulimia and Impulse Regulation subscales of the EDI for both male and female samples (see Table 4-2). For Bulimia, the variance accounted for by the VHQ was higher for men than for women (21% vs. 3%); in fact, the prediction equation for women reached only marginal significance ($F(1,123) = 3.57$, $p < .07$). In contrast, large percentages of the variance in Impulse Regulation were accounted for by the VHQ in both male and female samples (12% vs. 17%; F's > 7.42, p's $< .01$). Violence did not predict the Drive for Thinness variable.

The two dissociation subscales (the total DES and the Extremes subscale) incremented variance accounted for only in bulimia and only in the female subsample. The final R-squared values, reported in Table 4-2, exceed 10% for male and female samples on Bulimia and Impulse Regulation.

TABLE 4-2
Multiple Correlations (R^2) for EDI Subscales
Predicted by Violence History and Dissociation

	Violence History	Dissociation Variables	Dissociation and Violence
Bulimia			
Females	.03*	.08***	.10***
Males	.21***	.03	.26***
Impulse Regulation			
Females	.17***	.01	.17***
Males	.12***	.04	.15**
Drive for Thinness			
Females	.01	.02	.03
Males	.02	.03	.05
Bulimia × Impulse Regulation			
Females	.11***	.01	.11***
Males	.12***	.02	.16**

Note. Female n = 126, Male n = 57.
*p < .10; **p < .05; ***p < .01

The results of the hierarchical regressions (Table 4-2) and the final beta weight equations (see Table 4-3) are supportive of a role for *both* dissociation and violence history in the prediction of Bulimia, but not in the prediction of Impulse Regulation or Drive for Thinness. It is interesting to note that the dissociation scales were related to violence history in the female sample only ($F(2,122)$ = 3.46, p <.05).

An interaction variable, Bulmia × Impulse Regulation, was created to assess the role of violence history and dissociation in predicting subjects high on both variables. This new measure, theoretically linked to violence history by Lacey (1990), was highly associated with scores on the VHQ (see Tables 4-2 and 4-3) for both men and women.

Previous research in this area has suggested that violence history may be linked to the severity as well as the presence or absence of bulimic symptoms (Abramson & Lucido, 1991; Waller, 1992). In order to assess the VHQ and DES as predictors of severity of symptoms, the regressions described above were recalculated for Bulimia and Impulse Regulation using only those subjects who reported some symptoms (see Tables 4-4 and 4-5). The VHQ remained a powerful predictor of Bulimia and Impulse Regulation for women and approached significance for men. In women, the VHQ captured more variance as a predictor of severity than it had as a predictor of population symptomatology.

TABLE 4-3
Final Regression Weights for Violence and Dissociation Variables

	Violence History	DES Extremes	DES Total
Bulimia			
Females	.13	.29***	−.05
Males	.48***	−.24*	.05
Impulse Regulation			
Females	.42***	−.03	.01
Males	.34**	−.14	.21
Drive for Thinness			
Females	.03	.14	.02
Males	.17	−.20	.09
Bulimia × Impulse Regulation			
Females	.34***	.08	−.09
Males	.37***	−.20	.06

Note. Female n = 126, Male n = 57.
*$p < .10$; **$p < .05$; ***$p < .01$

TABLE 4-4
**Multiple Correlations (R^2) for Violence History and
Dissociation Variables Predicting Severity of Symptoms**

	Violence History	Dissociation Variables	Dissociation and Violence
Bulimia			
Female (*n*=43)	.12*	.10*	.19**
Males (*n*=13)	.35*	.21	.47
Impulse Regulation			
Females (*n*=62)	.28***	.00	.30***
Males (*n*=38)	.10*	.07	.17*

*$p < .10$; **$p < .05$; ***$p < .01$

TABLE 4-5
Final Regression Weights for Predictors of Symptom Severity

	Violence History	DES Extremes	DES Total
Bulimia			
Females (*n*=43)	.73***	−.06	.12
Males (*n*=13)	.51*	−.48	.31
Impulse Regulation			
Females (*n*=62)	.60***	−.14	−.04
Males (*n*=38)	.32**	−.23	.30

*$p < .10$; **$p < .05$; ***$p < .01$

DISCUSSION

The intriguing results of a survey study such as this one raise as many scientific questions as are answered. Both violence history and dissociation were implicated in the prediction of the EDI subscale of Bulimia for women, but the pattern was not clearly mediational. Dissociation did aid in the prediction of Bulimia for women, but the significance of the beta weight for the VHQ remained essentially stable. Mediation would predict a drop in VHQ beta weight significance (Pedhazur, 1982). Violence history was a strong predictor of impulse dysregulation for both men and women, and neither variable was an important predictor of Drive for Thinness. Replicating Bailey and Gibbons (1989), childhood violence history predicted both presence of bulimic symptomatology and severity of it, as it did presence and severity of impulse dysregulation.

Although the smaller male sample limits the conclusions that one may draw from this work, the sex differences that did emerge are interesting. For impulse dysregulation, violence history accounted for 12% of the variance for men ($p < .01$) and 17% for women ($p < .01$). Eliminating the zeros from the data (examining the effects of violence and dissociation on severity of symptoms), the corresponding figures were 10% ($p < .10$) and 28% ($p < .01$) with respectable sample sizes (38 men and 62 women). In contrast, violence in the full sample predicted 3% of the variance in bulimic symptomatology for women ($p < .10$) and 21% for men ($p < .01$); eliminating zeros, the figures were 12% ($p < .10$) and 34% ($p < .10$), with a questionable sample size for men (13 men and 43 women). Overall, more variance in impulse dysregulation is accounted for by violence in the female sample as compared to the male group, while the opposite is true for bulimia. Here, more variance in male bulimic symptomatology is accounted for by violence than in female bulimic symptomatology. Given this difference, one wonders, since bulimic symptoms are historically less common (and perhaps less acceptable) in men, whether serious trauma may be more prominent in their etiology. Since society may be less condemning of bulimia in women, the threshold for the behavior may be lower and the affective precursors less extreme than would be true for men. The same would be true for the male who is impulse disordered; since society is less disapproving, less serious or traumatic preconditions may be necessary to produce the behavior.

The sex difference in dissociation also is interesting. Dissociation predicted only one of the three EDI scales, Bulimia, and the increment was significant only for women. Although consideration of type 1 error risk should be made, the sample size and significance levels both suggest that this single relationship is worth pursuing. Again, it is possible that social desirability pressure against admitting dissociative symptoms differs in strength for men and women, or, in keeping with Spiegal (1984), that the predisposition to dissociation is biologically or genetically determined (and X chromosome-linked). As was true for the other measures discussed, dissociation is a complex phenomenon which was measured here in a fairly simplistic way. At least one study (Duvenage & Dalenberg, 1992), which is in the process of replication, has demonstrated that subscales of the DES may separately predict abuse-related phenomena (state dependent amnesia) in significant and *opposite* directions within the same analysis. Similarly, McCallum et al. (1992) found results for the DES in the prediction of self-harm using only the Depersonalization factor, while the full scale showed less significant results. Our own research direction at present is in modification of the DES to better assess *types* of abuse-related dissociation.

The mechanism whereby physical abuse exerts its effect on bulimia, assuming for the moment this causal direction, is discussed but rarely tested in the literature. For instance, Root and Fallon (1988, p. 170) state that it is simplistic to regard physical victimization as a ''cause'' of bulimia; rather, ''physical victimization experiences contribute to a woman's vulnerability to developing bulimia . . . as a way to cope with her anger, powerlessness, and depression following physical boundary violations.'' This suggests that particular cognitive-affective mediators between violence history and bulimia may be found rather than a direct link. It is thus interesting that Bailey and Gibbons's (1989) single-item measure of a perceptual label, which may or may not be a result of violence (''Were you ever physically abused as a child?''), *was* a powerful predictor of bulimia; our instrument, which asks the subject to report frequency and type of parental violence without subjective evaluation of its abusiveness, is also a predictor. Our own work with the VHQ has established that the cutoff for subject self-label of ''abused child'' is highly individual, and that the two measures (self-reported frequency of violent discipline and self-reported label of abuse) are surprisingly orthogonal. Forty-two percent of subjects reporting ''nonordinary violence'' (defined as types of parental violence utilized by less than 20% of the normative sample of Gelles and Straus, 1988) in our largest sample ($n = 226$) did not self-label as abused, despite multiple occurrences of parental discipline through burning, biting, kicking, or beating with an object.

The fact of abuse and the interpretation of it may well function separately to enhance the likelihood of abuse-related symptomatology such as bulimia and impulse dysregulation. Two recent dissertations from our research team (Jacobs, 1989; Post, 1990) have verified that "meanings" given to physical and sexual abuse correlate with the magnitude and type of symptoms displayed by adult victims of abuse (see Dalenberg & Jacobs, 1993). Dissociation and bulimia may develop then as a method of continuous effort to remain unaware of the emotional reactions to such meanings. In this way the bulimia itself becomes a dissociative mechanism using obsessions with food and weight in addition to bingeing and purging as a primary way of splitting off feelings and memories related to traumatic experiences (see Root, 1991). This route is supported by Heatherton and Baumeister's (1991) work on binge eating as an "escape from self-awareness." Escape through bulimia also may allow the individual to reexperience the affects associated with the trauma while exerting some control over the event.

On the other hand, certain routes from physical abuse to dissociation seem less meaning dependent. Dissociation as a means of separating self from body is a normal human response (and quite an effective one; see Giolas and Sanders, 1992); it is possible that those regularly subjected to physical pain become habitual dissociators. Here the dissociation would be related to the likelihood or severity of pain rather than the meaning given to the abuse. Dissociation learned as a response to physical pain thus may reduce the aversive aspects or qualities of bulimic episodes and allow one to more easily engage in this behavior.

It also should be noted that the DES is not a clinical instrument designed to differentiate between DSM-III-R diagnoses. The dissociative disorders may be more reliably identified through use of the Dissociative Disorders Interview Schedule (DDIS: Ross et al., 1989) or the Structured Clinical Interview for DSM-III-R Dissociative Disorders (SCID-D: Steinberg et al., 1990). In future research, use of a subgroup of subjects identified as dissociative by either of these diagnostic instruments would be particularly interesting.

Further work on the connection between bulimia, impulsivity, and physical abuse thus might fruitfully examine the multiple potential causal pathways by including specific assessment of frequency and severity of violence, subject labeling of the experience as abusive, and subject understanding of the perpetrator's act. Similarly, it is possible that certain types of bulimic patients (e.g., multi-impulse disordered patients, see Lacey, 1990) may be more likely to show violence history as an important etiological factor. Briere (1992) has made a cogent argument for use of instruments that are more abuse-specific, written precisely to measure the pathology most likely to stem from a physical or sexual abuse history.

In addition to use of more sophisticated measures of both violence and eating disorders, examination of potential mediators of the violence-bulimia connection is needed to address the methodological problems inherent in research designs such as ours. For instance, it has long been known that alcohol abuse is quite frequent in the physical abuse perpetrator population (Kempe & Kempe, 1978). More recently, elevated rates of alcoholism and alcohol abuse have been reported by researchers of bulimia (e.g., Bulik, 1987; Hudson et al., 1983). Thus, it is possible that the bulimia-abuse connection is not causal at all, but is an artifact of the joint connection of these phenomena with alcohol misuse (Pope & Hudson, 1992). While certainly plausible, it should be noted that both alcohol misuse by a parent and child physical or sexual abuse at the hands of an adult are more prevalent than is bulimic symptomatology, particularly among males, and research still must answer the question of why some children of violent and alcoholic homes develop bulimic pathology while others do not.

Finally, note should be taken of the use of a nonclinical population to assess the dissociation-abuse connection. Using college populations with near 100% participation has great advantages in making such assessments (see Haugaard & Emery, 1989); however, such nonclinical populations may need to be much larger than was utilized here in order to contain sufficient numbers of extreme eating-disordered or abused individuals. Use of a clinical population, a method subject to sampling bias and labeling bias, provides a different and perhaps more distorted picture, but allows more depth in the analysis of severity and pathology. In a larger nonclinical sample, it may be found that the abuse-dissociation connection, and the abuse-bulimia connection, if they exist, may be nonlinear, such that a certain threshold of violence or dissociation must be reached before the combination would precipitate pathology. Further, a larger sample would allow separate regression analyses within ethnic groups, testing for the possible mediational properties of culturally related attitudes toward eating and violence.

In conclusion, the results of this research strongly support the role of violence history in the prediction of bulimic symptomatology and impulse dysregulation. Although dissociation did play a significant part in the prediction of bulimia for women, the role of dissociation as a mediator of abusive events is less clear. At this point, gender-specific investigation, particularly work that acknowledges and examines the societally distinct roles of men and women, is the best route to this knowledge. Further work requires more sophisticated measurement of each of the contributors to this equation—dissociation, child abuse history, and bulimia—as well as the examination of gender-specific models.

REFERENCES

Abramson, E. E., & Lucido, G. M. (1991). Childhood sexual experience and bulimia. *Addictive Behaviors, 16,* 529–532.

American Psychiatric Association. (1987). *Diagnostic and statistical manual of mental disorders* (3rd ed., rev.). Washington, DC: APA.

Bailey, C. A., & Gibbons, S. G. (1989). Physical victimization and bulimic-like symptoms: Is there a relationship? *Deviant Behavior, 10,* 335–352.

Beckman, K. A., & Burns, G. L. (1990). Relation of sexual abuse and bulimia in college women. *International Journal of Eating Disorders, 9,* 487–492.

Bernstein, E. M., & Putnam, F. W. (1986). Development, reliability, and validity of a dissociation scale. *Journal of Nervous and Mental Disease, 174,* 727–735.

Briere, J. N. (1988). Controlling for family variables in abuse effects research: A critique of the "partialling" approach. *Journal of Interpersonal Violence, 3,* 80–89.

Briere, J. N. (1989). *Adults molested as children: Beyond survival.* New York: Springer.

Briere, J. N. (1992). *Child abuse trauma: Theory and treatment of the lasting effects.* Newbury Park, CA: Sage.

Bulik, C. M. (1987) Drug and alcohol abuse by bulimic women and their families. *American Journal of Psychiatry, 144,* 1604–1606.

Bulik, C. M., Sullivan, P. F., & Rorty, M. (1989). Childhood sexual abuse in women with bulimia. *Journal of Clinical Psychiatry, 50,* 460–464.

Calam, R. M., & Slade, P. D. (1988). Sexual experience and eating problems in female undergraduates. *International Journal of Eating Disorders, 8, 391–397.*

Chu, J. A., & Dill, D. L. (1990). Dissociative symptoms in relation to childhood physical and sexual abuse. *American Journal of Psychiatry, 147,* 887–892.

Connors, M., & Morse, W. (1993). Sexual abuse and eating disorders: a review. *International Journal of Eating Disorders, 13,* 1–11.

Dalenberg, C. J. (1982). *Violence history questionnaire: Psychometric evaluation.* Denver: Institute of Child Abuse and Neglect Monograph.

Dalenberg, C. J., & Jacobs, D. A. (1993). Attributional analyses of child abuse episodes: A response to Hunter, Goodwin and Wilson, 1993. Manuscript submitted for publication.

Demitrack, M. A., Putnam, F. W., Brewerton, T. D., Brandt, H., & Gold, P. W. (1990). Relation of clinical variables to dissociative phenomena in eating disorders. *American Journal of Psychiatry, 147,* 1184–1188.

Duvenage, C. A., & Dalenberg, C. J. (1992, January). Child abuse, hypnotizability, and dissociation as predictors of amnesiac barrier strength in a normal population. Paper presented at the San Diego Child Maltreatment Conference.

Finn, S. E., Hartman, M., Leon, G. R., & Lawson, L. (1986). Eating disorders and sexual abuse: Lack of confirmation for a clinical hypothesis. *International Journal of Eating Disorders, 5,* 1051–1060.

Garner, D. M., & Garfinkel, P. E. (1979). The eating attitudes test: An index of the symptoms of anorexia nervosa. *Psychological Medicine, 9,* 273–279.

Garner, D. M., Olmstead, M. P., Bohr, Y., & Garfinkel, P. E. (1982). The eating attitudes test: Psychometric features and clinical correlates. *Psychological Medicine, 12,* 871–878.

Garner, D. M., Olmstead, M. P., & Polivy, J. (1983). Development and validation of a multidimensional eating disorder inventory for anorexia nervosa and bulimia. *International Journal of Eating Disorders, 2,* 15–34.

Gelles, R. S., & Straus, M. (1988). *Intimate violence.* New York: Simon & Schuster.

Giolas, M. H., & Sanders, B. (1992). Pain and suffering as a function of dissociation level and instructional set. *Dissociation: Progress in the Dissociative Disorders, 5,* 205–209.

Groth-Marnat, G., & Schumaker, J. F. (1990). Hypnotizability, attitudes toward eating, and concern with body size in a female college population. *American Journal of Clinical Hypnosis, 32,* 194–199.

Halmi, K., A., Falk, J. R., & Schwartz, E. (1981). Binge eating and vomiting: A survey of a college population. *Psychological Medicine, 11,* 697–706.

Haugaard, J. J., & Emery, R. E. (1989). Methodological issues in child sexual abuse research. *Child Abuse and Neglect, 13,* 89–100.

Heatherton, T., & Baumeister, R. (1991). Binge eating as escape from self-awareness. *Psychological Bulletin, 110,* 86–108.

Hudson, J. I., Pope, H. G., Jonas, J. M., Yurelun-Todd, D., & Frankenburg, F. R. A controlled family history study of bulimia. *Psychological Medicine, 17,* 883–890.

Jacobs, D. A. (1989). A schematic analysis of child physical abuse. Unpublished doctoral dissertation, California School of Professional Psychology, San Diego.

Kempe, R. S., & Kempe, C. H. (1978). *Child abuse.* Cambridge, MA: Harvard University Press.

Lacey, J. H. (1990). Incest, incestuous fantasy and indecency; A clinical catchment areas study of normal-weight bulimic women. *British Journal of Psychiatry, 157,* 399–403.

McCallum, K. E., Lock J., Kulla, M., Rorty, M., & Wetzel, R. D. (1992). Dissociative symptoms and disorders in patients with eating disorders. *Dissociation, 5,* 227–235.

Oppenheimer, R., Howells, K., Palmer, R. L., & Chaloner, D. A. (1985). Adverse sexual experience in childhood and clinical eating disorders: A preliminary description. *Journal of Psychiatric Research, 19,* 357–361.

Pedhazur, E. J. (1982). *Multiple regression in behavioral research: Explanation and prediction.* New York: Harcourt, Brace, Jovanovich.

Pettinati, H. M., Horne, R. J., & Staats, J. (1985). Hypnotizability in patients with anorexia nervosa and bulimia. *Archives of General Psychiatry, 42,* 1014–1016.

Pope, H. G., & Hudson, J. I. (1992). Is childhood sexual abuse a risk factor for bulimia nervosa. *American Journal of Psychiatry, 149,* 455–463.

Post, C. L. (1990). Incest and depression: An attributional analysis. Unpublished doctoral dissertation, California School of Professional Psychology, San Diego.

Powers, P., Schulman, R. G., Gleghorn, A. A., & Prange, M. E. (1987). Perceptual and cognitive abnormalities in bulimia. *American Journal of Psychiatry, 144,* 1456–1460.

Root, M. P. P. (1991). Persistent, disordered eating as a gender-specific, post-traumatic stress response to sexual assault. *Psychotherapy, 28,* 96–102.

Root, M. P. P., & Fallon, P. (1988). The incidence of victimization experiences in a bulimic sample. *Journal of Interpersonal Violence, 3,* 161–173.

Root, M. P. P., & Fallon, P. (1989). *Bulimia and related eating disorders screen.* Seattle: Bulimia Treatment Program.

Ross, C., Heber, S., Norton, G., & Anderson, G. (1989). Differences between multiple personality and other groups on structured interview. *Journal of Nervous and Mental Disease, 177,* 487–491.

Sanders, S. (1986). The perceptual alteration scale: A scale measuring dissociation. *American Journal of Clinical Hypnosis, 29,* 95–102.

Sands, S. (1991). Bulimia, dissociation, and empathy: A self-psychological view. In C. L. Johnson (Ed.), *Psychodynamic treatment of anorexia nervosa and bulimia* (pp. 34–50). New York: Guilford Press.

Smith, M., & Thelen, M. (1984). Development and validation of a test for bulimia. *Journal of Consulting and Clinical Psychology, 52,* 863–872.

Smolak, L., Levine, M. P., & Sullins, E. (1990). Are child sexual experiences related to eating-disordered attitudes and behaviors in a college sample? *International Journal of Eating Disorders, 9,* 167–178.

Spiegal, D. (1984). Multiple personality as a post-traumatic stress disorder. *Psychiatric Clinics of North America, 7,* 101–110.

Steinberg, M., Rounsaville, B., & Cicchetti, D. (1990). The Structured Clinical Interview for DSM-III-R Dissociative Disorders: Preliminary report on a new diagnostic instrument. *American Journal of Psychiatry, 147,* 76–82.

Torem, M.S. (1986). Dissociative states presenting as an eating disorders. *American Journal of Clinical Hypnosis, 29,* 137–142.

Vanderlinden, J., Vandereycken, W., van Dyck, R., & Vertommen, H. (1993). Dissociative experiences and trauma in eating disorders. *International Journal of Eating Disorders, 13,* 187–194.

Waller, G. (1992). Sexual abuse and the severity of bulimic symptoms. *British Journal of Psychiatry, 161,* 90–93.

5

Sexual Barrier Weight: A New Approach

EDWARD J. WEINER

LARRY STEPHENS*

An eating disorder may have part of its roots in sexual abuse and/or trauma. We studied 42 women with eating disorders, two-thirds of whom gave histories of sexual trauma. By graphic analysis, age vs. weight, we have shown that fluctuations in body weight have followed sexually significant life events. This is especially significant in victims of rape and termination of a sexual relationship. We suggest that sexually traumatized persons may resist a specific body weight due to fear of sexual attractiveness or impulses relating to specific sexual trauma that occurred at that weight. Further study is necessary to confirm these hypotheses.

In working with eating disorder patients, it has been observed by these investigators that sexual issues arise at particular weights. The Sexual Barrier Weight Graph and Questionnaire are useful tools where significant life events (e.g., sexual trauma, marriage, termination of a relationship, hysterectomy) are plotted against the patient's weight history. The Sexual

---

*Special thanks to Jon Blachley, M.D. for technical assistance.

Barrier Weight event refers to the weight at which various life experiences occur. As patients near these trigger weights, past traumatic issues may surface for them.

Case Example. A 35-year-old woman, under treatment for compulsive overeating, reported fear and anxiety when her weight declined from 168 to 158 pounds. Her compulsive eating recurred until her weight increased to 162 pounds, and the fear resolved. She related that at 160 pounds she experienced indiscriminate and frightening sexual impulses. This cycle repeated three times until it was ultimately learned that she had been sexually abused by a family member at age 13 years, at which time she weighed 160 pounds.

When looking at a group of female anorectic and bulimic patients, Oppenheimer and colleagues (1985) applied a strict definition of sexual abuse and found that two-thirds of the group of 78 females qualified as having been abused. Oppenheimer and colleagues stated: ''Our work has persuaded us that there are often important links of meaning in the patient's mind between such experiences and subsequent eating disorders. Frequently the sexually molested subject has feelings of inferiority or disgust about her own femininity and sexuality. These may come to be entangled with concern about her body weight, shape and size.''

Sexual abuse is one of the more common initiators of a sexual barrier weight. Lindberg and Distad (1985) state that the average time for recollection of sexual trauma memories is 17 years; it may be longer if the events are associated with physical violence or the threat of physical violence. The issue has been raised whether the recollection of sexual abuse is real or imagined. Herman and Schatzow (1987) have shown that at least 75% of women who thought they were sexually abused were able to locate secondary proof of the trauma.

Bulimic, anorectic, and compulsive overeating patterns may partially be related to the previous sexual assault. In a group of patients studied by Hall and colleagues (1989), bulimia was triggered by anger toward male authority figures. Anorectic patients would strive to lose enough weight to appear ''skeletonized'' to ''disgust'' the perpetrator. The compulsive overeater would strive to gain as much weight as possible to become ''nonsexual.'' While only one of the anorectic patients was considered promiscuous, 46% percent of the bulimic patients reported promiscuous behavior.

Not all sexually traumatized individuals develop eating disorders, and some eating disorder patients have not been sexually abused. As a result, it is ''clear that sexual abuse or incest is neither necessary nor sufficient for the development of eating disorders'' (Sloan & Leichner, 1986). Reasons that an individual might maintain an eating disorder include avoidance of sexual feelings, sex-role conflicts, sexual activity, and sexual appearance (i.e., a wish to avoid an adult female form).

Physical sexual abuse is the most dramatic of the events that create a sexual barrier weight. However, other events that are symbolic for specific sexual issues may create a sexual barrier weight as well. Some examples of events include the first sexual experience, birth of a child, a parent having an affair, hysterectomy, divorce, or termination of a sexual relationship. Since one has many life experiences, one can also have many sexual barrier weights corresponding to each event.

METHODOLOGY

Subjects

Surveys were distributed to female outpatient and inpatient eating disorder patients during 1992.

Questionnaire and Graphic Analysis

The survey contained 18 questions, six of which were related to demographics. Ten questions concerned abuse events, and two questions were included to allow the description of events not covered by the questionnaire. All respondents were given a blank graph and were asked to plot their life span in years to the present time on the axis and their weight in pounds on the ordinate. Examples of completed Sexual Barrier Weight Graphs for four patients are included in the chapter appendix. The heading contained a promise of confidentiality and informed consent was obtained.

Data Analysis

Average weight fluctuation (AWF) following a significant life event was calculated as the difference between the weight three months before and 12 months after the event. Changes are reported as simple percentages. Weight gains and losses were treated identically.

RESULTS

A total of 42 surveys was obtained. All were female, with the youngest age 16, the oldest age 61, and a mean age of 37. The average height for

TABLE 1
Summary of Sexual Barrier Weight Data
N=42

Event	Number Reporting	Mean Age Event Occurred	Average Weight Fluctuation (AWF)
Involuntary Sex	12	23	15%
First Voluntary Sex	39	18	8.84%
Hysterectomy	14	40	9.53%
Sexual Abuse	22	7	7.94%
Termination of a Sexual Relationship	29	24	13.65%

the sample was 65 inches, the mean ideal weight was 135 pounds, and the mean current weight was 175 pounds. Thirty-two claimed to be compulsive overeaters, 23 bulimics, 6 anorectics, 14 alcoholics, 8 chemical dependents, and 25 sexual abuse survivors.

Involuntary sex was reported by 12 women, while 22 indicated sexual abuse. For purpose of this study, involuntary sex was considered to have happened over age 13 and sexual abuse occurred under 13. Involuntary sex was associated with the largest AWF (15%) and occurred at an average age of 23. Sexual abuse occurred at an average age of 7 with an AWF of 8%. Termination of a sexual relationship accounted for the second greatest AWF, at 14%. This group included 29 of the respondents. Hysterectomy included 14 women and first voluntary sex 39 women. Table 1 shows the mean weight fluctuation between three months before the event and 12 months after the event.

DISCUSSION

Previous studies (Oppenheimer et al., 1985; Sloan & Leichner, 1986) have suggested a link between sexual trauma/abuse and the subsequent development of eating disorders. However, until now, the long-term influence of sexual trauma on weight homeostasis was largely unknown.

The patients' individual weight graphs suggest that at least some who suffer eating disorders avoid a specific body weight that corresponds to specific emotional events that have sexual overtones. Though this was difficult to quantitate in the data, the graphs imply that weight changes may provide intolerable emotional upheavals, thus leading to marked resistance to voluntary weight change. This may also explain the "yo-yo" nature of weight loss-gain in many individuals in whom weight loss below a certain figure cannot be sustained. Further study is needed to determine the effect of nonsexual, significant life events among individuals who are not affected by eating disorders. Further, a longitudinal study would allow for objective weight measurement and would not rely on patient recollection.

These individual weight graphs were used both diagnostically and therapeutically with each patient. Patients had a sense of great relief when they were able to see their weight changes correlating with specific events. This understanding helped each patient feel less guilty about her own weight fluctuations. The interpretations are hypothesized based on life events and weight; as more history becomes available these often change.

It was not surprising that the event with the greatest change was an involuntary sexual experience; however, the small fluctuation in weight caused by childhood sexual abuse is difficult to explain. It is possible that because of the young age that the sexual abuse occurred, repression and dissociation are responsible for the small change in weight. Another explanation is that most people do not remember their childhood weights or that weight changes in childhood are expected. It is not unusual for a child to gain 4–7% in one year, which would make the AWF of 7.94% statistically insignificant. A future study should look at these individuals and weight fluctuations later in life. The termination of a sexual relationship had a dramatic effect on weight fluctuation that could be attributable to this event being a pure measure of abandonment issues.

Another study is needed where a control group is matched to patients with eating disorders to support the sexual barrier weight hypothesis. It is likely that through future research, a person's weight change can be estimated by the nature of the event. This information would be of great value to professionals in dealing with patients who are either currently experiencing a trauma or trying to understand why they cannot control their eating behavior.

There are some limitations to this study. It was a skewed sample, since 70% of the sample came from inpatient treatment facilities across the country, which would bias the data toward a more traumatic background. There may have been a leading of patients to correlate weight with events that have no relationship. Also, there is no way to confirm whether the stated weights are the real weights or the stated traumatic events really occurred. In this study the patients self-reported their own eating disorder behavior rather than using strict DSM-III-R criteria.

In summary, the strength of the sexual barrier weight theory is that by reviewing a patient's weight history compared to life trauma history, one can predict which issues may escalate eating disorder symptoms. It can also be used as a tool to help patients understand their years of inability to control their approach to food. Thus this theory can be used both diagnostically and therapeutically.

APPENDIX

Patient #1

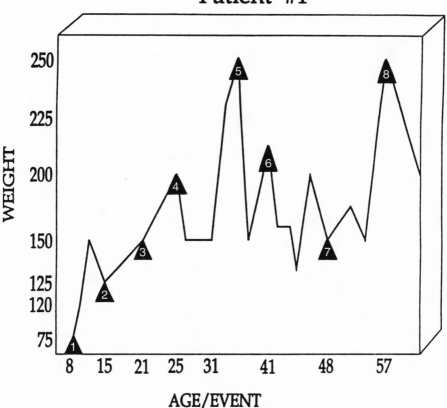

1. age 8—molested by 14-year-old boy neighbor
2. age 15—learned of father's affair of two years before
3. age 21—first marriage
4. age 25—divorced
5. age 31—second marriage; 75-pound gain over next two years
6. age 41—sold house and mother has heart attack
7. age 48—two sexual partners
8. age 57—eating disorder treatment

Interpretation: The molestation at age 8 causes the first weight gain, her father's affair causes the second sexual trauma and binge eating. The divorce causes another sexual barrier weight (SBW). The second marriage causes the fourth SBW.

Patient #2

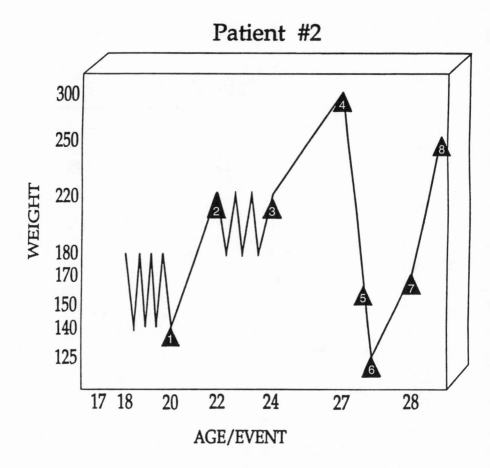

WEIGHT

AGE/EVENT

1. father dies; patient moves in with mother
2. moves out into own apartment
3. mother diagnosed with cancer; moves back in with mother
4. fasting program starts
5. feels very effective; successful dieter
6. seeks medical evaluation for "unexplained weight loss"; abuse memories begin but does not disclose
7. binge eating; does not seek treatment
8. overwhelmed by memories; hospitalized

Interpretation: This example demonstrates several sexual barrier weights. Numbers 1 and 3 signify engulfment by mother. Number 6 signifies sexual abuse memories that make maintenance of weight impossible. Treatment of the eating disorder must deal with engulfment and the sexual abuse.

Patient #3

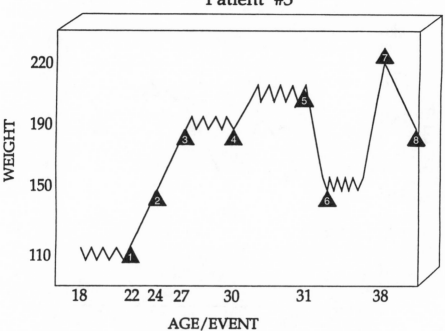

1. marries; husband distant
2. physical abuse by husband begins
3. major depression; put on antidepressants
4. divorce
5. fasting program
6. memories of sexual abuse; panic attacks
7. hospitalized at eating disorder unit
8. current status—in therapy working on eating disorder and incest issues

Interpretation: The sexual neglect plus the physical abuse caused initial weight gain from 110 to 190 pounds. Divorce caused additional gain to 210. Inability to go below 150 pounds may be the result of sexual abuse memories and would explain her choice of an abusive mate.

Patient #4

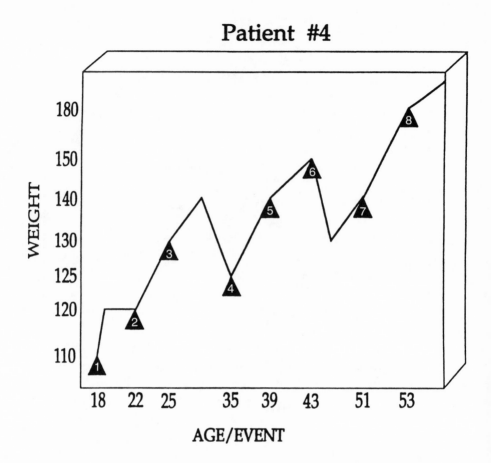

1. age 18—started college; initial sexual experience; date raped 6 months later
2. age 22—daughter born; had affair 4 months afterward
3. age 25—son born; had affair 8 months afterward
4. age 35—divorced; multiple sexual partners
5. age 39—hysterectomy
6. age 43—attempted suicide; divorced; moved back to Dallas
7. age 51—called off marriage plans; resumed sexual relations after 8-month abstinence
8. age 53—major depression

Interpretation: Date rape created the first SBW, the affair after her daughter was born created the second SBW, the affair after her son was born created the third SBW, the divorce is the catalyst to go below the third SBW, and she consequently acts out with food and sex. The hysterectomy creates the fourth SBW.

REFERENCES

Hall, R. C. W., Tice, L., Beresford, T. P., et al. (1989). Sexual abuse in patients with anorexia nervosa and bulimia. *Psychosomatics,* Winter, 73–79.

Herman, J. L., & Schatzow, E. (1987). Recovery and verification of memories of childhood sexual trauma. *Psychoanalytic Psychology, 4,* 1–14.

Lindberg, F. H., & Distad, L. J. (1985). Post-traumatic stress disorders in women who experienced childhood incest. *Child Abuse & Neglect, 9,* 329–334.

Oppenheimer, R., Howells, K., Palmer, R. L., & Chaloner, D. A. (1985). Adverse sexual experience in childhood and clinical eating disorders: A preliminary description. *Journal of Psychiatric Research, 2*(3), 357–361.

Sloan, G., & Leichner, P. (1986). Is there a relationship between sexual abuse or incest and eating disorders? *Canadian Journal of Psychiatry,* Oct., 656–660.

6

Sexual Abuse, Eating Disorders, and Prevention: Political and Social Realities

LANA STERMAC

NIVA PIRAN

PETER M. SHERIDAN

The prevalence of both sexual abuse and eating disorders has been linked to sociocultural factors that maintain and promote the manipulation and exploitation of the female body. This chapter identifies and discusses some of these factors and examines attempts at intervention and prevention. It is argued that the majority of sexual abuse prevention programs, which target children as the main agents of deterrence, reflect these social and political factors. The problems with this approach and possible alternatives are discussed.

The problem of childhood sexual abuse has received increased attention over the past decade (Briere, 1992), resulting in greater awareness of the nature and extent of this social problem. Sexual abuse is seen to violate the physical, psychological, and spiritual space of a developing individual (Root, 1991) and, therefore, to disrupt psychological and interpersonal development in a major way (Cole & Putman, 1992). Sexual abuse is a violent act against an individual that occurs within the context of an extreme power imbalance. Studies of survivors of childhood sexual abuse who present for treatment reveal an extensive list of severe symptomatology, including depression, suicide attempts, self-mutilation, substance abuse, eating disorders, dissociative phenomenon, and multiple identities (Courtois, 1979). Sexual assault of an adult has been found to be associated with some shared symptomatology, particularly depression, self-harm, poor self-esteem, and, at times, eating disorders (Root, 1991).

Clinical reports of a high incidence of past sexual abuse in individuals seeking treatment for eating disorders have led to a considerable number of studies that compared the incidence of reported past sexual abuse in individuals with or without eating disorders (for a meta-analysis of this body of research, see Mallinckrodt et al., 1993). Results vary depending on a number of relevant factors. One important factor is the composition of the comparison groups; for example, the reported incidence of past sexual abuse within individuals treated for an eating disorder seems comparable to that of a sample of individuals treated for substance abuse (Rohsenow et al., 1988).

Other factors include the co-occurrence of different abusive situations, the nonspecificity of measures, and the different definitions of sexual abuse or of eating disorders (Briere, 1992; Reppucci & Haugaard, 1989). Clearly, research methodology employing correlational investigations of retrospective data disallows the inference of a causal relationship between sexual abuse and eating disorders.

One should view the potential contribution of this research either to theory development or to the planning of therapeutic or preventative interventions in perspective. Eating disorders can be seen as only one form of expression of a core disturbance in an individual's experience of her or his body, along with other forms of expression of the same core disturbance such as substance abuse, self-harm, dissociative experiences anchored in different bodily experiences, psychosomatic pain, sexual difficulties, or odd eating or dressing habits. An eating disorder may occur when the core disturbance interacts with destructive social messages. Root (1991) gives a broad account of possible interactions between social messages and the trauma of sexual abuse that could result in the phenomenology of eating disorders. The association between eating disorders and past sexual abuse, however, may reveal a small segment of the trauma experience and its effect and should not obscure the much broader picture of victims' severe disturbance in their experience of themselves and their bodies. Similarly, the exclusive focus on child sexual abuse, a most severe violation of an individual's body, should not obscure the larger picture of violations of children's and women's bodies, including aggressive assaults, sexualization, and exploitation.

SOCIAL AND CULTURAL FACTORS

Social and cultural messages about children's bodies and their sexuality contribute not only to individual symptomatology but also to the phenomenon of sexual abuse itself. Feminist analysis of childhood sexual abuse (e.g., Brickman, 1992; Herman, 1981) has emphasized the dynamics of power, gender, and age as contributing to the early sexualization of children, particularly female children, who become the victims of sexual abuse. Sociocultural factors such as the sexual depiction and exploitation of children through art, literature, and media reflect ingrained attitudes and beliefs that may contribute directly to the way we interact with and treat children. The image of children's and women's bodies as sexual vehicles has been a significant part of this portrayal.

It may be argued that permissive and negative attitudes resulting from these sociocultural factors play a role in the promotion and legitimization of myths about women and children. It is further proposed that negative stereotypes and myths contribute to a culture that maintains sexual abuse and that also shapes the nature and focus of our intervention and prevention programs. The examination of these factors is critical to understanding the continued victimization of children in our society. Although considerable work has been done examining the role of negative and stereotypic attitudes in aggression against women, much less emphasis has been placed upon examining sociocultural factors influencing sexual abuse of children. The identification of negative attitudes can assist us in challenging the stereotypes as well as in designing clinical and educational interventions for both perpetrators and survivors of sexual abuse. This includes, among other things, the examination of social, cultural, and political factors (Driver & Droisen, 1989). We will address the relative paucity of work in this area and attempt to demonstrate that negative and stereotypic attitudes that underlie sexual aggression toward women are common also to myths about children.

Permissive attitudes and the promotion of adult sexual activities with children can be found in several areas of society (Stermac et al., 1990). Evidence of negative and stereotypic views regarding children and women among sexually aggressive men and others is well documented (Abel et al., 1984). Anecdotal evidence of permissive beliefs about sexual behavior and the behavior of children can be found among sexually abusive men (Stermac, 1988a). This may be seen in one of the most damaging of myths about children's behavior, which is that the victim wants sexual contact and even encourages her victimizer.

The prevalence of "victim blame" in our society can be seen even in some early professional literature about adult sexual contact with children (e.g., Cooke & Howells, 1981; Resnick & Wolfgang, 1972). Popular literature similarly supports permissive and stereotyped views of children. Along with such classics as Nabokov's *Lolita* (1966), whose heroine has come to symbolize a seductive child, the visual depiction of children in popular outlets such as advertisements in magazines further reinforces existing stereotypes. It is certainly well known that men who have sexual contact with children, namely, child molesters, believe, rationalize, or otherwise deceive themselves into thinking that children are seductive (like women), seduce them, and want to have sex with them (Segal & Stermac, 1990). These views are reinforced in media portrayals of children as provocative, enticing, and sexually available (Stermac, 1988b).

Other aspects of society also influence and perpetuate the myth of victim responsibility in sexual abuse. Lawyers, judges, and others involved in the judicial process respond to survivors and perpetrators within the context of their personal understanding of sexual abuse. Victim blaming and other negative attitudes toward children can be seen among criminal justice officials who raise the question of children's complicity in sexual assault (Driver, 1989). A number of reports (e.g., Becker & Shah, 1986; Stermac & Segal, 1989) have documented the existence of social attitudes consistent with the belief of victim responsibility in regards to the sexual abuse of children. One recent study of child molesters' cognitions (Stermac & Segal, 1989) addressed this issue by examining cognitions and attitudes among sexual offenders and professional and community groups toward adult sexual contacts with children. Stermac and Segal presented vignettes showing differing amounts of sexual contact between adult males and female children and varied the child's responses to the sexual contact (crying, smiling, and no reaction/passive). The authors found that in the vignettes where the child smiled, subjects from various occupational and social groups perceived the child as having more complicity in the behavior, attributed less responsibility to the adult, and rated more potential benefit to the child than in the other two conditions. It was noted that all nonoffender groups saw children as having some responsibility and deriving some benefit from sexual contact with an adult when the child did not actively resist and when the contact did not involve disrobing. The authors concluded that their data supported the mediating role of the victims' behavior in perceptions of adult sexual contacts with children and provided support for the belief that lack of resistance on the part of victims implies consent and minimizes the seriousness of adult sexual contacts with children.

Another common and damaging belief about sexual abuse, also tied to the victims' behavior, is the attribution of positive response and benefit to victims of sexual abuse and assault. As with victim responsibility, this myth asserts that women and children enjoy any form of sexual attention from males, and may even benefit from it through special attention and education (O'Hare & Taylor, 1983). This notion has been advanced through various theories, such as affection theory, Freud's seduction theory, and the "special" daughter theory (O'Hare & Taylor, 1983). One common perception is that children's desires encourage or provoke a sexual advance from an adult (Peters, 1977). This myth deals with incest as a child's fantasy rather than an adult's behavior and stems from the Freudian perception that all children experience sexual desires for their parents. Such "child seduction" theories fail to examine the sexual behaviors and feelings of parents toward their children or that "seductiveness" may be learned, possibly from prolonged incestuous abuse. Although these notions have been seriously challenged in recent work (e.g., Brickman, 1992), such views can be seen in the disposition and sentencing of perpetrators (Driver & Droisen, 1989).

Many clinicians and researchers have challenged these damaging views of the effects of sexual abuse of children and the belief that this is a benign and nonviolent activity that victims enjoy and benefit from. Stermac, Hall and Henskens (1989), for instance, carried out a study examining the characteristics of child molesters and of the offenses they committed. Twenty-five incest offenders and 27 nonfamilial sex offenders against children were compared in terms of the types of offenses committed, the degree of violence involved in their offenses, and the effects of their behavior on the victims. The authors found that penetration was involved in approximately 50% of the offenses, physical force was used extensively by perpetrators, and a substantial number of injuries sustained by the children required medical attention. Although the subject samples were biased in terms of psychiatric diversion and other factors, the results, nevertheless, challenge the notion of nonviolence among incest perpetrators.

These myths about the provocation and complicity of children have power over the way children who experience sexual abuse are treated by the educational and legal systems. In both overt and covert manner, our society fails to discourage male intimidation and sexual aggression/abuse toward both women and children. In general, women are not taught how to resist men's intimidation and violence, which they are confronted with and must avoid daily in many aspects of their lives. Women are often warned of the potential bodily harm that resistance to sexual aggression might encourage, despite research suggesting that women who physically resist are more likely than nonresisters to avoid being raped, without necessarily increasing the rapist's level of violence (Bart & O'Brien, 1984). It is certainly perplexing then that many sexual abuse prevention programs for children specifically target the child as the agent of deterrence and resistance.

PREVENTION STRATEGIES

One way to assess the systemic nature of a worrisome social phenomena is to explore suggested means for its prevention. A review of programs for the prevention of sexual abuse, which have mushroomed in the past 20 years, reveals that most programs focus exclusively on children (Reppucci & Haugaard, 1989). Moreover, in these programs children are asked to make distinctions between concepts such as good touch versus bad touch (Kearney-Cooke, 1988), trusted adults versus nontrusted adults (Conte' et al., 1984; Kearney-Cooke, 1988), and sexual touch versus nonsexual touch (Finkelhor, 1986; Madak & Berg, 1992). These concepts have been found in research to be difficult, if not outright impossible, to distinguish, especially for younger school-age children (Reppucci & Haugaard, 1989). It has also been suggested that negative effects have not been studied thoroughly enough and warrant further exploration (Reppucci & Haugaard, 1989). Negative effects may be particularly challenging in a culture where the topic of sexuality is taboo and fears regarding sexual feelings and experiences are not typically addressed (Finkelhor, 1986).

Outcome studies reflect limited support for the efficacy of sexual abuse prevention programs; a slight increase of knowledge about sexual abuse has been found in older school children (Reppucci & Haugaard, 1989). In their review, Reppucci and Haugaard (1989) state that there is no evidence that children exposed to a program are able to resist an abusive situation. On the other hand, there is some information that suggests adverse reactions to prevention efforts. This information has not discouraged the use of prevention programs. Reppucci and Haugaard (1989) describe them as "programs that make adults feel better but do not protect children" (p. 1274). There is some indication, however, that even relatively short programs may increase reporting of sexual abuse by children.

The programs that focus on intervention with children often do not seem to resonate with the life experience of the child (Reppucci & Haugaard, 1989; Tennant, 1988). Children describing their victimization elaborate on the confusing nature of the abuse and on their inability to view their abuser as untrustworthy (Tennant, 1988). They also comment on the sense of threat and fear (Cole & Putman, 1992). Children's reports correspond with the accounts of perpetrators who trap children into compliance typically through a process of confusing, conflicting messages of care and threat (Cohn, 1986). "Prevention" efforts may, therefore, be betraying the child further. For example, adults around the child may feel relieved by the child's exposure to the program and may become less vigilant in assessing risks their child may confront (Reppucci & Haugaard, 1989; Tennant, 1988). This combines with the documented tendency on the part of parents to deny the possibility that their child may be at risk for sexual abuse (Tennant, 1988; Wald & Cohen, 1986).

New directions for sexual abuse prevention programs have been advocated (Cohn, 1986; Tennant, 1988). Comprehensive preventive measures must address and challenge the social structures and cultural messages that promote the manipulation of children's and women's bodies and maintain sexual exploitation. For that purpose, further study of perpetuating factors should be pursued. Specific myths and stereotypes regarding children, especially female children, and sexuality have been identified in this paper. These and other myths and stereotypes have to be addressed publicly. Examples of corrective messages that could be conveyed by the media or be part of all educational programs include: sexual molestation of children is a crime; sexual molestation of children involves an abuse of power and trust and is based upon coercion and intimidation; a child is unable to give consent; the prevention of sexual abuse is the exclusive responsibility of adults; and sexual molestation is damaging to children. The way in which myths, prejudices, and the patriarchal power system may affect reporting and sentencing should be explicitly conveyed as well. Such messages in the media will help create an environment in which different preventive programs and concepts will be effective (Cohn, 1986).

Adults, rather than children, should be the main target group for intervention (Cohn, 1986). This group includes potential perpetrators, parents, teachers, and institutional personnel. Such a shift in focus places moral, ethical, and legal responsibility where it should be, with the adults surrounding the child. The goal should be to reach out to the potential abusers and help them to understand the impact of their behavior, to control their behavior, and to develop alternative and more appropriate behaviors

(Cohn, 1986). There is no particular profile of the sexual abuser; therefore, prevention efforts cannot be restricted to individuals who are thought to be high-risk sexual abusers (Cohn, 1986). Delivering prevention programs through places of employment or community service clubs may be effective (Finkelhor, 1986). Some men might be discouraged from becoming abusers if they believe that other adults or children are likely to detect and/or report sexual molestation.

Parents, teachers, volunteers, and administrative and other staff should all be educated in the detection, handling, and reporting of child sexual abuse. Their education should address resistance toward discussing sexual concerns with children and identifying or reporting sexual abuse where it occurs (Tennant, 1988). Parents and designated school staff should discuss healthy sexuality with children and form an opportunity within this positive context to identify abnormal and destructive sexual situations. In the field of prevention of eating disorders, Piran (1992) has found that the personal availability of the group educator at the school has aided disclosure by both students and staff of a variety of symptomatology and of a past history of abuse. First-time parents compose a particular target group for intervention; they should be given information about appropriate and inappropriate touching and how to detect in oneself and one's mate the inclination toward inappropriate touching and what to do about it (Cohn, 1986). Parents and other adults should train themselves to form a protective environment for their children. Adults and children should be aware of the lack of any particular characteristics of potential abusers, the high incidence of sexual abuse within the family or by other close relations, the tendency to deny the occurrence of abuse, and the tendency to rely on school prevention efforts. Careful institutional staff selection, ongoing monitoring, and reporting procedures will help form a protective environment.

Interventions with children should be guided by further study of the experience of the child. Such study will help clarify the conditions and processes conducive to the deterrence and reporting of sexual abuse (Reppucci & Haugaard, 1989). The effect of a child's cognitive and emotional stage on these conditions and processes should be clarified as well. Processes involved in the reporting of sexual abuse may differ from those involved in its deterrence. This topic should be explored as well since some data suggest greater success of existing prevention programs with the goal of secondary rather than primary prevention. Similar to Cohn's (1986) suggestion for intervening in the prevention of sexual abuse, Piran (1992), working in the prevention of eating disorders, has found that the creation of a supportive environment through interventions with adults prior to intervening with children can be crucial to the children's experience of support and to sustaining a positive impact.

To conclude, sexual abuse is a systemic problem rather than an expression of abnormal pathology; therefore, attempts at prevention should identify the systemic factors and work against them. Adults carry the moral, ethical, and legal responsibility to become involved with prevention activities, and the outcome of such activities depends on their involvement. Research grounded in the experience of children and addressing systemic factors should be conducted.

REFERENCES

Abel, G. G., Becker, J. V., & Cunningham-Rathner, J. (1984). Complications, consent, and cognitions in sex between children and adults. *International Journal of Law and Psychiatry, 7,* 89–103.

Bart, P. B., & O'Brien, P. H. (1984). Stopping rape: Effective avoidance strategies. *Signs, 10,* 82–101.

Becker, J. V., & Shah, S. A. (1986). The sexually abused child. In W. J. Curran, A. L. McGarry & S. A. Shah (Eds.), *Forensic psychiatry and psychology: Perspective and standards for interdisciplinary practice* (pp. 315–338). Philadelphia: F. A. Davis.

Brickman, J. (1992). Female lives, feminist deaths: The relationship of the Montreal massacre to dissociation, incest, and violence against women. *Canadian Psychology, 33,* 128–150.

Briere, J. (1992). Methodological issues in the study of sexual abuse effects. *Journal of Consulting and Clinical Psychology, 60,* 196–203.

Cohn, A. (1986). Preventing adults from becoming sexual molesters. *Child Abuse and Neglect, 10,* 559–562.

Cole, P. M., & Putman, F. W. (1992). Effect of incest on self and social functioning: A developmental psychopathology perspective. *Journal of Consulting and Clinical Psychology, 60,* 174–184.

Conte, J. R., Rosen, C., & Saperstein, L. (1984, September). An analysis of programs to prevent the sexual victimization of children. Paper presented at the Fifth International Congress on Child Abuse and Neglect, Montreal.

Cooke, M., & Howells, K. (Eds.) (1981). *Adult sexual interest in children.* London: Academic Press.

Courtois, C. (1979). The incest experience and its aftermath. *Victimology, 4,* 337–347.

Driver, E., & Droisen, A. (Eds.) (1989). *Child sexual abuse: A feminist reader.* New York: New York University Press.

Finkelhor, D. (1986). Prevention: A review of programs and research. In D. Finkelhor and associates (Eds.), *A sourcebook on child sexual abuse.* Beverly Hills: Sage.

Herman, J. (1981). *Father-daughter incest.* Cambridge, MA: Harvard University Press.

Kearney-Cooke, A. (1988). Group treatment of sexual abuse among women with eating disorders. *Women and Therapy, 7,* 5–21.

Madak, P. R., & Berg, D. H. (1992). The prevention of sexual abuse: An evaluation of "Talking About Touching." *Canadian Journal of Counselling, 26,* 29–40.

Mallinckrodt, B., McCreary, B. A., & Robertson, A. K. (1993, August). Co-occurrence of eating disorders and incest: The role of attachment, family environment, and social competencies. Paper presented at the annual conference of the American Psychological Association, Toronto.

Nabokov, V. (1966). *Lolita.* New York: Berkley Medallion.

O'Hare, J., & Taylor, K. (1983). The reality of incest. In R. J. Robbins & R. Josefowitz Siegel (Eds.), *Women changing therapy: New assessments, values and strategies in feminist therapy* (pp. 215–229). New York: Harrington Park Press.

Peters, J. (1977). Children who are the victims of sexual assault and the psychology of the offender. *American Journal of Psychotherapy, 30,* 398-421.

Piran, N. (1992, April). Can a subculture change? A trial of prevention in a high risk setting. Paper presented at the 5th International Conference on Eating Disorders, New York.

Reppucci, N., & Haugaard, J. (1989). Prevention of child sexual abuse. *American Psychologist,* October, 1266-1275.

Resnick, H. L., & Wolfgang, M. E. (Eds.) (1972). *Sexual behaviors: Social, clinical, and legal aspects.* Boston: Little, Brown.

Rohsenow, D. J., Corbett, R., & Devine, D. (1988). Molested as children: A hidden contribution to substance abuse? *Journal of Substance Abuse, 5,* 13–18.

Root, M. P. (1991). Persistent, disordered eating as a gender-specific, post-traumatic stress response to sexual assault. *Psychotherapy, 28,* 96–102.

Segal, Z. V., & Stermac, L. (1990). The role of cognition in sexual assault. In W. L. Marshall, D. R. Laws, & H. E. Barbaree (Eds.), *Handbook of sexual assault: Issues, theories, and treatment of the offender* (pp. 161–174). New York: Plenum Press.

Stermac, L. (1988a, February). Child sexual abuse: Myths and realities. Paper presented at the annual meeting of the Ontario Psychological Association, Toronto.

Stermac, L. (1988b, February). Sexual stereotyping: New challenges to old myths. Paper presented at the annual meeting of the Ontario Psychological Association, Toronto.

Stermac, L., Hall, K., & Henskens, M. (1989). Violence among child molesters. *Journal of Sex Research, 26,* 450–459.

Stermac, L., & Segal, Z. V. (1989). Adult sexual contact with children: An examination of cognitive factors. *Behavioral Assessment, 20,* 573–584.

Stermac, L, Segal, Z. V., & Gillis, R. (1990). Social and cultural factors in sexual assault. In W. L. Marshall, D. R. Laws, & H. E. Barbaree (Eds.), *Handbook of sexual assault: Issues, theories, and treatment of the offender* (pp. 143–159). New York: Plenum Press.

Tennant, C. (1988). Preventive sexual abuse programs: Problems and possibilities. *Elementary School Guidance and Counseling, 23,* 48–53.

Wald, M. S. & Cohen, S. (1986). Preventing child abuse: What will it take? *Family Law Quarterly, 20,* 281–302.

PART II

Clinical Perspectives and Treatment Strategies

7

Physical and Sexual Abuse and Neglect and Eating Disorder Symptoms

MARK F. SCHWARTZ

PAULA GAY

For eating-disordered patients with a history of posttraumatic stress, childhood abuse and neglect, and dissociative disorder, eating behavior symptoms may function as a rational response to unmetabolized traumatic experiences. This chapter will review trauma-based theory, dissociation, abreactive, and ego-state therapy as they apply to eating disorder patients.

Numerous studies have documented a correlation between eating disorder and a history of physical and sexual abuse in selected clinical samples (see Table 1). Studies have also correlated eating disorder with dissociative disorder and multiple personality disorder (see Table 7-1). We (Schwartz & Gay, 1993) have also identified a subset of eating disorder patients who have dissociative disorder as defined by significant scores on psychological instruments such as the Dissociative Experiences Scale (Bernstein & Putnam, 1986) and Dissociative Disorder Interview Schedule (Ross et al., 1989). We therefore initiated a specialized treatment

TABLE 7-1
Studies Looking for a Correlation Between Eating Disorders and Trauma

Study	Topic
Abramson & Lucido, 1991	Childhood Sexual Experience and Bulimia
Bailey & Gibbons, 1989	Childhood Abuse and Bulimia
Beckman & Burns, 1990	Sexual Abuse and Bulimia
Bulik, 1987	Abuse and Bulimia
Bulik et al., 1989	Sexual Abuse and Bulimia
Demitrack et al., 1990	Dissociation and Eating Disorders
Finn et al., 1986	Sexual Abuse and Eating Disorders
Folsom et al., 1993	Sexual and Psychic Abuse and Eating Disorders
Hall et al., 1989	Sexual Abuse and Anorexia and Bulimia
Hudson et al., 1987	Child Abuse and Bulimia
McCallum et al., 1992	Child Abuse Dissociation and Eating Disorders
McClelland et al., 1991	Sexual Abuse and Eating Disorder
Oppenheimer et al., 1985	Sexual Abuse and Eating Disorder
Palmer et al., 1990	Sexual Abuse and Eating Disorder
Pope & Hudson, 1992	Sexual Abuse and Eating Disorder
Root, 1991	Posttraumatic Stress and Eating Disorder
Root & Fallon, 1988	Victimization and Bulimia
Smolak et al., 1990	Sexual Abuse and Eating Disorder
Steiger & Zanko, 1990	Sexual Trauma and Eating Disorder
Stuart et al, 1990	Abuse and Bulimia
Torem, 1986	Dissociation and Eating Disorder
Vanderlinden et al., 1993	Dissociation and Eating Disorder
Waller, 1991, 1993	Sexual Abuse and Eating Disorder
Williams et al., 1992	Sexual Trauma and Eating Disorder

program four years ago for individuals who present clinically with eating-disordered symptoms and a history of posttraumatic stress and dissociative disorder. This chapter is a review of our clinical experience over the past four years utilizing ego-state therapy with a subset of eating disorder patients with dissociative symptoms.

EATING DISORDER TRAUMA:
TRAUMA-BASED THEORY

Trauma-based theory redefines the pertinent question as "What happened to" rather than "What's wrong with." Compulsivity symptoms are thereby reconceptualized as distorted survival strategies to overwhelming stressors. Whenever caregivers are dangerous and incapable of providing affection, the child becomes terrified in response to internal signals. Children have a miraculous capacity to dissociate, that is, to think, "this is not happening, it's not happening to me, it didn't happen at all." The following description depicts one survivor's dissociative experiences watching the act from afar:

> My room was dark, my thoughts were dark, and my vision was blurred from tears swelling in my eyes. My small body lay heavy in my bed as if I were dying. I thought I was dying for my thoughts had turned me into stone and my body was numb. I turned my head and looked out the window, and I caught a glimpse of the moon. I imagined sitting on that great big bluish grey object. Then the squeak of my door opening startled my peaceful thoughts. I clutched my covers close to my face squeezing them as hard as I could, as though if I let go I would fall. I knew I was in danger and my body began sending me messages of fear. My father walked in naked smoking a cigarette. I pretended I was asleep, but my attempt to pretend had failed me. My father was angry. I could tell by the way he tore back my covers. Terror struck my body and I couldn't move. He ordered me over and over again to take off my PJs, but even trying to lift my head was like lifting a boulder.

If the event is remembered, the individual might then rearrange cognitions to believe "I made it happen, I deserved for it to happen, I was chosen for such abuse because of my badness." In this manner, a sense of having been in control is preserved, and the abuser can remain "safe" and "good." In the context of this belief system, the child is unlovable, but the caretakers are loving; therefore, hope remains alive. Often trauma survivors describe out-of-body experiences in which they can watch from the ceiling the experience of being raped, and then depersonalize, that is, they think, "It didn't happen to me, it happened to my 'body' or to my 'sex organs.' " With extreme dissociation, multiple personality disorder DID (Dissociative Identity Disorder) may develop and alter personalities, personality fragments, or ego states may unfold that will communicate to the host personality, "I experienced that event because you could never have survived it." In such cases, the person dissociates by a part of self splitting off and becoming separate, insulating the person in certain instances through amnesic barriers. In many cases of trauma, the amnesic barriers are not complete, and ego states exist encapsulated, but less rigidly, yet still frozen in time and only accessible in trance work. Such fragments may speak in a child's voice and still manifest the child's fear. As an example, they may fear that the perpetrator can get them or the mother will punish them for telling, even though the client is now adult and the abuse occurred during childhood. Unlike MPD patients, however, there is not a complete personality with a separate developmental history or impermeable amnesic barriers, so such patients are diagnosed as atypical dissociative disorder (now DDNOS) (Braun, 1986). Fragmentation of personality can permit double-bind beliefs to coexist, so survivors can both know and not know that they were sexually abused, simultaneously feel as though they both love and hate their parents, and firmly believe that the abuse both was and was not their fault. Since memory can be stored within these ego states, the phenomenon reflects what has been described as state-dependent learning. In state-dependent learning, contextual stimuli can directly activate stored memories so that the individual automatically experiences a "flashback" or the feelings, thoughts, sensations, or cognitions of the frightened child. Various events or triggers, drugs, or therapeutic experiences can disinhibit and thereby reactivate memories.

The result of this trauma-generated dissociative process is that the individual will be unintegrated. He or she may feel like an imposter: the person everyone knows is not consistent with impulsive urges, behaviors, or self-knowledge. Such people may forget many years of their lives and function moment-to-moment without the benefit of previous models or experiences. They experience constriction and isolation from others and an "empty hole" in their stomach that is unfillable. They may describe feeling like objects or robots, functioning well with a job and job description, but feeling inept and childlike in social situations or roles. Often they will continue as adults to dissociate or space-out automatically and without control in various situations as a way of defending against shame or the intrusion of old memories.

EATING DISORDER SYMPTOMS AS FUNCTIONAL

As a child, the survivor struggles in a dissociative fog to thrive and begins to search for transitional objects of safety. Eating disorder symptoms function as distorted survival strategies within the context of this dissociative defense. Some of the functions of eating disorder symptoms are listed in Table 7-2. Eating is a ritual that some families frequently use to signify "We are loving and caring parents because we provide for our children and we sit at the table as a family." This nourishing with

TABLE 7-2
Adaptive Function of Eating Disorder Symptoms

Comfort/Nurturance
Numbing
Distraction
Sedation
Energizer
Attention—Cry for Help
Rebellion
Discharge Anger
Identity and Self-Esteem
Maintain Helplessness
Control and Power
Predictability and Structure
Establishment of Psychological Space
Reenactment of Abuse (Repetition/Compulsion)
Self-Punishment or Punishment of the Body
Containment of Fragmentation
Dissociation from Intrusive Thoughts, Feelings, Images
Cleanse or Purify the Self
Attempt "to Disappear" (Anorexia)
Create Large Body for Protection
Create Small Body for Protection
Avoidance of Intimacy
Release Tension Built Up From Hypervigilance
Symptoms Prove "I Am Bad" Instead of Blaming Abusers

food can easily be pointed to as proof to the unloved child or the parent that the family is a loving one. Thus, food comes to represent a substitute for affection: "I know I have love if I'm fed." Such parents can also use food to mask an incapacity for genuine affection. Parents incapable of caring will often caretake and establish a dependency-reversal in that they transform their own tremendous unmet dependency needs into obsessive caretaking of others. The child senses the parents' inability to care and accepts the caretaking instead, always inchoately aware that something is not right, but attributing the problem to self rather than parent.

If such families have sit down meals, frequently there is such verbal abuse and uproar that eating is itself associated with terror and fear. In homes where children are not permitted to express emotions and are treated unfairly, then prohibited from expression of the natural frustrations and anger related to daily injustice, rage begins to develop. Because the natural responses are suppressed, strong emotions must seek release in indirect and surreptitious ways. Strong emotion can be suppressed and sated by eating behavior. Thus, "I am frustrated and overwhelmed" =

"I am hungry"; "I am out of control" = "control food intake"; "I am lonely and afraid" = "I am hungry." This destructive eating behavior can be functional above and beyond the original causes that initiated the destructive coping.

Finally, when there is sexual abuse, frequently the body, sexuality, and gender (i.e., masculinity and femininity) become the enemy. The survivor may think, "I was abused because of my femaleness, attractiveness, vagina, breasts. . . ." Similarly, a distorted survival strategy is to make the body unattractive in order to keep abuse away.

When an individual is molested, the capacity to say no is injured. When a girl is molested at age six, for example, learned helplessness is established and she discovers that she continues to be unable to say no. When solicited, she dissociates and feels as if she has no choice, no control—only one outcome seems possible. She is therefore motivated to maintain an unattractive body as her only means of saying no to others who might want to date and eventually have sex.

Using eating disorder symptoms to contain fragmentation has been reported by McFarlane, McFarlane, and Gilchrist (1988), who found a reciprocal relationship between posttraumatic imagery and the intensity of preoccupation with food. They suggest that intrusive trauma memories are displaced by food or weight obsession and provide internal structure of dissociative states or aspects of self. In our experience, we have observed that when dissociative clients decrease their eating disorder symptoms, there may well be a subsequent increase in dissociation and fragmentation. One eating disorder client described herself as "an empty paper bag." She stated, "I feel like I am out of control. I get blown whichever direction the wind blows. When I stuff my body full of food, the paper bag can stand up and stay in one place." Root (1991) has observed that for some clients, eating disorder symptoms are a disguised posttraumatic stress response. If they relinquish their symptoms prior to adequately addressing the trauma, there may be an increase in other trauma-related symptoms such as flashbacks, self-mutilation, and suicidality.

Another very important function of the eating disorder symptom can be providing concrete, visible proof that "I am bad." As long as the victim believes she is defective and deserving of the abuse, she can avoid acknowledging that she was helpless and avoid recognizing that her parents were abusive or neglectful. Believing that "I am to blame" is much more tolerable than "I am helpless and there is no one to protect me." Changing this belief unleashes vast stores of anxiety, since the entire foundation of one's beliefs about oneself and one's world must be dismantled and reexamined. In order to tolerate the anxiety, the client needs to have a sense of safety and empowerment in her present life.

Eating disorder symptoms can serve multiple functions for the trauma-tized client. Once the more obvious functions, such as providing comfort or numbing pain, are understood, more subtle functions can be addressed (see Table 7-2). Understanding the symptoms in the context of dissocia-tion and as a symptom of posttraumatic stress disorder allows us to treat these clients more effectively. If the client can accept her symptoms as functional and experience an acceptance of aspects of herself she may have previously disowned, the foundation for further resolution of the abuse can be established.

REENACTMENT AND REVICTIMIZATION

Whenever an individual experiences an overwhelming stress, the body naturally responds with cycles of numbing and intrusion. During the numbing, the central nervous system appears to change in some individu-als, who manifest syndromes resembling the clinical effects of a narcotic. They experience analgesia to pain, clinical symptoms of dissociation, and even a ''high'' in response to what a nontraumatized individual might perceive as physically painful. Following the numbing, there is intrusion of memory and affect, characterized by terror, anxiety, sadness, and hyp-ervigilant symptoms. If the individual is able to express the intrusive symptoms verbally and create safety, eventually he or she will work through the trauma sufficiently to have resolution. If unable to master and resolve the overwhelming stressor, the individual will dissociate and potentially repress the event, and the numbing and intrusion cycles will continue throughout life, but they will be ''disguised'' and misattributed since the person is unable to remember the original cause. Such individu-als will feel disturbed and believe they are sick and need doctors and medication, instead of recognizing their need to resolve the original trauma.

Whenever they feel numbing, they often will feel the need to harm themselves to get out of the dissociative fog, and thereby no longer feel like an object. One self-cutter stated:

Picking up the razor was like picking up my ticket to death. I sat with it in my hand as I looked at my wrists and imagined myself slicing open my newly healed arms. Just thinking about the razor sinking into my skin brought me a chill of pleasure. For me to just feel the wet red blood trickling down my arm, but even more to see the little red droplets fall into the water and slowly disappear, would be like spending a day at Disneyland. I would come out happy. Then suddenly a little voice rings through my head asking the ultimate question: Why do I want to do this?

I am afraid, afraid of the truth, afraid of revealing more than I know or revealing more than I want someone to know. But to keep this a secret gives it power and permission to grow stronger.

To think about my father raping me and his sweat dripping on my small body only begins to turn me into stone. While all this happened I was stone, I was dead, I was gone, yes gone far beyond imagination. Far into a world where I walked around like a ghost. I was in this world where life passed me by. I only hoped to come out, and come out alive. But as it seems I am alive, and I did come out alive. But my question is, Am I alive, am I living? I feel like I'm not. But the truth is I live on other people. I live depending on other people to see me to the end. Now where does that leave me? The cutting makes me real, it helps me fulfill the need for pain. Because without the pain I don't think I would think I was real.

Another means of self-harm is starving the body, overeating, or throwing up. Such symptoms seem to function as an unconscious reenactment—the body is abused, but with the illusion of control: "This time I do it to myself rather than being so powerless." Thus, whenever an individual is completely out-of-control, he or she feels the illusion of control.

When individuals experience the intrusion phase of the numbing-intrusion cycle, they typically feel overwhelmed. Thus, they are motivated to take some action so as to not think or feel in order to reinstate the numbing. They use addictive behavior in general toward this end. Therefore, as soon as the intrusion of thinking or feeling begins, they binge or purge, which distracts them, provides some illusion of control and ultimately sedates them in a sense. When they begin abstinence, they often are predictably very overwhelmed with the affect they have suppressed for years.

Whenever they begin having success in life or in love relationships, it upsets the equilibrium. They are confronted with the reality that they are not bad, evil, or as damaged as they originally thought. The thinking and feeling initiate an intrusive cycle and create anxiety, which results in self-destructive behavior to reestablish equilibrium. The result is a very delicate system in which eating is used to maintain the intimacy disorder.

Once a child suffers a traumatic stress, there is injury to the sense of personal boundaries, esteem, trust, power and control; and if the abuse is sexual, to the genital sexuality, gender, and pair-bonding capacities. As adults, whenever they move into an intimate relationship, they automatically shut down, disconnect from others, and experience a sense of depersonalization, of feeling like a robot. Dissociation in this context acts as an automatic insulating device. The original dissociation from early trauma insures that they remain unable to recall what happened to them. Instead, they respond to being vulnerable in subsequent relationships with anger and destructive behavior, which then recreates the distance required to feel safe. Dissociation thereby functions as a defense to prevent them from being destroyed in a close relationship and defends against shame, enabling them to maintain a sense of control.

Eating, bingeing, purging, or starving are all automatic, self-destructive responses, which function to create numbing and keep the trauma from intruding or to escape the intolerable feelings of depersonalization. The symptoms are functional, "punish the body" for being bad, and keep some partners at a distance.

Typically, the eating disorder patient will cycle between overcontrol and out-of-control cycles; acting-out and acting-in cycles. The eating disorder patient acts with a rigid sense of beliefs and boundaries that allows her to organize the world by being angry at self and projecting and displacing the anger onto others. The result is interpretation of all transactions as one's own fault, avoiding and complying with others, and a sense of helplessness and powerlessness to solve problems or change.

Some acting-in individuals will instead develop unrealistic perfectionist righteousness and will channel their rage into taking care of others. They have such a great sense of neediness, which simultaneously evokes terror of allowing someone close enough to meet their needs, that they solve the dilemma by projecting their needs onto others and finding helpless children/creatures to take care of compulsively.

Acting-out individuals may move against and exploit self and others, directly or indirectly. Often they will physically abuse children or neglect them, often alternating with smothering them. They will find themselves in frequent power struggles, insidiously directing their anger at several of their "enemies," while simultaneously feeling like the victim.

EGO-STATE THERAPY WITH EATING DISORDERS

The use of ego-state therapy with eating disorders has been described in the literature by Watkins (1992) and Torem (1986). We have found that ego-state therapy provides a conceptual framework that makes intuitive sense to our clients and provides therapists with a useful structure for individual and group treatment.

Ego-state theory proposes that the presence of more-or-less separate ego states is part of the normal development of the self. These ego states frequently correspond to different roles and responsibilities in our lives, for example, a "mother ego state," a "daughter ego state," a "teacher ego state," a "supervisor ego state." Optimally, there is a conscious awareness of these various ego states and the ability to direct which ego state assumes executive control. For example, a therapist might be in a treatment team meeting at work, when a phone call is received from her child at home. Observers might notice a shift in voice tone, vocabulary, posture, and emotion as the therapist moves from a "therapist ego state" into a "mother ego state" and back again. Ideally, there are also communication and compromise among ego states. For example, a "therapist ego state" might want to throw a temper tantrum and refuse to perform a task suggested by her supervisor, but an "adult employee ego state" would modulate the emotional and behavioral reaction and respond appropriately in the workplace.

When ego states have been formed defensively due to environmental threat, there is less conscious awareness of the ego state, less ability to communicate and compromise with the ego state, and less ability to consciously move in and out of the ego state. For example, if a client grew up in a family where the expression of anger was not permitted, she might form an "angry ego state" to be the reservoir of angry feelings that are relatively hidden from herself and others. At some point, this ego state might experience emotional release as a result of self-induced vomiting or the satisfaction of expressing anger through rebellious binge eating. Because the eating symptom is highly reinforcing, and temporarily powerful in addressing her anger, it gets repeated compulsively and becomes entrenched.

This client could be described as having an "eating disorder ego state," which is organized around eating symptoms. A whole complex of emotions, experiences, beliefs, and memories underlies the eating disorder symptom. The eating disorder ego state could be described as a "subpersonality" that is triggered by anger. Because the client perceives that this ego state is not acceptable, the boundary around the ego state is relatively impermeable. The client has little awareness or understanding of the emotions, beliefs, and memories that underlie her eating disorder symptoms. She may view her symptom as an indication of her defectiveness or as an uncontrolled demon within that "takes over." Her internal experience is one of conflict and chaos due to not understanding how and why this ego state is triggered and how the symptom is a functional adaptation to her internal pain.

The goal of ego-state therapy is to identify the ego state responsible for the symptom, link the symptom to the individual's unique history, and develop communication and a cooperative relationship with the ego state. In the example above, the eating disorder ego state was formed to serve as a reservoir for the client's anger so that she could continue to live in a family where anger was not acceptable. In another client, the eating disorder ego state might have as its function the sexual protection of the client through the creation of a large body. Helping the client understand that the eating disorder has had an adaptive function as a response to stress or pain helps her to see the symptom not as a problem, but as an attempted problem solution. This reframing of the symptom is necessary as a precursor to establishing empathic communication with the ego state. When the eating disorder ego state can be viewed as a "protector," rather than a "persecutor," the client is better able to acknowledge and explore this aspect of self.

Ego-state therapy is a term that describes any intervention aimed at addressing the conflict between ego states within an individual (Watkins & Watkins, 1988). Group therapy, couples therapy, and family therapy techniques can often be easily translated into useful ego-state therapy techniques. Initially, the therapeutic task in a system is to align with the system and develop a working relationship with its members. The same is true in ego-state therapy, where the therapist empathizes and validates various ego states, identifies the conflict, and promotes communication and problem solving.

Although it may appear very basic, the first principle of treatment is to assume that the client has a strong need for her symptoms and for the therapist to communicate respect and empathy for that need. For the client to be able to identify and explore this aspect of herself, it is of utmost importance that the therapist model acceptance of her eating-disordered self. This is invariably a tricky balancing act, since the symptoms can be very dangerous and their presence inhibits the patient's ability to access feelings and memories. One might think of the therapy as a "braiding" technique. The therapist must focus clearly on the meaning of the symptoms and show respect for this aspect of the client's self, while at the same time addressing containment of the symptoms and alternative modes of expression. The message to the patient is: "This part of you is a valued and necessary aspect of your personality. We need to understand and acknowledge the feelings, beliefs, and experiences behind the symptoms. Let us also explore whether this part of you might choose to express itself in ways that are more adaptive for all aspects of yourself."

With this as a general philosophy, the next step in treatment is to link the eating disorder symptoms to the patient's individual history and experience, including her trauma. This allows the patient to have a more continuous identity, so that the split between her eating disorder ego state and other aspects of self is less disruptive and there are more awareness, cooperation, and acceptance among the various aspects of self. One author has described this as being "like the director of a play, the aware ego decides which subpersonality will be allowed on stage at any given time. It must also be aware of which 'actors' are lurking around backstage (the disowned or shadow selves, as Jung called them)" (Capacchione, 1991). Linking the symptom to the patient's history and experience increases the cohesiveness of her sense of self and promotes self-acceptance.

Experiential, expressive, and hypnotic techniques appear most effective in addressing and exploring the eating disorder state. Before any exploration can begin, it is necessary for the client to have a sense of both internal and external safety. For example, binge eating may have helped damp down intrusive memories, or restricting may have provided the client with a false sense of control or power. In order for the client to be able to risk becoming more distant from her symptoms as a way to view them more objectively, she must have something else in her life that provides safety. The therapist may provide safety through such interventions as helping the client to use imagery to visualize an internal safe place or to learn to set appropriate boundaries. A client's sense of emotional and environmental safety is dictated by her unique needs and experiences, and must be firmly in place as the foundation for change. These techniques seem to bypass some of the patient's cognitive defenses and help access affect as well as unconscious beliefs, experiences, and memories. In addition, these techniques are very useful in separating out and highlighting a specific aspect of self so that it can be explored.

Guided imagery is useful in treatment to help the patient explore and acknowledge this aspect of self. We have adapted inner-child guided imageries to address the eating-disordered aspect of self. In addition, during guided imageries we ask patients to visualize recent and past episodes of symptomatic eating behavior as though they were watching a video, and to use their observing self to communicate what the eating disorder ego state is feeling.

Other techniques designed to increase the communication and alliance between different aspects of self include drawings and collage. We routinely have patients draw their eating disorder ego state. One useful way to do this is to have patients draw themselves as they think others see them and then to draw themselves as they see themselves. Some people find it more useful to draw themselves with their nondominant hand. Another technique we use is to ask patients to let their eating-disordered selves express themselves through a collage. They are asked to cut out images that have meaning for them and glue them to a large posterboard without a specific final product in mind. We then ask them to interpret their collage, in a group or individual setting, as a telegram from their eating disorder ego state and to decode the message.

Journaling is another technique that is useful in developing an understanding and acceptance of the eating disorder ego state. Many patients find it useful to write a dialogue between their eating disorder ego state and other aspects of self. Through written dialogue the patient can ask questions of the eating disorder ego state, such as its functions, fears, memories, and what situations or emotions trigger eating symptoms.

Role-playing or empty-chair techniques are also used to define and explore the eating disorder ego state. Using their own written dialogues or journal exercises as a script, patients can role play their eating disorder ego state with other patients playing another aspect of themselves.

Writing out dialogues or role-playing conversations between the patient and her body are also helpful techniques for defining the eating disorder ego state. The patient is asked to visualize her body seated in an empty chair in front of her. Questions from the therapist or from the group can help her to articulate her feelings about her body, why those feelings exist, and what her body needs.

Another technique is to have the patient put her drawing of her eating-disordered self on an empty chair, and then have her express her feelings toward that aspect of herself. Usually this exercise accesses the shame that she feels about that aspect of self. Another exercise would be to have the patient write and read a letter of thanks to her eating-disordered self, acknowledging the protective functions she has served.

After increasing the cohesiveness of the self through exploration and acceptance for the eating-disordered self, the next step is to help the patient take responsibility for future choices and growth. One intervention we have used to address this goal is to develop the aspect of self called the "good mother," "future self," or "higher self." The same techniques of guided imagery, drawing, collage, written dialogue, and role-playing are useful in defining and developing this aspect of self. The patient experiences herself nurturing and guiding her eating-disordered self. This reinforces the concept that there is an internal, rather than external, solution in internal conflict.

We use a psychodrama technique called "The Dining Table" (Goldman & Morrison, 1984) to help patients develop a direction for positive change in their current family. The patient chooses group members to portray her present family. She then positions them at her dining table.

The therapist then asks her to describe each family member in a precise and limited fashion. Questions such as "What two words would you use to describe your husband?" or "What is the main message your daughter is giving you?" can help her to clarify her experience of family members. While dramatizing how the family interacts, the patient is asked to articulate and explore her feelings about their interactions. Then the patient reverses roles and changes places with other family members in an effort to understand the family on a different, deeper level.

Next the patient reproduces her family of origin and goes through the process of describing them and role-playing their interaction. In processing this experience, the patient works on linking her affect with cognition.

The patient is helped to understand how current interactions may be connected to dynamics in her family of origin. She is able to identify how her behaviors may help maintain dysfunction in her current family. She works on defining other choices or options that would be more adaptive in her present life.

ABREACTION AND CATHARSIS

Techniques of abreaction aimed at restoring memories of the original trauma, reconnecting the feelings associated with the trauma, and revising the cognitive distortion it produced, become integral to any successful treatment of the dissociated eating disorder client. In abreaction, the person combines the adult ego state's capacities to reason, to resolve the long-standing trauma-generated confusion of the encapsulated child ego state. This cut-off-self part at last experiences the reparative corrective experience of an adult to champion it. Abreaction thereby allows reassociation of the split-off cognitions, affect and sensation, as well as a restructuring of the attributions and belief systems that arose out of the destructive traumatic environment.

Abreaction consists of an intensive reliving of a traumatic experience in which the experience is reassociated into consciousness and thereby made known to self and others. The vivid reliving typically involves a catharsis, a profound release of the emotions, ideas, and associations that have been encapsulated in the traumatic experience. The release of these at last completes the stress response cycle set in motion by the trauma (Horowitz, 1976). This application of patients' own (and their therapist's) adult understanding of the early events allows them to break free from the perfectly reasonable, yet badly distorted, conclusions of the traumatized child: the attitudes and beliefs that bind survivors to the trauma, causing them to repeatedly reenact the trauma in their adult lives.

Typically, the parts of self or ego states that absorbed the traumatic experience are accessed in hypnosis. Once a degree of safety and trust is established, the traumatic experiences of those parts of self are shared by asking clients to share, detail by detail, their experiences, with "one foot in the past and one foot in the present," this time in the safety and company of the adult ego state's knowledge and experience.

Sexual trauma involves simultaneously knowing and not knowing. Many adults who suffered from sexual trauma during their childhoods have partial or total amnesia regarding the abuse incidents, or else minimize and distort their histories. Some have no recall of the abuse at all; others may have vague, shadowy suspicions, but no substantive, detailed memories. Due to their dissociation from the knowledge of the abuse, the sensations and affect they experienced in the course of the abuse, and/ or their own behavior during or after the abuse incidents, some survivors experience and express little or no emotion in relation to the trauma. Dissociation, which protected survivors from suffering the full impact of the trauma, simultaneously prevented them from ever resolving the trauma, thereby bonding their lives to the trauma. This hidden, yet powerful, trauma bond becomes the major force that shapes their lives. The bulk of the survivors' energies is spent protecting the wound that no one—not even they themselves—can see.

To utilize a metaphor apropos of eating disorder, to a small child, the experience of sexual trauma is incomprehensible, undigestible. When this traumatic material is forced on a child, it cannot be processed. The material just sits there, deep inside, unseen and undigested. A foreign body of undigested, unabsorbed bulk, the traumatic material does not pass through the system, but rather plugs it up, blocking normal functions and connections.

In order to integrate this traumatic material, survivors must "metabolize" the trauma. Since the material is so massive, it cannot be swallowed whole without choking. In order to avoid overwhelming or revictimizing the survivor, the traumatic material must be broken down into small pieces of work, each piece building on the mastery and digestion of the last. Survivors must chew on the material, working it over more than once in order to break it into absorbable components. They need to recognize and accept the abuse they suffered in the past, finally allow themselves to express the intense feelings and fears locked away inside these memories, and correct the accommodated beliefs and other cognitive distortions formed regarding the childhood trauma (Schwartz et al., 1993).

Child victims of sexual abuse refuse even to acknowledge their traumatic losses, because these losses threaten their very survival. Yet this disavowal prevents survivors from mourning the physical, material, and psychological losses sustained through sexual trauma. For this reason, grief work is one of the cornerstones of abreaction. Our model for abreactive work, derived from earlier grief work, embraces the concepts of reliving, revising and revisiting:

Reliving—the abreactive work of revivification: recalling the details of the abuse and reexperiencing the traumatic affect—the subjective fears, somatic responses, and feelings associated with the trauma

Revising—the cognitive work of abreaction: reattributing responsibility to the abuser instead of the victim; correcting accommodated beliefs, ways of thinking, and attitudes; and recognizing the numerous revictimizations of self and others as repetitious of the original traumatic event(s)

Revisiting—going back to the original trauma with a new perspective and no longer needing revenge or acceptance from caregivers; developing new boundaries with a renewed sense of power, control, esteem, trust, and intimacy or of impending danger

Abreaction allows an adult survivor to register the totality of childhood wounds in manageable allotments; not just sexual trauma, but also physical, emotional, and gender abuse—all of the negative existential messages that have been internalized. Remembering childhood abuse of this kind evokes significant losses—of safety, of trust, of innocence, of virginity, of idealized images of the parent or other perpetrator, etc.—losses denied by the child because they were too unbearable. Grieving over these losses—allowing themselves to feel the pain, anger, sadness, and fears of the child who suffered these losses—must also be experienced as a part of abreaction. For many survivors, merely describing in detail the abuse and putting their fears and feelings into words will cause eating disorder symptoms to remit, at least temporarily.

SUMMARY AND CONCLUSIONS

Selected eating disorder clients have developed symptoms as functional, yet distorted, survival strategies to overwhelming, chronic, inescapable stress and acute trauma in childhood. By accessing the dissociated parts of self, and hypnotically facilitating abreaction and catharsis, there can be trauma resolution and the eating disorder symptoms become no longer functional. Once breaking this trauma bond, client are more able to benefit from cognitive-behavioral, systemic, gestalt, and 12-step approaches to superimposed factors that maintain and perpetuate the symptomatology. They are then able to learn to overcome long-term patterns of self-revictimization, learned helplessness, and low self-esteem and to utilize their own efforts and accomplishments to solve problems, thereby feeling more powerful and effective. In addition, they can then establish healthy relationships and sexual interaction, no longer feeling terrified by their vulnerability and dependency in intimate relationships.

REFERENCES

Abramson, E. E., & Lucido, G. M. (1991). Childhood sexual experience and bulimia. *Addictive Behaviors, 16,* 529–532.

Bailey, C. A., & Gibbons, S. G. (1989). Physical victimization and bulimic-like symptoms: Is there a relationship? *Deviant Behavior, 10,* 335–352.

Beckman, K. A., & Burns, G. L. (1990). Relation of sexual abuse and bulimia in college women. *International Journal of Eating Disorders, 9,* 487–492.

Bernstein, E. M., & Putnam, F. W. (1986). Development, reliability and validity of a dissociation scale. *Journal of Nervous and Mental Disease, 174,* 727–735.

Braun, B. G. (1986). *Treatment of multiple personality disorder.* Washington, DC: American Psychiatric Press.

Bulik, C. M. (1987). Drug and alcohol abuse by bulimic women and their families. *American Journal of Psychiatry, 144,* 1604–1606.

Bulik, C. M., Sullivan, P. F., & Rorty, M. (1989). Childhood sexual abuse in women with bulimia. *Journal of Clinical Psychiatry, 50,* 460–464.

Capacchione, L. (1991). *Recovery of your inner child.* New York: Simon & Schuster.

Demitrack, M. A., Putnam, F. W., Brewerton, T. D., Brandt, H., & Gold, P. W. (1990). Relation of clinical variables to dissociative phenomena in eating disorders. *American Journal of Psychiatry, 147,* 1184–1188.

Finn, S. E., Hartman, M., Leon, G. R., & Lawson, L. (1986). Eating disorders and sexual abuse: Lack of confirmation for a clinical hypothesis. *International Journal of Eating Disorders, 5,* 1051–1060.

Folsom, V., Krahn, D., Nairn, K., Gold, L., Demitrack, M. A., & Silk, K. R. (1993). The impact of sexual and physical abuse on eating disordered and psychiatric symptoms: A comparison of eating disordered and psychiatric inpatients. *International Journal of Eating Disorders, 13,* 249–257.

Goldman, E. E., & Morrison, D. S. (1984). *Psychodrama: Experience and process.* Dubuque, IA: Kendall/Hunt.

Hall, R. C. W., Tice, L., Beresford, T. P., Wooley, B., & Hall, A. K. (1989). Sexual abuse in patients with anorexia nervosa and bulimia. *Psychosomatics, 30,* 73–79.

Horowitz, M. J. (1976). *Stress response syndromes.* Northvale, NJ: Jason Aronson.

Hudson, J. I., Pope, H. G., Jonas, J. M., Yurelun-Todd, D., & Frankenburg, F. R. (1987). A controlled family history study of bulimia. *Psychological Medicine, 17,* 883–890.

McCallum, K. E., Lock, J., Kulla, M., Rorty, M., & Wetzel, R. D. (1992). Dissociative symptoms and disorders in patients with eating disorders. *Dissociation, 5,* 227–235.

McClelland, L., Mynors-Wallis, L., Fahy, T., & Treasure, J. (1991). Sexual abuse, disordered personality and eating disorders. *British Journal of Psychiatry, 158 (Suppl. 10),* 63–68.

McFarlane, A., McFarlane, C., & Gilchrist, P. (1988). Post-traumatic bulimia and anorexia nervosa. *International Journal of Eating Disorders, 7,* 937.

Oppenheimer, R., Howells, K., Palmer, R. L., & Chaloner, D. A. (1985). Adverse sexual experience in childhood and clinical eating disorders: A preliminary description. *Journal of Psychiatric Research, 19,* 357–361.

Palmer, R. L., Oppenheimer, R., Dignon, A., Chaloner, D. A., & Howells, K. (1990). Childhood sexual experiences with adults reported by women with eating disorders: An extended series. *British Journal of Psychiatry, 156,* 699–703.

Pope, H. G., Jr., & Hudson, J. I. (1992). Is childhood sexual abuse a risk factor for bulimia nervosa? *American Journal of Psychiatry, 149,* 455–463.

Root, M. P. P. (1991). Persistent, disordered eating as a gender-specific, post-traumatic stress response to sexual assault. *Psychotherapy, 28,* 96–102.

Root, M. P. P., & Fallon, P. (1988). The incidence of victimization experiences in a bulimic sample. *Journal of Interpersonal Violence, 3,* 161–173.

Ross, C. A., Heber, S., Norton, G. R., & Anderson, G. (1989). Differences between multiple personality disorder and other diagnostic groups on structured interview. *Journal of Nervous & Mental Disease, 177,* 487–491.

Schwartz, M., Galperin, L., & Masters, W. (1993). Dissociation and treatment of compulsive reenactment of trauma: Sexual compulsivity. In Hunter, M. (Ed.), *The sexually abused male* (Vol. 3). Lexington, MA: Lexington Books.

Schwartz, M. F., & Gay, P. (1993). Unpublished manuscript.

Smolak, L., Levine, M. P., & Sullins, E. (1990). Are child sexual experiences related to eating-disordered attitudes and behaviors in a college sample? *International Journal of Eating Disorders, 9,* 167–178.

Steiger, H., & Zanko, M. (1990). Sexual traumata among eating-disordered, psychiatric and normal female groups. *Journal of Interpersonal Violence, 5,* 74–86.

Stuart, G. W., Laraia, M. T., Ballenger, J. C., & Lydiard, R. B. (1990). Early family experiences of women with bulimia and depression. *Archives of Psychiatric Nursing, 4,* 43–52.

Torem, M. S. (1986). Dissociative states presenting as an eating disorder. *American Journal of Clinical Hypnosis, 29,* 137–142.

Vanderlinden, J., Vandereycken, W., Van Dyck, R., & Vertommen, H. (1993). Dissociative experiences and trauma in eating disorders. *International Journal of Eating Disorders, 13,* 187–193.

Waller, G. (1991). Sexual abuse as a factor in eating disorders. *British Journal of Psychiatry, 159,* 664–671.

Waller, G. (1993). Association of sexual abuse and borderline personality disorder in eating disordered women. *International Journal of Eating Disorders, 13,* 259–263.

Watkins, J. G. (1992). Psychoanalyse, hypnoanalyse, ego-state therapie: Auf der suche nach einer effektiven therapie. (Psychoanalysis, hypnoanalysis and ego-state therapy: In search of an efficient therapy). *Hypnose und Kognition, Band 9,* 125–143.

Watkins, J. G., & Watkins, H. H. (1988). The management of malevolent ego states in multiple personality disorder. *Dissociation, 1,* 67–72.

Williams, H. J., Wagner, H. L., & Calam, R. M. (1992). Eating attitudes in survivors of unwanted sexual experiences. *British Journal of Clinical Psychology, 31,* 203–206.

8

Body Image Disturbance in Eating Disorders and Sexual Abuse

CAROLYN COSTIN

> The truth about our childhood is stored up in our body and although we can repress it, we can never alter it. Our intellect can be deceived, our feelings manipulated, our perceptions confused and our body tricked with medication.
>
>   But someday the body will present its bill, for it is as incorruptible as a child who, still whole in spirit, will accept no compromises or excuses, and it will not stop tormenting us until we stop evading the truth.
>
> —Alice Miller*

Eating disorders represent ways in which the body presents its bill. Anorexia and bulimia nervosa can be seen as creative responses to developmental deficits, trauma, or other psychological stressors in a society that is obsessed with the body. In our thin-is-in society, what you weigh seems more important than who you are, and being thin is a measure not only of beauty, but of success and happiness as well. Given this climate, the body becomes an obvious place for a suffering will to do battle. An anorexic's body becomes the trophy that society willingly awards her, envious of what is perceived as her triumph of mind over body, her self-discipline, self-restraint, and control.

---

*Quotation from Alice Miller provided by a patient, source unknown.

Issues involving body self-pathology must be addressed in all individuals seen in therapy, but nowhere is this more profoundly apparent than in the treatment of individuals with eating disorders, especially those who have been sexually abused. If the "body is the temple of the soul," what are we to expect when that temple is violated, damaged, and left in ruin, as happens with sexual abuse? And what are we to make of those who tear down, fail to supply materials for, or completely disregard the need to care for their own temple, as is the case with eating-disordered patients? The similarities seen in how sexually abused patients and those with eating disorders view and treat themselves and their bodies have led to a better understanding of the experience and effects of nonintegration of mind and body. A significant correlation between sexual abuse and eating disorders has been mentioned elsewhere in this volume, but it is important to reiterate that not all patients who have been sexually abused develop eating disorders and that not all eating disorder patients have been sexually abused. However, the understanding and treatment of sexual abuse have significantly facilitated and enhanced the treatment of eating disorders, and vice versa. Furthermore, in learning how to treat the most difficult cases, the sexually abused and eating disordered, we become more adept at understanding and treating all others. Working with these patients has brought needed attention to the developmental issues that must be acknowledged and repaired in order for a cohesive body self and psychological self to exist.

BODY IMAGE DEVELOPMENT AND DISTURBANCE

To develop and maintain a healthy sense of self, a cohesive, distinct, accurate body self is necessary. Conceptualizations and representations of the body self become the body image. A succinct definition of the term "body image" can be found in *Body Image and Personality* by Fisher and Cleveland: " . . . a term which refers to the body as a psychological experience, and focuses on the individual's feelings and attitudes toward his own body" (Fisher & Cleveland, 1968).

Our feelings and attitudes toward our body, ultimately how we form our body image, are built on the interest, caring, and respect that others, particularly our caregivers, give our body when we are growing up. What an infant's body experiences and feels leads to a sense of body self (the discerning of self from nonself and the functions and kinesthetic experiences entailed). It was Freud who first recognized the ego as "first and foremost a body ego" (Freud, 1923/1961), as bodily experiences are the center around which the ego is developed. It is through our bodies that we come to know and experience ourselves as distinct, separate entities in the world. A healthy body image involves a good sense of body boundaries—feeling separate from but equal to others. Intrusive or neglectful caregiving will result in poor body boundaries, a poorly defined body self, and thus a poor mental representation of the body self or body image. Poorly formed body boundaries result in a lack of body awareness or an attempt to create boundaries in other ways. There are countless forms of intrusion and neglect, ranging from physical beatings to neglecting a child's wet diaper or cry for food. An extreme form of intrusion is sexual abuse. In sexual abuse, the body, the psychological self, and the sexual self are all violated in a seductive, confusing, and secretive way. In most cases, the perpetrator is someone who is supposed to love, take care of, and protect, which renders the child not only unable to understand but unable to discuss the abuse. The child will likely not have any visible wounds to show for it either.

THE PSYCHE AND SOMA SPLIT

Patients who have been sexually abused provide the most extreme examples of a conscious and sometimes unconscious need to gain control over or distance themselves from their body. To varying degrees, people who have been sexually abused perceive themselves as separate from their bodies. They have become split off from the body self as a way of protection. The abused may say, ''I don't remember feeling anything, it was as if the abuse was happening to someone else,'' and eating disorder patients may say, ''It was as if someone else was doing the bingeing and purging and I was an observer.''

The separation of the psychological self from the body self is an overriding feature of eating disorder patients and those with sexual abuse histories, with the most extreme cases being those who have both. How the body/mind separation becomes manifest is crucial and points to the need for the body self to be directly part of the treatment. Manifestations include:

Dissociation. Dissociating from the body is a form of protection that allows one to separate the self from the trauma: ''It happened to my body, not to me.'' Dissociation is not always the result of a defensive splitting off; in many cases, there was never a real integration of the mind and body to begin with: ''I have no idea how my body feels, hunger and fullness are foreign to me.'' It is common to hear patients refer to their bodies as separate from them or as monsters or as foreign creatures over which they have no control:

> "I look in the mirror, the reflection I see
> Half my weight stares back at me
> Where once was a smile is now just a frown
> Could that monster I see there be me?''
>
> —22-year-old bulimic patient

Numbness. If a person cannot physically get away from the abuse s/he can, in some sense, get away from it by becoming numb. Numbing serves the purpose of repressing a trauma or bad experience, or at least allowing one not to feel it. Bingeing, purging, compulsive exercising, and starving are all used by eating disorder patients to numb out either past or current events. Unfortunately, numbing leads to the avoidance both of pain and of pleasure: "When I'm bingeing I don't have to think about or feel anything else.''

Somatisization. Physical symptoms often substitute for psychological feelings—"I'm not good enough" equals "I feel hungry," or "I feel angry" equals "I feel fat," or "Everything agitates me, and I experience every agitation as a sensation of hunger, even if I have just eaten.'' The body may become the only container for the abuse with all cognitive memory repressed. The body retains such things as smells, sensations, sounds, and tastes from the trauma. These are referred to as body memories and are held in the body even when the incident is blocked from conscious awareness.

Reenactment. A reenactment refers to when an abused person becomes abusive and rageful toward others or self, reenacting abuse using his or her body or another's body with the illusion of being in control. For example, some say that they realize that bingeing and vomiting 20 times a day is harmful to their bodies, but at least they are in control of the harming. Self-starvation may be used as a means of keeping "harmful, dirty things'' out of one's body. (Mark Schwartz and Paula Gay discuss this phenomenon in Chapter 7.)

Repetition. The body may be used as currency to get needs met; for example, a sad lonely child who turns to food for comfort in an environment of neglect may continue this behavior into adulthood with no conscious understanding of what is taking place. If bingeing provides a self-soothing function, the individual will have to go back continually to this behavior to get comfort because the underlying deficit or neglect is not repaired by the bingeing. The ability to sooth one's self is not internalized, therefore, returning to the external behavior (bingeing) remains necessary as an adaptive function and an addictive pattern is set.

EATING DISORDERS AS ADAPTIVE FUNCTIONS

When the body is mistreated, neglected, or violated, one experiences a loss of control over it and a need somehow to get control back. Eating disorders represent a tenuous feeling of control, which has been achieved through the body. Controlling the body, and what goes in and out of it, becomes an adaptive and defensive reaction to past neglect, abuse, and developmental deficiencies. Starving, bingeing, and purging may be used to ward off an impending sense of fragmentation and thus serve as adaptive functions for a disordered self. Disordered eating patterns are, in part, attempts to resist with the body and to define, establish, or restore a sense of self. Through selective eating, an individual can decide and control what is taken in or released from the body. As one patient put it, "Eating or not eating is a way for me to control my body. I am the master of it. I am in charge of what goes in or out. Even if it isn't good for me, I am the one doing it, I am the one in control." Feeding and caring for the body may feel like a betrayal of one's self. The body is the enemy because it has turned on the individual, by being abused. A patient explains, "If it weren't for this body, I would have been Okay."

An anorexic who maintains extremely rigid control over her body may be expressing the fear of interpersonal contact. Fear of intrusion or losing controls fuels her will to defy her own needs: "I don't need food, I don't need you, I don't need anybody." A binge eater, on the other hand, may fear abandonment so much that she desperately attempts to fill the emptiness with food. A bulimic with fear of intrusion and abandonment seeks control of what goes in to the point of purging in order to keep things out. Clinicians have observed that similar to those who have been sexually abused, "The anorexic, the bulimic, and some compulsive overeaters experience a dreaded state of feeling that their bodies, indeed their self organization, is easily invaded, influenced, exploited, and overwhelmed by external focus (especially important people)" (Krueger, 1989).

One patient's journal described this event: "She binged and I went home and took laxatives, it is as if I don't know where my body stops and someone else's begins, I needed to purge for what she did. Not only do I not need anyone else to abuse me, now that I do it myself, I don't even need to binge to have my purging cycle triggered to an intense degree . . . help!''

Connecting abuse to body image disturbance and dissatisfaction is significant for patients and helps them begin to understand why and how their eating disorder developed as an adaptive function or response. Therapists can provide insight by explaining, for example, that in sexual abuse the child's body not only is violated, but, in a sense, is used as a weapon against her, and that an abused child may internalize an abusive attitude toward herself or her body, thinking ''I must be bad'' or ''My body is bad.'' A sexually abused anorexic offers: ''Every waking minute it seems I spend hating my body. Everything about my body is linked to pain and violence. Everyone says I have to eat and that they are trying to keep me alive, yet I feel like they are trying to kill me. I feel dirty and ugly and fat. I can never be thin enough. I'm not eating or drinking again. It scares me, it hurts me, and I hate it. Maybe I'm making a bad choice, but it's my choice.''

A task for the therapist working with such a patient would be to explore how she had turned the blame for the abuse toward her own body instead of toward the abuser. Blaming the body is extremely common in individuals whose bodies responded to the abuse with a physical sensation of pleasure: ''My body betrayed me, how could it have felt pleasure from such a vile disgusting act. It sickens me and I cannot forgive it. I stuff it all day long to keep it quiet.''

It is easy to understand how hatred, disgust, shame, and fear of the body are all results of sexual abuse and how controlling the body and what goes in and out of it becomes an adaptive and defensive reaction to such feelings. Understanding the importance of the development of the body self and body image helps us explore and treat nonabused eating disorder patients who feel similarly. Katryn Zerbe notes in *The Body Betrayed* that eating disorder patients in general believe their bodies are malevolent: ''Their sense of the body as a good and worthwhile container is impaired'' (Zerbe, 1993).

''My body is a useless burden, it will never be good enough, it is not worthy of attention or nurturing. Anything that enters my body, even food, could hurt me and over it I will have no control'' (17-year-old anorexic patient).

UNDERSTANDING BODY SELF AND BODY IMAGE DEVELOPMENT AND DISTURBANCE

To understand and treat the body self, we can begin by assessing (see the appendix) and empathically understanding the patient's body image.

Hilda Bruch was the first to point out: "Body image disturbance distinguishes the eating disorders, anorexia nervosa and bulimia nervosa, from other psychological conditions that involve weight loss and eating abnormalities and its reversal is essential to recovery" (Bruch, 1973). Research in the field of eating disorders has shown that body-image dissatisfaction is a better predictor of eating attitudes and behaviors and dieting pathology than other variables, such as self-esteem, depression, and social anxiety combined (Gross & Rosen, 1988). Furthermore, continued body dissatisfaction is associated with relapse and the poorest patient prognosis (Garfinkle et al., 1977).

The notion of a disturbed body image is complex. To understand body image is to understand the psychology of the body self, including physical appearance in both subjective and objective representations. As Cash and Pruzinsky (1990) point out, the concern with external, objective attributes of physical appearance is different from the concern with the internal, subjective representations of physical appearance and bodily experience. Both are important aspects of body image work. "I look fat," "I feel fat," and "I am fat," are very different experiences. As one patient describes it: "As long as the feeling is still there, it doesn't matter how thin I look in the mirror, because it's not thin enough to make me feel thin."

The diagnostic criteria relating to body image criteria for anorexia nervosa in the *Diagnostic and Statistical Manual of Mental Disorders*, Fourth Edition (DSM-IV) state: "Disturbance in the way in which one's body weight or shape is experienced, undue influence of body weight or shape on self-evaluation, or denial of the seriousness of the current low body weight" (DSM-IV, 1994, p. 545).

In 1980 when bulimia nervosa was first officially recognized, body image disturbance was not even included as a feature. The diagnostic criteria now states: "Self-evaluation is unduly influenced by body shape and weight." (DSM-IV, 1994, p. 550).

What constitutes "disturbance," "undue influences," or "denial"? Body image disturbance and overconcern with body image are common and even considered normal in this society but this does not mean that they are healthy. In eating disorder patients, it is not body-image dissatisfaction alone that is significant, but rather the importance placed on weight and shape in determining self-worth, and the measures they are willing to take to manipulate and control their bodies in order to conform to some standard or self-imposed body image.

Body image disturbance must be seen as a multidimensional phenomenon that involves three main components: perception, attitude, and behavior. In assessing body image, each of these components needs to be considered:

Perception. That is what a person actually sees when looking at him- or herself directly or in the mirror. Perceptual distortion is a common feature of eating disorders. Most anorexics and many bulimics actually see themselves as fat even though they are normal weight or even emaciated: ''I look into the mirror and a fat person stares back, even though the scale reads 65 pounds.'' An obese binge eater may also have a distorted body image, for example, expressing shock and disbelief upon seeing her reflection in a window.

Attitude. The attitude toward one's body expresses the meaning given to one's perception, and reflects the investment of self-worth in appearance. It is not the body itself, but rather the attitude toward it, that causes someone to feel and act in certain ways. Significant changes in our culture have led to an overfocus on the female body in general, with the idealization of a lean body type over the last 30 years. Young women today are being exposed to this image from birth, their mothers having already been indoctrinated to worry about getting fat. Girls often approach puberty carrying a negative attitude toward their mother's body and their own. The influence of maternal attitudes on the daughter's body image was illustrated in a *Glamour* magazine survey of 33,000 women conducted in 1984. The survey found that when mothers were critical of their daughter's bodies, the daughters showed poorer body images, a greater use of severe dieting practices, and a higher incidence of bulimia.

Behavior. It is important for both therapist and patient to understand that such behaviors as fasting, self-induced vomiting, compulsive exercise, and bingeing are, in part, based on perception and attitude. Changing the behavior alone most likely will do nothing to change the perception or attitude. (An exception to this would be when upon refeeding an anorexic, her visual distortion and her obsession with food diminish due to an adequate nutrient supply.) Changing perception and attitude, however, will result in changes in behavior. If a patient no longer sees herself as fat, unacceptable, easily invaded, and likely to go out of control, the need to starve decreases. It is important to note that by influencing cognition, behavior reflects body image: ''I must starve this unacceptable fat body''—and affects body image: ''If I exercise or don't eat, I feel good about my body.''

UNDERSTANDING THE EATING DISORDER SELF

Overconcern with weight and shape no doubt is a partial result of our cultural idealization of thinness and a major contributing factor to the rise in eating disorders. However, in today's climate of "thin is in," in which most women are dissatisfied with their bodies, we must remember that not all women develop eating disorders and that eating disorders are not just about food and weight. Probing beneath the surface of an obsession with food and weight, we find a disordered self, usually one that is split off from nature, separated in mind from body, and divided in thought from feeling.

Patients need our help to understand their obsession, to learn that they are not monsters or diseased but rather that they have been injured, that something bad or monstrous was done to them, or that something that was supposed to happen to them did not. They need help in understanding how they developed a split-off self when their early needs were not responded to, and how, at some point, eating, not eating, or purging became a substitute for responsiveness from caregivers because of previous disappointment or abuse. Patients must be helped to recognize that their body has been recruited through the eating-disorder symptoms to enact their deepest needs, for example, bingeing as an expression of the need for nurturance or connectedness and purging as the need for self-definition. How often have eating disorder therapists heard some version of these statements from patients—"I can trust food," "Food doesn't ask anything of me," "Food is always available," "Food doesn't talk back," "Food fills up my emptiness," "Food gives me what I expect."

In *The Obsession*, Kim Chernin describes one of the first detailed accounts of a woman suffering from anorexia nervosa, who was originally written up in 1944 and referred to as Ellen West (Chernin, 1981). Ellen's struggle still provides insight into this disorder as we come to understand how she eventually gave up all of her strivings and longings to be replaced by her obsession for being thin. Her internal conflicts shifted from the real and vital issue of her own development to the symbolic issue of the size of her body and the amount of food she ate. Like Ellen West, our patients need to gain a meaningful understanding of their condition. In Ellen's own words, "I am in prison and cannot get out. It does no good for the analyst to tell me that I myself place the armed men there, that they are theatrical figments and nor real. To me they are very real. Perhaps I would find liberation if I could solve this puzzle: the connection between eating and longing" (Chernin, 1981).

The armed men represent the forces with which those suffering from eating disorders are struggling, the forces that those hoping to treat them must identify and reckon with. What was said about Ellen West in 1944 can be said about sexually abused eating-disordered patients suffering now: "Her rage, which arose initially because of the restrictions imposed upon her self-development, is now directed, through her body, at the "inner self" which hungers for its development. It is a costly and tragic reversal . . . her obsession with her body is, fundamentally, an expression of violence towards her soul" (Chernin, 1981).

My personal experience with anorexia nervosa and my work with eating disorder patients over the last 15 years have led me to the conclusion that all eating-disordered patients, to a greater or less degree, have an eating disorder self with a different set of feelings, needs, perceptions, and behaviors than that of the patient who initially walks through the door and presents for the session. For example, patients will describe internal dialogues between one self who wants to eat and another who cannot allow it. Understanding the concept of an eating disorder self has been enhanced through work with dissociative patients so severely sexually abused that they develop parts of self, or alters, that are distinct from and not readily accessible to the core self or to others.

CONTACTING THE EATING DISORDER SELF

It is not enough for therapists to explore with patients their distorted perception, thinking, or the function of eating disorder symptoms. What is needed is to contact and transform the split-off eating disorder self or body self and integrate it back into the core. For those of us doing this work, the response from our patients has been positive and overwhelming. When talking to patients about the part of them that does the bingeing rather than about the bingeing itself or the reasons behind the bingeing, a new dimension is opened up in the treatment and patients feel understood like never before. This technique is not intended to absolve patients from responsibility for their behavior; rather, it is meant to help them accept, understand, and express that they have a separate part of self that functions differently from the self they usually present to others, and to help them to get in contact with this part of self, and accept responsibility for it. By not contacting this part of self, the patient and therapist make the mistake of not accepting it and of pushing it further out of awareness and thus further out of control. For full recovery to take place, it is a psychological imperative that the eating disorder self be empathized with and integrated into the whole psyche, just as it is for the integration of traumatic memories into the psyche of those who have been abused, otherwise its motives and behaviors will proceed untransformed.

New strategies have been developed in order to contact and work with the eating disorder self. These strategies take into account that this self's ability to communicate verbally is minimal, if not altogether unrealized, as it is a mute feeling, body self, split off from the rest of self, and it very likely was developed before verbalization was part of the patient's repertoire. Techniques that utilize expressive therapies, such as art, movement, dance, guided imagery, and hands-on-body work (like massage), are used to integrate issues of body image and the body self into the larger context of psychotherapy for eating disorders. Detailed treatments developed to deal with the effects of sexual abuse, such as ego-state therapy, abreaction, and presentification, are also useful in healing body-image disturbance. These treatments are described in this volume and elsewhere (Schwartz & Gay, 1993).

The expressive and experiential techniques can be powerful in elucidating body image disturbance, bringing out the eating disorder self, and uncovering stored feelings and body memories because they deal in the realm of sensations and images. Some of this work flows freely from the patients because they are less experienced in doing these activities, and thus they are less likely to have developed guards and resistances. However, proper precautions must be taken. Patients must feel safe and supported to do this work. The intensity of this type of treatment ranges from creating a piece of artwork, which is fairly nonthreatening, to actual body massage, which can cause painful and frightening memories to be relived and released.

Examples of Expressive and Experiential Strategies

Journaling and Writing

Have patients write letters to or dialogue with their eating disorder selves or body selves.

Have patients write dialogues between their eating disorder selves and some other parts of the selves.

Have patients write what they are feeling immediately before a binge or purge.

Do interviews with their bodies or have them interview their body selves.

Art

Have patients express their feelings and thoughts through colors or pictures.

Have patients draw how they feel about or how they see their bodies.

Have patients make a life-size drawing from memory of their bodies and then trace their real bodies.

Have patients draw or otherwise represent their mind/body split.

Have patients draw or otherwise visually present certain feelings in their bodies.

Using collage work, ask patients to: create images of their eating disorder selves, both positive and negative; create box collages with their "presenting" selves on the outside and eating disorder selves inside; create a story of all the things that have influenced their body images.

Eating with Patients

Have patients bring "problem" foods to eat during the session.

Have a meal with the patient.

Using Analogies

Patients have an easier time relating to an abstract but analogous concept than directly discussing their own bodies. Over the years I have developed a variety of useful analogies, some examples of which follow.

Garden Hose. When patients first begin to eat and keep down adequate amounts of food, even after only one meal, they may experience a weight gain, which makes them feel as if they are out of control, getting bigger, and reinforces the "food makes me fat" fear. The analogy of a garden hose offers an alternative: "If I pick up and weigh an empty garden hose, and then I fill it with water and weight it again, I will find that the hose weighs more when it is filled, but it hasn't gotten any bigger. This is what it is like to now have food in your intestines." I explain to patients that they will weigh more after eating until the food is digested and burned up, as when you put wood in a fireplace (another analogy).

Sun Burn. Patients think that because they cannot see or feel the damage happening to their body, it is not going on. It can be suggested to the patient that it is as though she is lying on the beach on a sunny day without sunscreen and others are trying to tell her that she is burning her skin, which they know from experience. Because she cannot see her skin getting red or feel it burning, she does not believe it is happening. Tell her that those who care about her are trying to protect her from herself and the harm that will eventually show up. The goal is not to take the suntan away from her, but to show her how to be in the sun without burning her skin.

Heart Surgery. Patients almost always feel worse as they begin to decrease their use of eating disorder symptoms. Without the numbing or distracting functions that the symptoms served, real feelings surface and are felt more deeply than before. At this point in therapy, patients may express such sentiments as "This feels worse than having the eating disorder, I can't continue treatment." One can use the analogy of a patient who goes in for heart surgery and wakes up on the operating table. Seeing the state his body is in and feeling the pain from which he was supposed to be anesthetized, he screams, "Get me out of here, I'm in much more pain now than I was when I came in." Tell patients that as with heart surgery, things seem to get worse before they get better and that they must not leave treatment just when they are opened up and ready for the surgery; they must stay until the damaged parts are fixed and they are closed back up again. Explain that they need to stay around for the stitches to be removed and the final healing to take place. A scar may always remain, but not necessarily the need for continued treatment.

Body Work

Some therapists believe that the body itself needs help in overcoming the damage of abuse, and they promote hands-on physical body work, such as massage, in conjunction with psychotherapy. There are numerous forms of this kind of body work, including accupressure, rolfing, Alexander technique, Heller work, and polarity. Such books as *Your Body Never Lies* (Berry, 1993) and *Embodying Healing: Integrating Bodywork and Psychotherapy in Recovery from Childhood Sexual Abuse* (Timms & Conners, 1992) cite research from various sources, claiming that physical events have corresponding emotional responses experienced and stored in the body as body memories. As a result of childhood trauma, the body retains abuse memories and develops automatic response patterns, such as rigidity, inability to cry, constant tension, and headaches or stomachaches. Although more research is needed in this area, it appears that, in some cases, body work may facilitate the release of these stored body memories. Professional and ethical issues must be considered regarding the incorporation of body work into the therapeutic process.

Incorporating body self and body image work into treatment can be accomplished in a variety of ways. It can be separately focused on in workshops or intensives, and it should be part of ongoing therapy.

Part of Ongoing Therapy

Body image work and techniques can be woven into ongoing therapy. Specific sessions can be devoted to the topic and certain strategies can be utilized, or the topic can come up during any session and thus working on it can be incorporated into the moment. Patients provide opportunities for therapists to deal with their body image issues, and therapists too often let these invitations go by without or with minimal response. For example, an anorexic or a bulimic complaining of a fat stomach or of being fat while pointing to a slim or emaciated body might be told that, in fact, she is not fat. Although trying to reassure a patient or to challenge the distortion can be a useful approach, often left out are important questions, such as, "So what if your stomach was sticking out, what would that mean to you?" "What would happen if it were true?" "Who would love you or like you less?" "How would you be different?" "What are you willing to do about it?" "What is the price you are willing to pay for a flatter stomach?" Patients do not have a deep understanding of what their perception really means to them and too often are not even asked to explore it because the distorted perception itself is receiving all the attention.

An Example from My Own Practice

An invitation to deal with body image opens up when patients talk about their weight and always need to know what it is. In order to protect patients from themselves and their inevitable reactions to the number on the scale—whether they are overweight, underweight, or normal weight—I work hard to establish rapport and trust with patients such that they agree to weigh only in my office and to weigh with their back to the scale. Various arrangements are made between me and patients as to what and when I will tell them. For example, with an overweight patient I might say, "I will tell you when you've lost 10 pounds," whereas to an anorexic I might say, "I will tell you when you have gained five pounds." The agreement in itself is a great undertaking, one that in many therapy offices is often disregarded or left to another professional, such as the doctor or dietitian. In some cases, deferring weight issues to others is appropriate, but I caution therapists to be careful not to split the issue by referring to weight and food intake as material for the dietitian and not for therapy. If not handled carefully, therapists can reinforce a mind–body split, which works against the task at hand—to try to integrate mind and body. Whenever a client wants to know her weight, I use that opportunity to explore what her weight means to her and what she will do with the information whether she has gained, maintained, or lost weight. Patients often say they will be fine with the data and that they are just curious. Why? What does the information really tell them about themselves? What is the patient willing to do; in other words, what price is she willing to pay if the number on the scale is not to her liking? Going through this with a patient is critical. Quite often in the beginning of a conversation when a patient wants to know her weight, I disarm her by stating that I am willing to tell her her weight if she still wants to know after our discussion. Many times, after we have discussed the pros and cons of knowing the number on the scale and its significance in her life, the patient can accept my reluctance to tell her, and eventually she no longer needs to see or know that number. Part of my argument involves asking the patient to give up, or at least temporarily suspend, her focus on her body and begin to re-focus attention on her inner self.

SPECIAL CONSIDERATIONS FOR THE THERAPIST

If patients are to develop positive relationships with their bodies, therapists must assist them in challenging and correcting their distortions. The task of the therapist is to help the patient create a nurturing attitude and develop behaviors such that the body is no longer used as a battleground or to express hidden pain, but is accepted as a source of feelings and physical needs. In this endeavor, the therapist must serve as a role model for patients in terms of the therapist's regard for and care and feeding of his or her own body. The therapist must assist the patient while allowing her to accomplish whatever she can on her own. The task can be a difficult one: the more chronic and severe the symptoms, the more direct management of the symptoms is needed. Anorexics who appear self-sufficient and determined to do it their own are often allowed to drop to dangerous weights before more serious intervention takes place. On the other hand, we must keep in mind that removing a woman's choice concerning her own body can be both violating and disempowering. Our patients' problems already reflect disempowerment, and we must be careful not to reinforce it. Knowing when to allow the process to unfold and when to step in and take over represents the difference between the art and the technique of therapy.

In working with patients, therapists must continually ask, "Whose agenda am I attending to?" There is a fine line between taking over for a patient when she needs it and is silently asking for the container and protector that she never had, and controlling a patient, reenacting abuse or intrusiveness. Ultimately, the motivation to gain or lose weight, nourish the body, and discontinue purging or gorging oneself into numbness must be an internal one. External motivations will not endure alone. Often when threats or behavioral contingencies are employed, anorexics forced to gain weight, binge eaters forced to lose weight, or bulimics forced to stop purging go right back to their old behaviors as soon as the contingencies stop. Weight change is no guarantee of improved body image or of healing. One patient with anorexia nervosa, who had recently been discharged from a hospital program and immediately began losing the 15 pounds she had gained there, put it this way, "They taught me how to change my behaviors and put weight on, but they didn't help me learn to deal with it." A binge eater had a similar complaint, "Everyone was willing to help me lose weight, but no one prepared me for the real things that losing the weight would uncover. I didn't know how to deal with it."

Patients who change their body image often need to grieve the loss of an ideal, a focus and a preoccupation that gave them a sense of safety and purpose. They must confront reality and illusions about what their bodies can and cannot do. They must face the fear of accepting their bodies and face the fact that their compulsive activities produce only a temporary illusion of self and that a well-formulated identity still needs to be achieved.

As one young woman in recovery from anorexia stated, "I'm not sure who I am anymore, my only identity was with my body in terms of making it look a certain way and making it do what I wanted. I spent all my time wondering how I looked, was I thin enough, did I run far enough, was I attractive enough. It's as though my whole purpose has been taken away from me and I have to find something else."

Therapists must empathize with the sense of loss experienced by patients when giving up their eating disorder self and must help them with the grieving process, as well as with the establishment of a new, healthier identity and focus. The eating disorder most likely will not be given up unless something else exists to replace it. The idea of integrating the eating disorder self rather than getting rid of it provides a useful perspective. One patient on the road to healing put it this way in a letter to her bulimia.

You have a lot of strength, which I acknowledge and admire. Let's try to channel that strength into employing our newly learned coping skills, building a strong, healthy body free of the chains of the eating disorder. No one said I have to get rid of you. Just the opposite. Carolyn is hoping I can integrate your strength into me to create an even stronger, much healthier system. I'm not saying I don't need you; I'm just saying I need you in a new and different way, a healthier way, a way Carolyn is teaching us about and encouraging us to become. I certainly don't see you as all bad, Bulimia; I need your determination and your control, but I need it to be expressed in a healthy way. I'm tired of throwing up. I'm tired of the laxatives. I'm tired of always being dehydrated. I'm tired of living my life in the bathroom, sneaking in and out so no one knows or suspects. I'm tired of craving foods I know I'll just throw up if I eat one or two. And I'm no longer proud of the fact that I can throw up so quietly that no one hears. That's a part of your identity that I'd like to leave behind, replacing it with a strength such as knowing that to eat one or two forbidden foods won't kill us, and that we can be in control without being self-destructive. I need you, Bulimia, you're right; but I need the healthy aspects you can offer, without the destructive ones. That is my goal as the healthy self.

SUMMARY

Body image disturbance is a primary feature of eating-disordered, sexually abused individuals. Specific attention must be given to the body self-pathology and to the developmental deficits that caused or contributed to this pathology in order for a cohesive body self, encompassing body image acceptance and thus a healthy integrated psychological self, to exist.

Eating disorder behaviors are adaptive functions of a disordered self trying to cope. The task of the therapist is to provide insight into how the patient has become disconnected from her body, using it as a weapon against herself, and to respond to the patient's derailed developmental needs, assisting her in the development of more useful methods of coping. We must help our patients to understand that rather than giving up their eating disorder, they are integrated it into their core self. It is the ultimate task of the therapist to give the patients back to themselves, the body's bill having been paid.

APPENDIX

Assessment Techniques

A variety of body image assessment methodologies have been developed. The following two assessment tools are easy to administer, and to interpret and use with patients in either an outpatient or inpatient setting.

The Perceived Body Image Scale (PBIS) 21 is a visual rating scale consisting of 11 cards containing figure drawings, ranging from emaciated to obese. Subjects are given the cards and asked four questions that represent different aspects of body image. Subjects are asked to pick the figure card that best depicts their answer to each question. The question structure basically remains the same with the substitution of four different inserts: Which body best represents the way you—

think you look?

feel you are?

see yourself in the mirror?

would like to look?

The PBIS was developed for easy and rapid administering to determine which components of body image are disturbed and to what degree. The PBIS is useful not only as an assessment, but also as a tool in psychotherapy.

The Eating Disorder Inventory, 2 (EDI-2) (Garner, 1991) is another way to assess body image and related issues. It is a significant and respected tool used to determine several eating disorder behaviors and characteristics, many of which are important in understanding and treating body image. Three subscales of the EDI-2 are body dissatisfaction, drive for thinness, and interoceptive awareness.

> The *body dissatisfaction* subscale measures dissatisfaction with overall shape and dissatisfaction with the size of those regions of the body that are of greatest concern to eating disorder patients.

> The *drive for thinness* subscale measures excessive concern for dieting, preoccupation with weight, and fear of weight gain.

> The *interoceptive awareness* subscale is a useful indicator of how in touch a person is with emotional and physical sensations and feelings, including hunger and fullness. This subscale measures confusion and mistrust related to affective and bodily functioning.

This author's experience in testing patients with the EDI-2 has shown that high scores on the body image dissatisfaction subscale (BID) accompany high interoceptive awareness scores, and that in patients who have been sexually abused, both scores are extremely elevated, and much higher than for nonsexually abused patients. Smolak (1990) did not find these differences.

REFERENCES

American Psychiatric Association. (1994). *Diagnostic and statistical manual of mental disorders* (4th ed.). Washington, DC: Author.

Berry, C. (1993). *Your body never lies.* Berkeley, CA: PageMill Press.

Bruch, H. (1973). *Eating disorders: Obesity, anorexia nervosa, and the person within.* New York: Basic Books.

Cash, T., & Pruzinsky, T. (1990). *Body images: Development, deviance and change.* New York: Guilford Press.

Chernin, K. (1981). *The obsession.* New York: Harper & Row.

Fisher, S., & Cleveland, S. E. (1968). *Body image and personality* (rev. ed.). New York: Dover Press.

Freud, S. (1961). The ego and the id. In J. Strachey (Ed. and Trans.) The standard edition of the complete psychological works of Sigmund Freud (Vol. 19, pp. 3–66). London: Hogarth Press. (Original work published 1923).

Garfinkle, P., Molodofsky, M., & Garer, D. (1977). Prognosis in anorexia nervosa as influenced by clinical features, treatment and self-perception. *Canadian Medical Association Journal, 117,* 1041–1045.

Garner, D. (1991). *Eating Disorder Inventory-2.* Odessa, FL: Psychological Assessment Resources.

Gross, J., & Rosen, J. C. (1988). Bulimia in adolescents: Prevalence and psychosocial correlates. *International Journal of Eating Disorders, 7,* 51–61.

Krueger, D. (1989). *Body self and psychological self.* New York: Brunner/Mazel.

Manley, R., & LePage, T. (1986). *The Perceived Body Image Scale (PBIS).* Vancouver, BC, Canada: Childrens Hospital.

Schwartz, M., & Gay, P. (1993). Physical and sexual abuse and neglect and eating disorder symptoms. *Eating Disorders: The Journal of Treatment and Prevention, 1* (3, 4).

Smolak, L., Levine, M. P., & Sullins, E. (1990). Are child sexual experiences related to a college sample? *International Journal of Eating Disorders, 9,* 167–178.

Striegel-Moore, R. H., Silberstein, L. R., Frensch, P., & Rodin, J. (1989). A prospective study of disordered eating among college students. *International Journal of Eating Disorders, 8,* 99–509.

Timms, R., & Conners, P. (1992). *Embodying healing: Integrating bodywork and psychotherapy in recovery from childhood sexual abuse.* Brandon, VT: Safer Society Press.

Zerbe, K. (1993). *The body betrayed.* Washington, DC: American Psychiatric Press.

9

Medical Presentations of Covert Sexual Abuse in Eating Disorder Patients

PHILIP S. MEHLER

KENNETH L. WEINER

A subpopulation of patients with eating disorders has also experienced sexual abuse. Medical symptoms in that subpopulation can, at times, represent an embellishment of true organic pathology or a physical way of remembering past trauma ("body memories"). Organic disease must be ruled out by the use of specific and appropriate tests. A thorough history and a detailed physical examination are imperative so that the patient is not subjected to unnecessary, expensive, and/or often invasive tests, which may only worsen or complicate the patient's condition. Medical personnel and therapists alike should be direct their attention to the connection between unusual physical symptoms and a history of sexual abuse in patients with eating disorders.

A distinct subpopulation of eating disorder patients has been sexually abused (Connors & Morse, 1993; Hall et al., 1989; Hudson et al., 1987; Pope & Hudson, 1992). Sexually abused patients with bulimia and anorexia nervosa frequently present with medical symptoms that may be difficult to explain. Differentiating bulimia, esophageal reflux, and psychogenic vomiting can often involve numerous costly medical tests. When the physical presentation has atypical characteristics, an underlying psychiatric conflict should be considered. At times, this is not a black-or-white equation, but rather the patient may be experiencing true organic pathology in an idiosyncratic fashion. At other times, especially in patients with a history of sexual and/or physical trauma, the patient may have symptoms representative of the unresolved conflict. Pain, cramping, nausea, vomiting, and fears of being infected can frequently be ways of remembering in a somatic rather than a cognitive fashion. Some therapists refer to these as "body memories." This chapter briefly discusses three patients with eating disorders who presented with unusual medical complaints. In all three cases, medical intervention was not helpful until the patients' sexual abuse histories were diagnosed and effectively treated

CASE REPORTS

Patient A is a 33-year-old female who presented with a nine-week history of recurrent vomiting in the setting of a few-year history of mild anorexia nervosa. She was evaluated by her psychiatrist who referred her to an internist. Her history was notable for a 10-pound weight loss, and the absence of abdominal pain or systemic symptoms. Physical examination was notable for a thin female, but was otherwise completely benign, as were her laboratory results including a complete blood count and chemistry panel. Despite the prescription of a vast array of different antiemetic medications, the vomiting and weight loss persisted. A CAT scan of the abdomen and brain were normal, as were an upper gastrointestinal series and abdominal ultrasound. The patient was then admitted to a psychiatric hospital where she was treated with bowel rest and intravenous fluids. During the course of her nine-day hospital stay, intensive psychotherapy and hypnosis revealed a remote history of severe incest, which was dealt with by her psychiatrist. The vomiting ceased soon thereafter, and the antiemetics were discontinued without recurrence of the vomiting.

Patient B is a 41-year-old female with a three-year history of severe anorexia nervosa. The initial precipitant seemed related to a pseudomonal lung infection.[1]* Thereafter, she became convinced that she had a candidal[2] throat infection concomitant with a strongyloides[3] bowel infection. Of note, this patient had formal training in microbiology. As a result

---

*Superior numbers throughout refer to items in the glossary at the end of this chapter.

thereof, she restricted her intake and lost 25 pounds. Her examination was normal, aside from severe cachexia. Stool examinations for blood, fecal leukocytes,[4] culture, and ova and parasites were all negative. Chest radiographs, sputum cultures, and bloodwork were also unremarkable. She was treated with total parenteral nutrition[5] for her severe and refractory anorexia nervosa. Intense psychotherapy revealed a latent history of incest and sexual abuse. Gradually, her weight was restored. She has been able to maintain her weight with regular eating habits and has recovered from her anorexia nervosa.

Patient C is a 36-year-old woman with a four-year history of anorexia and the fear that she had systemic candidiasis. These problems occurred shortly after the patient had a vaginal hysterectomy for a prolapsed uterus[6] and almost died from postoperative hemorrhaging. On presentation, the patient was convinced she had a systemic candidal infection which caused bloating and stomach pain. She also had chronic complaint of vaginal burning, itching, and lubrication similar to that one would experience with sexual excitement. She was also bothered by a burning in her chest, mouth, and tongue. The patient was hospitalized medically and underwent gynecologic, internal medicine, gastroenterological, neurologic, and allergy consultations. She had extensive bloodwork and endoscopy.[7] The results were all negative. Following years of extensive psychiatric treatment, a history of the patient having been incested by her father from age 7 to 16 emerged. The patient's eating disorder, posttraumatic stress disorder, depression, and panic disorder were treated aggressively, with cessation of anorexia, gastrointestinal, and gynecological complaints, and concerns about systemic candidiasis.

DISCUSSION

The victim of sexual abuse who has a concomitant eating disorder will frequently complain of predominantly physical ailments. It may be unclear to the physician or therapist whether the patient is suffering from a physical or psychiatric disorder. This dilemma is not uncommon; it is difficult to ascertain whether the complaint is a response to a primary physical illness or a symptom of underlying coexistent psychiatric disorders associated with sexual abuse (Barrett et al., 1988; Coulehan et al., 1990; Kathol & Petty, 1981; Rodin & Voshart, 1986). A number of articles have dealt with similar dilemmas. Perhaps, as in other depressed patients, survivors of sexual abuse report more severe physical symptoms and dysfunction, which further complicates the situation. This physical dysfunction may be a variant of a heterogeneous set of factitious disorders seen in a medical practice (Reich & Gottfried, 1983). In the cases described herein, we find this dilemma clearly manifested. These patients presented with predominantly physical complaints, seemingly indicative of an underlying medical condition. Yet, after an extensive negative evaluation, latent sexual abuse was found to be at the root of the symptoms.

With regard to the patient with incessant vomiting, Patient A, there may have been some clues, in retrospect, suggestive of a functional etiology. Perhaps, if these were heeded, the need for some of the medical evaluation and treatment might have been obviated. Specifically, although vomiting may be a manifestation of a wide variety of conditions, including gastrointestinal obstruction, pancreatitis,[8] peptic disease,[9] cholecystitis,[10] pregnancy, drug toxicity, hepatitis, increased intracranial pressure, and the Zollinger-Ellison syndrome,[11] to name a few, there are some clinical features that help the physician logically approach a patient with vomiting. If the vomiting occurs during or soon after a meal and relieves abdominal pain, peptic disease should be considered. Alternatively, if the vomiting is delayed at least one hour after eating, gastric obstruction or a gastric motility[12] disorder is likely. Vomiting of material eaten 12 hours earlier is pathognomic for an obstruction and excludes a psychogenic cause. Other general items to consider when evaluating a patient with vomiting are age, the presence or absence of weight loss, history of previous abdominal surgery, and the characteristics of the abdominal examination.

There are two distinct psychological entities that are heavily punctuated by vomiting, namely cyclical vomiting and psychogenic vomiting. Cyclical vomiting is defined by recurring attacks of intense vomiting that recur at regular intervals. Each episode begins suddenly and may last a few days. Psychogenic vomiting is characterized by vomiting that typically occurs soon after the meal has begun, after just a few bites, or soon after completion. This type of vomiting can be suppressed, if necessary, until the patient, for example, reaches a toilet, and does not usually affect appetite. However, weight loss can be profound (Wruble et al., 1982).

Similarly, with Patient B, there were definite clues that a diagnosis of a parasitic infection did not pertain to her. There was no eosinophilia[13] present on her blood count, multiple stools were negative for ova and parasites, and she never had documented diarrhea. With regard to her concern about a candidal infection in her throat and lungs, there was never any objective evidence to support this diagnosis. Her pharnyx was devoid of thrush,[14] she never had the odynophagia[15] which is found with esophageal candidiasis, and repeated culture of her sputum merely grew normal oral flora. This same negative evaluation was found with Patient C despite referrals to multiple subspecialists.

Thus, from a treatment vantage point, when dealing with this emotionally tenuous population, which frequently voices a multitude of physical complaints, organic disease must be ruled out by appropriate tests. It is imperative that the correct diagnosis be made with alacrity so that the patient is not subjected to unnecessary, expensive, and often invasive tests, which may only worsen or complicate the patient's condition. This is especially true in the group of eating disorder patients who have also been sexually abused. A thorough history and detailed physical examination must be accomplished to look for typical features of functional illnesses, as well as the presence of an objective disease process.

GLOSSARY OF TERMS

1. Pseudomonal lung infection—a severe type of pneumonia.
2. Candida—a type of yeast that causes different types of infections.
3. Strongyloides—a type of parasite that causes bowel problems.
4. Leukocytes—white blood cells.
5. Total parental nutrition—predigested nutritional solution infused through a catheter in a vein.
6. Prolapsed uterus—a condition where the ligaments holding the uterus in the pelvis become lax.
7. Endoscopy—looking into the stomach through a fiberotic scope.
8. Pancreatitis—inflammation of the pancreas which causes vomiting and abdominal pain.
9. Peptic disease—ulcers.
10. Cholecystitis—inflammation of the gall bladder.
11. Zollinger-Ellison syndrome—a stomach condition that causes ulcers.
12. Gastric motility—the act of the stomach contracting to empty the food within it into the intestines.
13. Eosinophilia—a type of white blood cell that indicates an allergic or parasitic disease process.
14. Thrush—a whitish coating of the throat that indicates a yeast infection.
15. Odynophagia—painful swallowing.

REFERENCES

Barrett, J. E., Barrett, J. A., Oxman, T. E., & Gerber, P. D. (1988). Prevalence of psychiatric disorders in primary care practice. *Archives General Psychiatry, 45,* 110–1106.

Connors, M. E., & Morse, W. (1993). Sexual abuse and eating disorders: A review. *International Journal of Eating Disorders, 1,* 1–11

Coulehan, J. L., Schulberg, H. C., Block, M. R., Janosky, J. E., & Arena, V. C. (1990). Medical comorbidity of major depressive disorders in a primary medical practice. *Archives of International Medicine, 150,* 2363–2367.

Hall, R. C. W., Tice, L., Beresford, T. P., Wooley, B., & Hall, A. K. (1989). Sexual abuse in patients with anorexia nervosa and bulimia. *Psychosomatics, 30,* 73–79, 1989.

Hudson, J. I., Pope, H. G., Yurgelun-Todd, D., Jonas, J. M., & Frankenburg, F. R. (1987). A controlled study of lifetime prevalence of affective and other psychiatric disorders in bulimic outpatients. *American Journal of Psychiatry, 7,* 257–267.

Kathol, R. G., & Petty, F. (1981). The relationship of depression to medical illness. *Journal of Affective Disorders, 3,* 11–121.

Pope, H. G., & Hudson, J. I. (1992). Is childhood sexual abuse a risk factor for bulimia nervosa? *American Journal of Psychiatry, 4,* 455–463.

Reich, P., & Gottfried, C. A. (1988). Factitious disorder in a teaching hospital. *Annals of Internal Medicine, 99,* 240–247.

Rodin, G., & Voshart, K. (1986). Depression in the medically ill. *American Journal of Psychiatry, 143,* 696–705.

Wruble, L. D., Rosenthal, R. H., & Webb, W. L. (1982). Psychogenic vomiting: A review. *American Journal of Gastroenterology, 77,* 318–325.

10

The Emerging Sexual Self of the Patient with an Eating Disorder: Implications for Treatment*

KATHRYN J. ZERBE**

Following a public lecture on the eating disorders, I received a call from a concerned long-time acquaintance and colleague. One of his patients had attended the lecture and was incensed that I had shown "pornographic slides of voluptuous, curvy, seductive" men and women to demonstrate particular cultural, psychodynamic, and biological themes. My colleague asked what pictorial representations I had used to highlight the suppressed aspirations and quiescent desires of the person with an eating disorder. What specific materials had been so shocking and riveting that his patient had been unable to sleep for two nights following the lecture? In effect, he asked if I had showed pornographic video clips or photographs.

After I clarified my selections and intent, the therapist noted that the patient's reaction had actually underscored the extent of psychological

*This chapter is based on the Hilde Bruch lecture presented at the Thirteenth Annual Conference on Eating Disorders, Columbus, Ohio, October 3, 1994.
**The author wishes to thank Kelli L. Holloway, M.D., for her insights into the clinical material and critical reading of this manuscript. She also gratefully acknowledges the support and encouragement of Laura Hill, Ph.D.

work left to be mastered in this discordant area. Apparently, the partially unclothed Rembrandts and Renoirs had pierced the defensive barriers of this primarily asexual woman. Relegating sexuality and femininity to the back burner of her twice-weekly sessions for the better part of two years, the patient had instead concentrated on her difficulty in sustaining friendships and maintaining cordial relationships with coworkers. She struggled with intermittent periods of self-starvation, bingeing, and laxative and emetic abuse, but never fulfilled the full DSM-IV (American Psychiatric Association, 1994) criteria for either anorexia nervosa or bulimia nervosa. Like that of many other patients, her eating pathology was on a continuum of disturbance (Zerbe, 1993a, 1993b) that occasionally took precedence in her treatment, but usually was not the focus of either her therapist's efforts or her own misery.

Married and the mother of an 11-year-old, this patient had refused to have sexual relations with her husband for more than five years. Although her husband remained quite supportive of his wife and her treatment, the patient felt ashamed that she could not be more sexually forthcoming and emotionally available to him. She attempted to hide her womanliness by wearing frumpy, baggy clothes, and she repeatedly expressed her hatred of the sight or the thought of nude male or female bodies. Even in college when she had been sexually promiscuous, she had experienced no emotional connection to any of her partners. Her years of psychological work on "other important matters in life, like my eating" were beginning to yield fruit in her family, however; she shyly but courageously told her therapist that she had recently begun to hug her husband and her child with real emotion. As she put it, "I'm finally beginning to feel my body in new ways and to reach out to others. Frankly, it scares the living daylights out of me."

What does this vignette suggest about the sexual liveliness or lack of it in many of our patients with eating disorders? Its uniqueness lies only in the manner in which it came to my attention. Most therapists who work with persons struggling on the continuum of eating-disordered behavior (Zerbe, Marsh, & Coyne, 1993; Zerbe, 1993b) are well aware of the variety of sexual and relationship concerns that befall this group. They are ever present, below the surface of the manifest eating disorder. My own practice confirms the summaries of other writers (Garfinkel & Garner, 1982; Hsu, 1990; Johnson & Connors, 1987; Keilen, Treasure, Schmidt, & Treasure, 1994; Raboch & Faltus, 1991): our patients lead unhappy and unfulfilling sexual lives, but are reluctant to share their difficulties. We often wonder why we hear so little about this issue and what we can do to help our patients address their secret, crippling conflicts.

Unfortunately, as clinicians are forced by managed-care constraints to spend less time getting to know their patients and more time on brief symptom-oriented interventions, we may by necessity learn much less about individuals as people, particularly about their erotic lives. Such gaps in our knowledge works to their detriment and to ours. Although more superficial symptomatology can be tackled—and occasionally even cured—other central issues that have an impact on the quality of life are rarely shared. Concomitantly, clinicians may find that lack of sexual fulfillment is often quite tenacious; hence, we may tend to avoid dealing with it bluntly and directly. Yet by bringing forward the dearth of pleasure and fulfillment in this crucial life domain, patients such as the one described are apt to teach us a great deal about what goes awry in human development. Because eating and sexuality are linked in the unconscious (Menninger, 1942), examining their association in individual treatment also heightens the capacity to truly effect change and to grow throughout the life cycle.

Several commonly encountered sexual themes may arise in the treatment of persons with eating disorders. The goal here is not to cover all the possible themes, but rather to encourage observation, thought, and debate with respect to this issue. In outlining some of the most commonly observed erotic stalemates and sexual concerns, I seek to encourage open dialogue among clinicians addressing this frequently neglected treatment issue.

SEXUAL DYSFUNCTION IN EATING DISORDERS

A variety of sexual dysfunctions may accompany an eating disorder (Hsu, 1990). Bruch (1973, 1978) and Palazzoli (1978) emphasized sexual inhibitions based on the patient's fears of growing up and subterfuge of parental conflict, whereas others (Crisp, 1980; Sours, 1980) underscored fears of sexual responsiveness. In the 1970s and 1980s, the relatively minor focus in the literature on the sexual difficulties of eating-disordered patients primarily underscored the developmental arrest that results in adult unresponsiveness.

More recently, Simpson and Ramberg (1992) discussed a paradoxical finding among a small group of eating-disordered patients. These patients requested sex therapy during inpatient treatment but were unable to follow through on its prescriptive techniques. Despite yearnings to remedy their sexual conflicts, they had inadequate psychological resources to call on even when given the opportunity.

In a commentary on the article, I (Zerbe, 1992) pointed out how a number of these patients felt quite guilty about becoming sexual; they believed they were doing something wrong by becoming more sexually alive, and their unyielding superegos needed additional therapeutic input to be mollified. Their identity concerns and their fear of losing their body boundaries in an intimate relationship contributed to their sexual dysfunction. In essence, their persistent belief that they would lose themselves in an uncontrolled symbiosis/merger with their partner led to the disruption of the sex therapy relationship.

Addressing this issue from a biological perspective, Tuiten et al. (1993) have suggested that hypogonadism (particularly low testosterone levels) brought on by malnutrition is the main cause of such sexual dysfunction. Although endocrine abnormalities and the starvation state have long been observed to contribute to impaired sexual responsiveness (Frankl, 1963; Keys et al., 1950), clinical practice suggests that the majority of eating-disordered patients with sexual dysfunction have more than just a medical/endocrine problem.

Tuiten et al. (1993) underscored what happens to the libido of starving people. Both the victims of concentration camps (Frankl, 1963) and experimental volunteers (Keys, 1950) who were starved thought obsessively about food, but lacked interest in sex or even in their families. These observations corroborate the maxim that sound nutrition is the keystone of total body integrity. Without it, no individual can function at maximum capacity in any chosen endeavor. However, the conscious use of food by starving, bingeing, and purging in a society where sustenance is readily available may be a marker of the linkage between two of life's most enhancing activities—eating and making love.

One need only look at contemporary novels and their cinematic versions to underscore the connections among love, friendship, food, and sex. *Like Water for Chocolate*; *Babette's Feast*; *Tampopo*; *Eating: A Very Serious Comedy About Women and Food*; *The Wedding Banquet*; *The Cook, The Thief, His Wife, and Her Lover*; *Delicatessen*; and *The Postman Always Rings Twice* are just some of the recent movies whose popularity rests on the intuitive notion that love and food are unconsciously connected (Menninger, 1942). In essence, eating is equated with being loved and with loving; refusing to eat or rejecting the wholesomeness of food is equated with rejecting love or the beloved.

"GOOD ENOUGH" SEXUALITY

Knowledge of what constitutes a mature sexual bond can further illuminate the commonly observed difficulties of eating-disordered patients.

What characteristics are implied in a mature, affirming sexual relationship? Among other qualities, the couple should be able to play with and to enjoy each other. Sexual excitement may always be heightened by sublimated aggression but should not be tainted with undue hostility (Stoller, 1979, 1985). Sexual interludes thrive when based on mutuality, balance, and love. Such a sexual encounter has the capacity to renew the bond between the couple and to help each individual recover from the disappointments and defeats of everyday life (Pines, 1994; Prozan, 1992; Scharff, 1982). Moreover, sexuality helps the individual prepare for and endure separations, it enhances self-image, and it conveys forgiveness for inevitable relationship disappointments, as well as acceptance of the partner's basic humanness (Kaplan, 1979; Person, 1988; Singer, 1983).

Because eating-disordered patients rigidly cling to their symptoms as a way of dealing with life's vicissitudes, they have fewer internal resources to draw on in their relationships. No wonder that at least one study (Raboch & Faltus, 1991) has reported that as many as 80% of anorexic patients lead impoverished sexual lives. Instead of using the eating disorder to assuage the pain of life and to fill their inner emptiness, these patients must be helped to develop a sense of mature dependence on people rather than inanimate objects such as food to regulate their feelings (Troop et al., 1994). The therapeutic relationship is often the first experience to challenge the eating disorder as the central organizer of the patient's life; other experiences are also gradually called on to arrest pain, fill emptiness, and lead to a fuller realization of the body's potential.

Before the patient can feel alive and real in a sexual relationship, she must be able to develop the capacity to play, negotiate separations safely, and feel confident that her aggression is not overwhelming. Developing a "good enough" sexuality is predicated on transforming her identity from that of an eating-disordered patient to that of a person willing to explore new, more mature modes of experiencing a vital, lively self.

FACTORS RESTRICTING THE SEXUAL SELF

Shame

Psychodynamic theory has made a belated but fortuitous shift toward giving equal weight to the etiological roles of guilt and shame in a variety of psychological illnesses (Broucek, 1991; Miller, 1985; Nathanson, 1992; Okano, 1994; Zerbe, 1994b). Eating-disordered patients usually minimize how often they binge or purge or engage in other inappropriate behavior, such as stealing, having temper or crying outbursts, and neglecting to take prescribed medication, because they are *ashamed* of what they perceive as failure. It is also quite humiliating for them to speak about the shame they feel toward their own or others' bodies. The patient described in the introductory vignette was able to suggest to her therapist that she abhorred the sight of her own body and her partner's nude body; but the extent of her body shame was apparent only after she attended a lecture where she felt mortified by slide depictions of classic nudes.

Extended clinical experience reveals that body shame can usually be traced to the earliest childhood messages imparted by parents or their surrogates (Broucek, 1991). American culture appears to accept nudity and sexual expression, as evidenced by salacious television shows, movies, and contemporary literature; but, in fact, our overt affirmation may be a counterphobic and subtly inhibiting expression of deeper fears, as suggested by many European and developing-country commentators. In reality, American men and women receive myriad mixed messages from the culture that augment developmental and patriarchal attitudes promoting body shame (Fallon et al., 1994).

Patients will usually be straightforward when asked about how their parents dealt with nudity and sexuality in the home. Sometimes sensitive questioning alone may be therapeutic in attenuating prudishness, because the patient has never before been given permission to address such concerns and memories. Encouraging honest expression in a safe relationship conveys the message that it is possible to be decent and respectable while openly discussing physical and sexual matters. Treatment provides a unique window of opportunity for the therapist to unabashedly correct early misconceptions. The sympathetic clinician who can openly discuss competing familial and cultural messages about sexuality diminishes patients' tendencies to denigrate their bodies.

Difficulties with Joy and Liveliness

Marriages that continue despite noxious bickering, argument, abuse, and derision are known to take their toll on children. Sequelae include the child's fear and inhibition in reaching out and finding mature relationships that sustain the self—for example, marriage (Coen, 1992; Scharff, 1982; Zerbe, 1993c). Although much is known about the negative consequences of bitter and unhappy marriages, less is known about the antithesis. What are the effects on individuals who grow up witnessing their parents as sharing a mutually satisfying, happy relationship filled with a modicum of joyful interludes and strengthened by each other's affirming, complementary contributions?

Eating-disordered patients are commonly fascinated with the friendships and marriages of their therapists. However, their voyeurism may be uncomfortable for the treater, who wishes to preserve good therapist–patient boundaries and so discourages pointed personal questions. These questions usually reflect the desire to acquire another picture of the world of relationships. Not being privy to a family where happiness, warmth, and the complementarity between the sexes was usually imparted, these patients have little knowledge about what a healthy partnership entails. The result is a psychological deficit with respect to their own ability to sustain life-affirming connections.

With respect to treatment, ascertaining the patient's perception of the parental relationship and the relationships of parental surrogates—grandparents or other primary caretakers—is often a crucial first step. The therapist must then educate the patient that what transpired in the family of origin is not necessarily the only model for life. At the same time, the therapist must guard against idealizing marriage and family life (the ''father knows best'' syndrome), because no family is ideal. (Interestingly, the children of divorced parents often maintain a positive view of marriage; perhaps they have been inoculated against negative messages by their parents' instruction, their own resiliency, or the benefits of growing up in the absence of verbal barrages.)

Patients may have such unshakable beliefs in the misery of family life that they must find and form new models. The therapist may assign realistic books, movies, or television shows that appeal to the abilities and interests of the patient, and then work concretely with the patient about the lessons depicted in them.

Patients will be attuned to the nuances of negative family interactions. This reaction gives the therapist an opportunity to counter assumptions by pointing out the fun, playfulness, and growth inherent in marriage. Thus the patient gains new models of identification.

Judiciously sharing the genuine pride the therapist takes in his or her own friendships or marriage can also prove instructive for many patients. By underscoring these relationships' many positive and fulfilling moments, the therapist points the way to the patient's eventual acquisition of a robust and playful sexual life; it must begin with the sense of a more positive, beneficent view of adult dyadic relationships, especially friendship.

Spiritual Malaise

Because eating-disordered patients focus almost exclusively on what does or does not go into their bodies, precious little time is left for them to develop spiritually. In pursuit of physical perfection, they lose sight of the quest for spiritual growth and higher ideals. They place so much emphasis on how they look that they neglect the vital significance of inner beauty and eternal values. They waste much time and many resources attempting to be other than who they really are.

Because the person whose life is centrally organized around eating cannot reach out and fully enjoy the experience of giving to others, the deepest source of sharing in physical union is precluded. Consider the individual who has regulated her feelings by sexual promiscuity and periods of bingeing and purging. In these ego states, she finds it impossible to seek her highest spiritual fulfillment. For the patient to grow beyond her eating disorder, she must learn that there is a greater purpose in life than seeking beauty. She must be repeatedly confronted by how this focus keeps her from finding more sustaining and reciprocal relationships.

The Role of Trauma

Trauma—particularly in the forms of sexual and physical abuse—has been linked in numerous contemporary reports to eating disorders (Chewning-Korpach, 1993; Connors & Morse, 1993; Esman, 1994; Herman, 1992; Kinzl et al., 1994; Miller, 1993; Rorty et al., 1994; Rorty & Yager, 1993; Schwartz, 1993; Schwartz & Gay, 1993; van der Kolk & Fisler, 1994; Waller et. al., 1993; Wooley, 1993; Zerbe, 1993a, 1993b). Recent reports have suggested that the adult trauma of rape may also contribute to an eating disorder and lead to psychopathology, including posttraumatic stress disorder and sexual dysfunction.

Although clinicians must never minimize the role of sexual trauma in the etiology of disordered eating or sexual experience, it is more critical to listen carefully to the patient's explanation of what happened to her and her perception of its impact. As Esman (1994) has noted, "It is wise, proper, and humane for us to hear what our patients tell us; it is unwise, improper, and hazardous for us to tell them what we want to hear" (p. 1102).

With respect to the experience of sensuality, many patients who have been abused lead full and satisfying sexual lives despite their belief that they cannot. In contrast, many women who have not been so tormented may struggle with a host of difficulties within relationships when they try to express themselves sexually. Clinicians wishing to help their patients traverse the sexual impasse will thus be best guided by maintaining an open ear and an open heart to the patient's perceptions of her past, her sexuality, and her goals.

An important lesson about one particular toll of abuse and loss is derived from the work of Ferenczi (1949) and Bowlby (1979). Ferenczi observed that the trauma is complicated by the multiple messages the family gives to the patient *not to talk about it.*

Concomitantly, Bowlby's research on families where a parent had committed suicide revealed that the surviving parent gave frequent and pervasive messages to the child to never discuss the suicide. These children suffered from a host of emotional difficulties. Central to their struggle was the sense that their own experience of loss was unspeakable and unknowable, which exacerbated their sense of shame and deviancy. The sense of being all alone with such a horrendous history equaled or exceeded the pathogenic power of the original tragedy.

The therapist's sensitivity to the patient's personal story and painful reminiscences, coupled with appropriate support and education, is the first step in eradicating this sense of emotional abandonment. Regardless of the specific events or perceptions of the past, it is crucial to pace the work at a rate set by the patient. It cannot be hurried, because the ''unspeakable truths'' have usually been buried for years. Open conversations with the therapist form the model for other open relationships where difficult, disquieting moments can be shared. Slowly and powerfully, the patient comes to realize that being with another person does not necessitate forsaking one's real thoughts and feelings.

Pregnancy

Some eating-disordered patients do become pregnant and successfully deliver. Although much remains to be learned about this important group of patients, the current literature underscores how some pregnant women experience a temporary remission of their eating disorder because of their concern about the emotional and physical well-being of the fetus (Edelstein & King, 1992).

After the baby is born, symptoms may reemerge or be projected onto the newborn. Body image concerns can interfere with the growth of the infant when the mother mistakenly experiences her child's baby fat as adipose tissue and resists feeding him or her.

For most women, motherhood reawakens conflicts with their own mothers. Since the maternal bond itself has been complicated as an etiologic component of eating disorders (Halmi, 1992; Zerbe, 1993b, 1994a), pregnancy is clearly a time to listen carefully for references to the earliest developmental struggles. If the patient's relationship with her spouse is supportive and nurturant, she is likely to do much better. In particular, giving permission for the couple to "fall in love with their baby" and to normalize the stress of this developmental period is often a useful and psychologically sensitive intervention.

It is also helpful to normalize any concerns with identity that may arise in the patient or couple during pregnancy. Particularly if the patient has been sensitive to boundary issues in her own family of origin or if she becomes anxious that she is becoming fused to her fetus, the therapist should reiterate how autonomous strivings are the norm for both mother and child throughout the life cycle (Coen, 1992; Zerbe, 1993b, 1994a).

Identity issues may become most apparent in dreams and in fantasies about mortality concerns. Some patients dream of lush growth in a jungle, floods washing over riverbanks, and physical residences expanding or shrinking. These dreams reflect the changing body image of the pregnant woman. Placing such dreams of unlimited growth in the patient's own particular life context, and reassuring her that they are reflective of the anxieties faced by all pregnant women, goes a long way toward reducing her anxiety.

When possible, group therapy with other pregnant eating-disordered patients can be helpful (Edelstein & King, 1992). Because the patient has not grown up in a family atmosphere where she can ask questions about sexuality and her body, she may be woefully ignorant about the most basic physical processes. At this time, education assumes a primary role in the therapy, providing the patient with emotional support she had not known before. The therapist's capacity to model flexibility will help the patient develop her own mothering capacities. To listen attentively to her concerns, to clarify and correct her misconceptions, and to help her understand her own struggles from the perspective of her own life experience all promote vitality and cohesion throughout pregnancy and thereafter.

Homosexuality

Whether or not lesbian women experience the same types of difficulties with expressing their sexual selves as do heterosexual women with an eating disorder remains to be determined. As yet, only a few articles have examined the whole issue of homosexuality and eating disorders (Brown, 1987; Herzog et al., 1992; Lancelot & Kaslow, 1994; Striegel-Moore, 1993; Striegel-Moore et al., 1990; Yager et al., 1988). These important works have emphasized how lesbians and homosexual men may differ from the general culture in how they view their bodies. Although these studies have produced conflicting results, there is some evidence that the sexual experiences of lesbian women may foster body image acceptance.

However, since particular clinical issues arise in the treatment of the homosexual patient (Striegel-Moore, 1990, 1993), therapists should be alert to the possibility of internalized homophobia. As members of a marginal minority group, homosexual women face special pressures that impede their development of a positive sense of self, which can naturally exacerbate any underlying sexual anxieties or difficulties. As Striegel-Moore (1993) concedes, homosexuals may appear to accept themselves, only to "still struggle with a profoundly negative attitude about their own sexual orientation" (p. 4).

It thus behooves clinicians who work with this population to remain open and sympathetic to the life and relationship concerns that are bound to arise, yet to be equally cognizant and accepting of the patient who chooses to remain closeted in the treatment. Even within the most open and accepting of therapeutic situations, the lesbian or gay man will find it difficult to override a personal sense of self-hatred. The therapist may suspect but not know for the longest time that the eating-disordered patient is also homosexual and thus struggling with additional relationship/ sexual difficulties because of that sexual orientation. Because these hidden struggles differ only in degree rather than kind from heterosexual ones, empathic resonance can promote acceptance and progress in the treatment.

When dealing with matters of sexual preference and taste, the therapist must always be alert for the element of surprise. For example, after more than a year of a highly expressive individual psychotherapy process, an extremely bright, professional man (whom I thought I knew quite well) finally confided that he felt most sexually alive when he dressed as a woman prior to having intercourse. Over many months, we came to understand this behavior as representing his desire to be accepted by women for his tender and feminine feelings. What I wish to stress here is my own startled reaction at being caught off guard by his revelation. Patients can thus amaze us by the secrets they hold dear. Such revelations require us to shift perspective as we revise our preconceived ideas and assimilate the new information.

The Older Patient

Our society tends to view older adults as being devoid of interest in sex. Statistical surveys and personal testimonials contest this notion. Rather, they suggest that most older adults maintain a healthy interest in sex and can be fully active, even if at a slightly slower pace, throughout the entire life cycle.

Middle-aged and older women who present with an eating disorder frequently also describe sexual difficulties and inhibitions. The eating disorder may be exacerbated or may occur for the first time at midlife or later as a result of marital strife or sexual dysfunction. The individual may sense that her partner's interests are waning as less emotional investment and physical affection are displayed in the relationship.

For the older patient with an eating disorder to reveal her sexual self, the clinician must first take a thorough history, paying close attention to details of erotic and sensual experience. At times, brief counseling, augmented by educational videotapes and books, is all the patient needs to reclaim the sexual self in her mature years. On other occasions, a focused sex therapy process, complemented by more intensive individual or marital work, is warranted. Should the patient be willing to accept referral to another clinician with specific expertise in sex therapy, the message from the primary treater is clear: sexuality is to be encouraged and sustained throughout the entire life cycle. Growth is possible. Because patients tend to view their treaters as having the omnipotent and omniscient authority of a parent, regardless of age (Epstein & Feiner, 1979), they project harshness and criticalness onto them. Clinicians will therefore find a benevolent, encouraging stance most efficacious.

Psychotropic Medication

It is generally conceded that psychotropic medication can be quite useful in the treatment of eating disorders, particularly bulimia nervosa. Increasingly, psychiatrists are finding ways of enhancing treatment with a range of psychotropic medications (Baldessarini, 1994; Brewerton et al., 1992). Because tricyclic antidepressants and, most recently, the selective serotonin reuptake inhibitors (SSRIs) have been utilized in the treatment of both depressed and nondepressed eating-disordered patients, therapists who treat patients who are on these medications must remember their potential to cause sexual dysfunction.

Although sexual side effects may be quite diverse, the most common difficulty of each class of antidepressants is decreased libido and delayed orgasm and anorgasmia (Gitlin, 1994). SSRIs tend to have a higher rate of sexual side effects, which may be correlated with a serotonergic effect. Should the patient experience diminished libido or other sexual difficulties, it is prudent to ask first about any changes that have occurred since medication was instituted. If medication is thought to be the culprit, the treatment plan can be modified by changing the dosage, changing the antidepressant, or monitoring the side effects to see if they abate over time (Gitlin, 1994).

Interestingly, the antihistamine cyproheptadine, which has been utilized in the treatment of anorexia nervosa, has sometimes been shown to reverse antidepressant-induced anorgasmia in both men and women. However, it is not yet widely employed to remedy sexual dysfunction in either depressed or eating-disordered patients.

COUNTERTRANSFERENCE ISSUES

Whenever the patient first begins to experience sexual aliveness, it will be met with a mixture of reactions by the therapist. Many times a patient will say, after months or even years of treatment, "I'm beginning to feel really good and like life is worth living. It's not that life is perfect, but I never dreamed that I could really feel this good." Therapists can and should take legitimate pride in their part in the patient's progress. However, there are some very real stumbling blocks that are bound to arise as the patient launches into this new phase.

Occasionally, therapists of either gender can find themselves worrying excessively, becoming unduly curious, or asking intrusive questions about the sexual lives of their patients. Therapists may become excessively preoccupied with their patients' comings and goings, much like the parent of an adolescent. Although genuine concern about such issues as pregnancy, AIDS, and peer relations may be acknowledged, therapists must recognize that their frequent or intense intrusions may be the result of countertransference feelings. (I have somewhat facetiously coined the term "proud mama" countertransference for such feelings of pride and accomplishment on the part of the therapist and the term "mama mia" countertransference for those occasions of excessive worry about the patient's safety in romantic matters.)

The parental paradigm sheds light on another countertransference concern: Just as parents must reckon with feelings of jealousy, envy, and competitiveness toward their adolescent children, so must therapists be aware that they, too, may be jealous and envious of a patient's talent, youth, attractiveness, and romantic possibilities. For the therapist at midlife, romantic interludes are usually neither as numerous nor as idealized as in younger years. Moreover, even professional aspirations become more limited with an increasing awareness of life's finiteness. We may find ourselves inadvertently coveting the newfound energy, enthusiasm, and excitement of our patients that remind us of our youth.

Lastly, a patient's involvement in a new relationship means that the therapist will play less of a central role in the patient's life. Instead, the patient is moving on to other life goals and personal adventures (Prozan, 1992). Just as we must help our patients to separate and mourn losses in their own lives, including, but not exclusively, the relationship to the treater, so must we also be aware that it is time—albeit potentially painful—to see patients mature and to let them go. A new relationship is clearly an important life achievement that reflects growth in treatment, but it also symbolizes inevitable loss and change that the therapist must acknowledge.

These countertransference paradigms are so commonplace as to be considered normal reactions. They are usually dealt with by limited self-reflection and honest self-scrutiny. Ongoing supervision or consultation with a trusted colleague is helpful; the practice should be encouraged and sustained throughout one's professional life. Although supervision means an investment in time, attention, and money, it enhances professional growth while helping to minimize significant countertransference difficulties.

On occasion, therapists have great difficulty monitoring their countertransference feelings and may transgress the ethical bounds of the therapeutic relationship (Collins, 1989; Collins et al., 1978; Gabbard, 1989). Gabbard (1994a, 1994b) and Gabbard and Wilkinson (1994) have discussed extraordinary countertransference situations aroused by more deeply disturbed patients. Although this seminal work does not specifically address patients with eating disorders, the description of what can arise in special, charged treatment instances is applicable here. According to Gabbard (1989, 1994a, 1994b), psychotherapists who transgress sexual boundaries fall into one of four groups: (1) psychotic disorders, (2) predatory psychopathy and paraphilias, (3) lovesickness, and (4) masochistic surrender.

Gabbard believes that the most commonly observed boundary violation arises from lovesickness on the part of the treater. Usually the therapist is a lonely middle-aged man who falls under the spell of the idealizing transference of a female patient. In my experience, eating-disordered patients often idealize their male therapists and may believe they are falling in love for the first time. Therapists must thus be especially alert to their own feelings.

As Gabbard has explained (1994b), the clinician believes that his feeling is very different from those experienced with other patients he has treated and that he is now truly in love. Usually, the therapist is struggling with problems in his own marriage or intimate relationships; Gabbard believes that the most effective way for therapists to avoid lovesickness is to take care of their own personal lives. A healthy personal relationship helps them avoid the temptation of falling in love with a patient.

Predatory psychopathy may be distinguished from lovesickness by the number of patients who have been involved with the treater. The lovesick therapist becomes involved with one individual and usually feels quite guilty and ashamed of the behavior. In contrast, predatory psychopaths have many victims. When practice restrictions are placed on them by one state's regulatory board, such therapists frequently move to another locale. As a result, regulatory agencies, licensing organizations, and subspecialty academies are being forced to take a more concerted, proactive approach to this blight on the profession.

In the meantime, we must be aware that eating-disordered patients who have not had meaningful sexual relationships may be at special risk for exploitation. Their typical brightness and vulnerability, combined with a notable capacity to idealize the therapist, may create an especially charged therapeutic climate. Their allure is a real strength that signals their potential for growth; a sensitive and savvy treater can be a catalyst for change, as long as firm boundaries are maintained and natural countertransference feelings are monitored.

In contrast to Wooley (1994), I do not believe that female treaters should be given greater latitude in expressing their emotions or in exhibiting physical expression toward their patients than is given our male counterparts. Not only can such sharing be misconstrued, but it may place the therapist on a "slippery slope" (Gabbard, 1994a) toward greater and greater self-revelation and boundary crossing. Realness is to be encouraged, but therapists must always remember that they are there for the patient; what appears to be a deviation from practice on her behalf may in reality be an attempt to fulfill an unmet personal need for the treater.

With respect to the vicissitudes of feelings that can erupt in any treatment process, therapists may rely on conferences, reading, consultation, and the arts to contain and metabolize the feelings brought to them by their patients (Epstein & Feiner, 1979; Gabbard & Wilkinson, 1994; Zerbe, 1988). Sexual aliveness on the part of the patient stirs a host of feelings in the therapist. The therapist who can listen, understand, and work with the meanings of these newfound sexual feelings can help the patient move away from years of aloneness toward a fuller participation in life. Such containment promotes the ambience of therapeutic safety—an essential element for strengthening the patient's selfhood. This very selfhood will then help launch the patient into an appropriate relationship that "holds forth the promise of unfolding—if we will only keep ourselves open to its challenge" (Person, 1988, p. 353).

TREATMENT CONSIDERATIONS

Erik Erikson once remarked that without the potential to see individuals as capable of unfolding and ripening over the course of life, psychotherapy remained a retrospective, traumatological psychology (Evans, 1967). Throughout this chapter, I have attempted to delineate some of the issues facing the patient with an eating disorder who strives to become more sexually alive. To do so, I have integrated a variety of treatment recommendations based on a broad theoretical base.

1. Encourage the formation and nurturing of friendships. Often our patients have experienced conspicuous parental possessiveness and a paucity of age-appropriate relationships. Mature love grows out of solid friendship. Forming strong platonic bonds teaches mutuality and will help establish the foundation for the patient's safe sexual expression.

2. Help the patient to mourn. Whatever has constituted the real or perceived deprivations of the past, the patient needs to move beyond them. Stress how the eating disorder has been the central organizer of her life. To become sexually alive, she will need to leave it behind and progress to other, more enhancing activities. Help the patient to find new ways to describe all her feelings, particularly those of sadness.

3. Model flexibility. When appropriate, enjoy a good laugh with the patient. Help her take life a bit less seriously. Remind her of her own humanness. This focus will enable her in future years to sustain the necessary resiliency to enjoy romance and love and to survive life's inevitable disappointments and losses.

4. Educate the patient that sexuality evolves over the life cycle. Even if she has had some early difficulties, love has the capacity to transform the self. As Person (1988) has also explained, "Love gives us one more chance" (p. 351) in life. The intensity, range, and depth of our undertakings may change over the course of a lifetime, but our erotic relationships should remain a vitalizing and affirming source of psychological nourishment.

5. Assist the patient in dealing with intense feeling states. Patients are often terrified of becoming emotionally overwhelmed, because they lack the capacity to symbolize their feelings. By naming feelings in the office, by encouraging exploration in journal writing and bibliotherapy, and by mirroring the patient's growth by tolerating her intensity, the therapist facilitates affect integration and initiates

communication. Fear of sexual response is rooted in the patient's worry that the passionate self will be perceived as crazy, debauched, wild, out of control, even monstrous. Learning to deal with strong feelings and positively identifying with others who have done so (e.g., female characters in short stories or novels) lays important groundwork for later growth in the relational and sensual domains. Expressive group therapy led by a seasoned clinician may be a particularly helpful, cost-effective tool for exploring and working through intense affect in a containing environment (Buchele, 1994).

6. When appropriate, encourage the patient to take advantage of experiential therapies (Hornyak & Baker, 1989). Although the particular modality must be chosen according to the patient's needs, working with one's body through movement therapy, psychodrama, relaxation procedures, and dance can augment the verbal therapies by increasing body awareness and acceptance. Referral to a reputable masseur or masseuse may be the patient's first experience of safe touch of the entire body. It may also potentiate healing by its effect on neuropsychological integration as well as on personal growth.

7. Above all else, maintain a sense of hopefulness. Reassure the patient that, although sexuality has been a painful and conflictual area in the past, it need not be so for a lifetime. Underscore how the eating disorder and other psychological symptoms not only have taken their toll, but have also been rigid ways of adapting to life. As more flexible coping strategies are instituted, and as the eating disorder no longer fills an emotional void or serves as a central organizer of the individual's life, other activities and relationships will naturally take its place.

By serving as a resource and role model in these ways, the therapist conveys the message that growth throughout the life cycle not only is possible, but is something to champion (Zerbe, 1994b). That perspective was abundantly represented in the life and pioneering work of Hilde Bruch (1973, 1978, 1988), and we build on her work and her memory whenever we undertake such an odyssey of personal unfolding with our patients. The implied inherent value of such psychiatric treatment is our wish that our patients not only be able to experience more of life—and of love—for themselves, but that they also become able to impart that new understanding, optimism, solace, and love to others. Their lives gain new meaning as they partake of the give-and-take of human bonds, including sexual ones. Emerging from the wretched aloneness of "The Golden Cage" (Bruch, 1978), they know the perspicacious truth embodied in the Hindu maxim, "Those who give have all things; they who withhold have nothing."

REFERENCES

American Psychiatric Association. (1994). *Diagnostic and statistical manual of mental disorders* (4th ed.). Washington, DC: Author.

Baldessarini, R. J. (1994). Enhancing treatment with psychotropic medicines. *Bulletin of the Menninger Clinic, 58*(2), 224–241.

Bowlby, J. (1979). On knowing what you are not supposed to know and feeling what you are not supposed to feel. *Canadian Journal of Psychiatry, 24*, 403–408.

Brewerton, T. D., Murphy, D. L., Lesem, M. D., Brandt, H. A., & Jimerson, D. C. (1992). Headache responses following m-chlorophenylpiperazine in bulimics and controls. *Headache, 32*(5), 217–222.

Broucek, F. J. (1991). *Shame and the self.* New York: Guilford Press.

Brown, L. S. (1987). Lesbian, weight, and eating: New analyses and perspectives. In Boston Lesbian Psychologies Collective (Eds.), *Lesbian psychologies: Explorations and challenges* (pp. 294–309). Chicago: University of Illinois Press.

Bruch, H. (1973). *Eating disorders: Obesity, anorexia nervosa, and the person within.* New York: Basic Books.

Bruch, H. (1978). *The golden cage: The enigma of anorexia nervosa.* Cambridge, MA: Harvard University Press.

Bruch, H. (1988). *Conversations with anorexics.* In D. Czyzewski & M. Suhr (Eds.). New York: Basic Books.

Buchele, B. J. (1994). Innovative uses of psychodynamic group psychotherapy. *Bulletin of the Menninger Clinic, 58*(2), 215–223.

Chewning-Korpach, M. (1993). Sexual revictimization: A cautionary note. *Eating Disorders: The Journal of Treatment and Prevention, 1*(3,4), 287–297.

Coen, S. J. (1992). *The misuse of persons: Analyzing pathological dependency.* Hillsdale, NJ: Analytic Press.

Collins, D. T. (1989). Sexual involvement between psychiatric hospital staff and their patients. In G. O. Gabbard (Ed.), *Sexual exploitation in professional relationship* (pp. 151–162). Washington, DC: American Psychiatric Press.

Collins, D. T., Mebed, A. K., & Mortimer, R. L. (1978). Patient-therapist sex: Consequences for subsequent treatment. *McLean Hospital Journal, 3*, 24–36.

Connors, M. E., & Morse, W. (1993). Sexual abuse and eating disorders: A review. *International Journal of Eating Disorders, 13*, 1–11.

Crisp, A. H. (1980). *Anorexia nervosa: Let me be.* London: Academic Press.

Edelstein, C. K., & King, B. H. (1992). Pregnancy and eating disorders. In J. Yager, H. E. Gwirtsman, & C. K. Edelstein (Eds.), *Special problems in managing eating disorders* (pp. 163–184). Washington, DC: American Psychiatric Press.

Epstein, L., & Feiner, A. H. (Eds.) (1979). *Countertransference.* New York: Aronson.

Esman, A. H. (1994). "Sexual abuse," pathogenesis, and enlightened skepticism (editorial). *American Journal of Psychiatry, 151*(8), 1101–1103.

Evans, R. I. (1967). *Dialogue with Erik Erikson.* New York: Harper & Row.

Fallon, P., Katzman, M. A., & Wooley, S. C. (Eds.) (1994). *Feminist perspectives on eating disorders.* New York: Guilford Press.

Ferenczi, S. (1949). Confusion of tongues between the adult and the child. *International Journal of Psycho-Analysis, 30*, 225–230.

Frankl, V. (1963). *Man's search for meaning: An introduction to logotherapy.* New York: Washington Square Press.

Gabbard, G. O. (1989). (Ed.) *Sexual exploitation in professional relationships.* Washington, DC: American Psychiatric Press.

Gabbard, G. O. (1994a). Sexual misconduct. In J. M. Oldham & M. B. Riba (Eds.), *Review of psychiatry* (vol. 13, pp. 433–456). Washington, DC: American Psychiatric Press.

Gabbard, G. O. (1994b). On love and lust in erotic transference. *Journal of the American Psychoanalytic Association, 42*, 385–403.

Gabbard, G. O., & Wilkinson, S. M. (1994). *Management of countertransference with borderline patients*. Washington, DC: American Psychiatric Press.

Garfinkel, P. E., & Garner, D. M. (1982). *Anorexia nervosa: A multidimensional perspective*. New York: Brunner/Mazel.

Gitlin, M. J. (1994). Psychotropic medications and their effects on sexual function: Diagnosis, biology, and treatment approaches. *Journal of Clinical Psychiatry, 55*(9), 406–413.

Halmi, K. A. (Ed.). (1993). *Psychobiology and treatment of anorexia nervosa and bulimia nervosa*. Washington, DC: American Psychiatric Press.

Herman, J. L. (1992). *Trauma and recovery*. New York: Basic Books.

Herzog, D. B, Neuman, K. L., Yeh, C. J., & Warshaw, M. (1992). Body image satisfaction in homosexual and heterosexual women. *International Journal of Eating Disorders, 11*(4), 391–396.

Hornyak, L. M., & Baker, E. K. (Eds.) (1989). *Experiential therapies for eating disorders*. New York: Guilford Press.

Hsu, L. K. G. (1990). *Eating disorders*. New York: Guilford Press.

Johnson, C., & Connors, M. E. (1987). *The etiology and treatment of bulimia nervosa: A biopsychosocial perspective*. New York: Simon & Schuster.

Kaplan, H. S. (1979). *Disorders of sexual desire and other new concepts and techniques in sex therapy*. New York: Brunner/Mazel.

Keilen, M., Treasure, T., Schmidt, U., & Treasure, J. (1994). Quality of life measurements in eating disorders, angina, and transplant candidates: Are they comparable? *Journal of the Royal Society of Medicine, 87*, 441–444.

Keys, A., Brozek, J., Herschel, A., Mickelsen, O., & Taylor, H. (1950). *The biology of human starvation*. Minneapolis: University of Minnesota Press.

Kinzl, J. F., Traweger, C., Guenther, V., & Biebl, W. (1994). Family background and sexual abuse associated with eating disorders. *American Journal of Psychiatry, 151*(8), 1127–1131.

Lancelot, C., & Kaslow, N. J. (1994). Sex role orientation and disordered eating in women: A review. *Clinical Psychology Review, 14*(2), 139–157.

Menninger, K. A. (1942). *Love against hate*. New York: Harcourt Brace.

Miller, K. J. (1993). Prevalence and process of disclosure of childhood sexual abuse among eating-disordered women. *Eating Disorders: The Journal of Treatment and Prevention, 1*(3,4), 211–225.

Miller, S. (1985). *The shame experience*. Hillsdale, NJ: Analytic Press.

Nathanson, D. L. (1992). *Shame and pride: Affect, sex, and the birth of the self*. New York: Norton.

Okano, K. (1994). Shame and social phobia: A transcultural viewpoint. *Bulletin of the Menninger Clinic, 58*(3), 323–338.

Palazzoli, M. (1978). *Self-starvation: From the individual to family therapy in the treatment of anorexia nervosa*. New York: Jason Aronson.

Person, E. S. (1988). *Dreams of love and fateful encounters: The power of romantic passion*. New York: Norton.

Pines, D. (1994). *A woman's unconscious use of her body*. New Haven, CT: Yale University Press.

Prozan, C. K. (1992). *Feminist psychoanalytic psychotherapy*. Northvale, NJ: Jason Aronson.

Raboch, J., & Faltus, F. (1991). Sexuality of women with anorexia nervosa. *Acta Psychiatrica Scandinavica, 84*, 9–11.

Rorty, M., & Yager J. (1993). Speculations on the role of childhood abuse in the development of eating disorders among women. *Eating Disorders: The Journal of Treatment and Prevention, 1*(3,4), 199–210.

Rorty, M., Yager, J., & Rossotto, E. (1994). Childhood sexual, physical, and psychological abuse in bulimia nervosa. *American Journal of Psychiatry, 151*(8), 1122–1126.

Scharff, D. E. (1982). *The sexual relationship: An object relations view of sex and the family*. London: Routledge & Kegan Paul.

Schwartz, M. F. (1993). Introduction. *Eating Disorders: The Journal of Treatment and Prevention, 1*(3,4), 197–198.

Schwartz, M. F., & Gay, P. (1993). Physical and sexual abuse and neglect and eating disorder symptoms. *Eating Disordes: The Journal of Treatment and Prevention, 1*(3,4), 265–281.

Simpson, W. S., & Ramberg, J. A. (1992). Sexual dysfunction in married female patients with anorexia and bulimia nervosa. *Journal of Sex and Marital Therapy, 18*, 44–54.

Singer, J. (1983). *Energies of love: Sexuality re-visioned*. Garden City, NY: Anchor Press.

Sours, J. A. (1980). *Starving to death in a sea of objects: The anorexia nervosa syndrome*. New York: Jason Aronson.

Stoller, R. J. (1979). *Sexual excitement: Dynamics of erotic life*. New York: Pantheon.

Stoller, R. J. (1985). *Observing the erotic imagination*. New Haven, CT: Yale University Press.

Striegel-Moore, R. H. (1993). Homosexuality and eating disorders. *National Anorexic Aid Society Newsletter, 16*(3), 1–6.

Striegel-Moore, R. H., Tucker, N., & Hsu, J. (1990). Body image dissatisfaction and disordered eating in lesbian college students. *International Journal of Eating Disorders, 9*, 493–500.

Troop, N. A., Holbrey, A., Trowler, R., & Treasure, J. (1994). Ways of coping in women with eating disorders. *Journal of Nervous and Mental Diseases, 182*(10), 535–546.

Tuiten, A., Panhuysen, G., Everaerd, W., Koppeschaar, H., Krabbe, P., & Zelissen, P. (1993). The paradoxical nature of sexuality in anorexia nervosa. *Journal of Sex and Marital Therapy, 19*(4), 259–275.

van der Kolk, B. A., & Fisler, R. E. (1994). Childhood abuse and neglect and loss of self-regulation. *Bulletin of the Menninger Clinic, 58*(2), 145–168.

Waller, G., Ruddock, A., & Pitts, C. (1993). When is sexual abuse relevant to bulimic disorders? The validity of clinical judgments. *European Eating Disorders Review, 1*, 143–151.

Wooley, S. C. (1993). Recognition of sexual abuse: Progress and backlash. *Eating Disorders: The Journal of Treatment and Prevention, 1*(3,4), 298–314.

Wooley, S. C. (1994). The female therapist as outlaw. In P. Fallon, M. A. Katzman, & S. C. Wooley (Eds.), *Feminist perspectives on eating disorders* (pp. 318–338). New York: Guilford Press.

Yager, J., Kurtzman, F., Landsverk, J., & Weismeier, E. (1988). Behaviors and attitudes related to eating disorders in homosexual male college students. *American Journal of Psychiatry, 145*, 495–497.

Zerbe, K. J. (1988). Walking on the razor's edge: The use of consultation in the treatment of a self-mutilating patient. *Bulletin of the Menninger Clinic, 52*(6), 492–503.

Zerbe, K. J. (1992). Why eating-disordered patients resist sex therapy: A response to Simpson and Ramberg. *Journal of Sex and Marital Therapy, 18*, 55–64.

Zerbe, K. J. (1993a). Selves that starve and suffocate: The continuum of eating disorders and dissociative phenomena. *Bulletin of the Menninger Clinic, 57*, 319–327.

Zerbe, K. J. (1993b). *The body betrayed: Women, eating disorders, and treatment*. Washington, DC: American Psychiatric Press.

Zerbe, K. J. (1993c). Whose body is it anyway? Understanding and treating psychosomatic aspects of eating disorders. *Bulletin of the Menninger Clinic, 57*, 161–177.

Zerbe, K. J. (1994a). Uncharted waters: Psychodynamic considerations in the diagnosis and treatment of social phobia. *Bulletin of the Menninger Clinic, 58*(2a, suppl.), A3–A20.

Zerbe, K. J. (1994b). The body betrayed: Integrating feminist and psychodynamic theory in the treatment of eating disorders. *National Eating Disorders Organization Newsletter, 16*(7), 1–4.

Zerbe, K. J., Marsh, S. R., & Coyne, L. (1993). Comorbidity in an inpatient eating disordered population: Clinical characteristics and treatment implications. *Psychiatric Hospital, 24*(1/2), 3–8.

11

Treatment of Childhood Sexual Abuse in Anorexia Nervosa and Bulimia Nervosa: A Feminist Psychodynamic Approach*

ANN KEARNEY-COOKE

RUTH H. STRIEGEL-MOORE

In this chapter a parallel is drawn between the psychological problems experienced by victims of childhood sexual abuse and by clients with eating disorders. In particular, we describe how sexual abuse has a significant and lasting effect on body image, identity, self-regulation, and interpersonal functioning. Treatment issues are outlined including the nature of the healing relationship, assessment of abuse, development of capacity for self-soothing, techniques for assisting in memory recall, sculpting of images, description and reenactment of abuse, dealing with shame, and ending the cycle of repeated victimization.

*Reprinted by permission of John Wiley & Sons, Inc. from *International Journal of Eating Disorders*, Vol. 15, No. 4, 305–319, copyright © 1994 by John Wiley & Sons, Inc.

"An unacknowledged trauma is like a wound that never heals over and may start to bleed again at any time" (Miller, 1984, p. 47).

Eating disorder experts are currently engaged in a heated debate concerning the role of childhood sexual trauma in the etiology of anorexia nervosa and bulimia nervosa. Although few would argue that sexual abuse is unrelated to the development of eating disorders, the disagreement centers around specificity of risk: Does sexual abuse constitute a specific risk factor for an eating disorder or is it merely a general risk factor for development of any psychiatric disorder? The former position is exemplified by Root (1991), who describes eating disorders as a form of gender-specific posttraumatic stress disorder (PTSD). In contrast, Pope and Hudson (1992) have concluded that eating disorders are not caused specifically by childhood sexual trauma. Although this debate is useful in stimulating research of the role of sexual abuse in the development of eating disorders, in our opinion the equally important question of how to treat victims of sexual abuse who have an eating disorder is not addressed adequately in the eating disorder literature. In this chapter, we will briefly summarize the arguments for and against the role of sexual abuse as a specific risk factor for eating disorders. Against this background, we will then introduce a set of therapeutic techniques that we have found helpful in treating women with an eating disorder who were sexually abused before the onset of the disorder.

IS SEXUAL ABUSE A SPECIFIC RISK FACTOR FOR EATING DISORDERS?

Proponents of the "specific link" hypothesis describe complex, multiple mediating mechanisms between sexual abuse and disordered eating. They emphasize the adverse effects of sexual abuse on body esteem, self-regulation, identity, and interpersonal functioning (Kearney-Cooke, 1988; Pribor & Dinwiddie, 1992; Root & Fallon, 1988). Sexual victimization, these proponents argue, has a direct effect on body image: The victim comes to see her body as a source of vulnerability, shame, and betrayal. In their efforts to understand and cope with the abuse, many victims attribute the cause of the abuse to aspects of their physical appearance and feel ashamed and guilty for the role they believe it played in the abuse. The connection between having been abused and experiencing one's body as deficient may not always be available to conscious awareness. In a culture that is saturated with messages that women's bodies must be changed to conform to a narrowly defined beauty ideal of thinness, striving to be thin may bring focus to the diffuse, yet pervasive, body loathing experienced by the victim of sexual abuse. On the other hand, for women who attribute sexual abuse to being too attractive, overeating may be a strategy in defense against further victimization.

The equation of eating disorders with arrested psychosexual maturity has long been a tenet of theory. In his widely accepted formulation Crisp (1980) regarded the central psychopathology underlying the weight phobia as related to avoidance of psychological maturity and to its concomitant problems. For the survivor of abuse, the phobic avoidance of normal weight, secondary sexual characteristics, and menstruation may be used in the service of denial, by producing a shutdown of sexual impulses and other physiological reminders of a painful and shame-bound sexual past. Also, feelings of pleasure experienced during the abuse may have heightened the child's sense of shame and guilt, thus increasing vulnerability to the development of an eating disorder. The intense need to lose weight and "get rid of the body" may be a defensive way of handling the shameful feelings. Bulimia can become a ritual of self-purification that provides the victim with hope that if she is "perfect," she will be cared for and no longer will feel ashamed. The failure of the weight loss to rid her of shame sets the foundation for further hopelessness and self-destructive behaviors.

According to Cole (1985) the violation of the victim's bodily integrity and safety teachers her that she has no control over her own physical space. The breaks in the continuity of the self, the discontinuity of memory resulting from dissociative states, the loss of self-control accompanying environmentally triggered states of consciousness such as flashbacks, panic attacks, and regressive states, all contribute to feeling out of control. It is widely accepted that issues of control are central in the etiology of an eating disorder. Bruch (1978) states that clients with anorexia nervosa seem to believe "that neither their bodies, nor their actions are self directed, or not even their own" (p. 38). Abuse victims may believe that if they control their appetite for food, sex, and human contact they will feel in control and competent. It has been proposed (Johnson & Connors, 1987) that from birth, children develop feelings of personal mastery by gaining control of their bodies. From the time they are able to reach out, grab things, crawl, walk, ride a bicycle, and so on, an important feedback loop exists between control of body and self-esteem. Given that our culture promotes the view that one can achieve control over one's life through thinness, it is not surprising that victims of abuse may attempt to regain control by changing the size and shape of their body through dieting, which in turn puts them at risk for the development of an eating disorder (Polivy, Herman, Jazwinski, & Olmsted, 1984).

Developing a secure, cohesive sense of self is central to psychological adjustment. As described by Cole and Putnam (1992), the pervasive, sustained stress of incest specifically affects self-development, particularly the development of self-regulatory processes, such as modulation of affect and impulse control. An eating disorder may become an adaptive effort to defend against self-regulatory deficits resulting from abuse. For the eating-disordered client, regaining the safety that was lost during the abuse becomes associated with being able to restrict "bad" foods and only take in "good foods." Moreover, reestablishing control is associated with needing no one, with isolating oneself on an "anorexic island," with becoming a self-contained system in which one will never feel vulnerable to the betrayal of others. The need to be "perfect" to cover up the "badness," "dirtiness," "ugliness," of abuse becomes associated with being in complete control over one's appearance (e.g., not a hair is out of place), over one's needs and feelings (e.g., never feeling the pangs of hunger for food, human contact, or sexuality), and over one's relationships with others (e.g., never being disappointed again). Thus the eating disorder represents an effort to develop a positive sense of self.

In our view, a basic goal of development is to establish and maintain meaningful relationships. The "self in relation" model (Surrey, 1985) of identity development assumes that other aspects of self (creativity, autonomy, assertion) develop within the context of meaningful relationships. Sexual abuse by a trusted adult violates the child's basic beliefs about safety and trust in relationships. It shatters her hopes for satisfying relationships in which she can feel loved and protected, and in which she can negotiate the fulfillment of her needs. The resultant hopelessness about human relationships then may be displaced into concerns about food, body, shape, and appetite. For example, the anorexic's denial of the need to eat may be a metaphor for her denial of the need for any other person because she learned through the abuse that others can be psychologically dangerous. Relying on food, a substance on which the bulimic can call 24 hours a day to soothe herself and make herself feel full, may become a survival tool that replaces the need for any other person.

In summary, sexual abuse has been described to have a significant and lasting effect on body image, identity, self-regulation, interpersonal functioning, and feelings of effectiveness in ways that echo the clinical issues encountered in clients presenting with an eating disorder, whether or not they have experienced abuse. As we will describe next, despite the compelling arguments that have been made in support of the specific link hypothesis, empirical evidence seriously challenges the notion that sexual abuse is a causal variable in the development of an eating disorder.

Opponents of the specific link hypothesis typically challenge explanations of eating disorders as caused by sexual abuse based on epidemiological studies that have failed to show that women with an eating disorder have suffered disproportionately higher rates of sexual abuse than women with other types of mental disorders (e.g., Fairburn, 1993; Pope & Hudson, 1992). As Pope and Hudson (1992) point out, studies that offer support for sexual abuse as a specific risk factor are characterized by methodological problems including failure to ascertain that abuse occurred prior to the onset of the eating disorder or absence of an appropriate control group. We would argue that existing studies of the association between sexual abuse and eating disorders do not do justice to the complexity of the issue at hand. Several researchers have described in detail the methodological issues involved in studying the impact of sexual abuse (e.g., Herzog, Staley, Carmody, Robbins, & van der Kolk, in press; Pope & Hudson, 1992; Wonderlich, 1993). Currently, there is no uniformly accepted definition of what constitutes sexual abuse, nor have researchers agreed upon a particular methodological approach to solicit information about sexual abuse. For instance, Herzog et al. (in press) argue that the nature of interview used to determine abuse may influence significantly rates of reported sexual abuse. Beyond these unresolved questions of definition and measurement of sexual abuse, to date, insufficient attention has been paid in the eating disorder literature to the fact that the specific impact of sexual abuse on mental health is determined by a wide array of factors including the age at which the abuse occurred, the severity of the abuse, the response of significant others to the abuse, and revictimization to name only a few (Burnam et al., 1988; Cole & Putnam, 1992; Herman, 1992; Waller, 1992). Lastly, we agree with Connors and Morse (1993), who argued that the role of sexual abuse in the etiology of eating disorders needs to be studied together with other variables thought to cause these disorders (e.g., Striegel-Moore, Silberstein, & Rodin, 1986). We believe that a simple determination of presence or absence of abuse is as inadequate toward furthering an understanding of etiology as is the simple determination of whether or not someone has been dieting (not all dieters become eating disordered). As Garber and Hollon (1991) argued in their recent paper on specificity designs, when examining a single variable in a specificity design, one can only rule out a single variable causal model. One cannot, however, extrapolate from results of a single variable model to a complex etiological model. Given these complex unresolved issues, it appears premature to offer a conclusion about the role of sexual abuse in the etiology of eating disorders.

To therapists working with eating-disordered clients who have a history of sexual abuse, the challenge to answer the question of specificity of risk may pale in comparison to the clinical challenges posed by these clients. Although clearly important, attention to the question of the etiological significance of sexual abuse in eating disorders seems to have eclipsed attention to another pressing question confronted daily by therapists working with victims of sexual abuse: How can the therapist facilitate recovery from sexual trauma? We will now turn to a description of steps and strategies aimed at facilitating recovery from sexual trauma in clients with an eating disorder.

COMPONENTS IN THE TREATMENT OF SEXUAL ABUSE

Our approach to the treatment of sexually abused clients with eating disorders has been influenced by the pathbreaking work of Herman (1981, 1992) and of Courtois (1988). As Judith Herman (1992) described, recovery from trauma involves three stages: establishing safety, remembrance and mourning, and reconnection with real life. Moreover, because traumatic experiences fundamentally involve disempowerment and disconnection from others, recovery is based on the empowerment of the survivor and the creation of new connections. To enable a client to move through the stages of recovery, we believe that treatment needs to encompass the following components: comprehensive assessment of the abuse, developing clients' capacity for self-soothing, enabling clients to recall and work through the abusive event, dealing with shame, and ending the cycle of victimization. Before describing each of these components, we will briefly comment on the type of therapeutic relationship most suited to the techniques we will suggest.

Nature of the Therapeutic Relationship

The therapeutic relationship is crucial to the success of therapy. It serves as a blueprint for the client's future relationships and as a vehicle through which to achieve change. We encourage therapists to approach the survivor as a partner on a journey of recovery and to refrain from entering the relationship as a silent expert or observer. For therapists, taking an active role in the relationship includes making an empathic connection with the survivor as well as allowing for disagreement and conflict. The therapist must be deliberate about his or her role of "bearing witness" (Herman, 1992) as well as about awakening the heroic potential of these often isolated clients who have been preoccupied with the pursuit of thinness and perfection. Conflicts between the therapist and the client must be out in the open; and the victim must learn that she can be separate, and that she can have a voice while keeping the connection with the therapist. She needs to learn that although the perpetrator did not take her needs seriously, the therapist does and that it is time for her to pay attention to her reactions, label them, and speak the truth. It is important to process breaks in empathy, incorrect interpretations, and other mistakes on the part of the therapist. Eating-disordered clients must learn that people, like bodies, are not perfect; they make mistakes and have flaws, but still are acceptable and worthy of care. Clients must learn that intimacy can be achieved without acting out physically or emotionally. The therapist must encourage the client to reclaim her power and competence, and must not collude with the client's sense that she lacks control of her symptoms. It is important to help the client make the connection between her eating-disordered symptoms and the feelings, thoughts, and memories related to her victimization experiences. This connection decreases the sense of powerlessness the client had experienced without such an understanding (Root & Fallon, 1989).

As therapy progresses, the therapist must send a clear, unambiguous signal that he or she is able to handle the client's growing sense of personal authority. The therapist can remind the client that she was not permitted to have a voice in the abusive relationship, but that she has a voice now and can practice using it within the therapeutic relationship. For example, a therapist suggested to a client in recovery from abuse who wanted to work on her sexuality that she read two books to begin this process. At the next session, the client said she was uncomfortable with the exercises in the books and preferred to view movies that introduced safe, healthy sexuality. The therapist commented on her courageousness in her ability to reclaim her sexuality at a pace and with the methods that felt right to her.

This type of relationship helps clients to develop a renewed sense of trust in others and leads to a hunger for relationships, food, and other forms of nourishment. With renewed hope in their ability to be their own person with their own set of needs, which can be expressed and negotiated in relationships, victims can let in food as well as other people. They can "climb out of the anorexic box," where power equals a perfect body and no needs, to a world of complex relationships. It is essential that the therapist develop a strong therapeutic alliance with the client before using the following techniques to treat abuse.

Initial Assessment

Research suggest that many victims of sexual abuse do not tell their therapists about their history of victimization (Pribor & Dinwiddie, 1992). As therapists we must ask ourselves these questions: Will we, like other significant people in the client's life, ignore the abuse? Or will we ask about it, believe it, and treat it? Bearing witness (Herman, 1992) is a central therapeutic task; and therapists must make it clear that they will be able to tolerate hearing about atrocities without becoming overwhelmed by the client's accounts. In our work with eating disorder clients, we routinely ask about sexual abuse as part of the initial assessment. We preface this inquiry with a reassuring statement that many clients with eating disorders had unpleasant or distressing childhood sexual experiences, and then ask whether anything of this nature happened to them. The fact that the therapists raises the matter during the initial assessment signals specifically that she/he is comfortable in dealing with sexual abuse, is knowledgeable about it, and regards it as an important issue to address in therapy.

The specific details of the abuse need to be explored, including the type of contact (e.g., exposure, touching, oral sex, intercourse), the degree of threat or violence involved, the victim's relationship to the offender(s), the duration of the abuse, the developmental stage at which the abuse occurred, whether the victim received any support from others in ending the abusive situation and/or dealing with its effects, and the meaning the victim attached to the event, to herself, and to others. Moreover, the therapist must "debrief" the client upon disclosure of this painful material. This includes exploring the client's reactions to having told about the abuse, making clear that the therapist will offer continued support, and beginning to examine what the client has done to cope with the trauma.

Many clients will be unable or unwilling to report sexual trauma early in treatment. Weisberg (1991) listed several indices of sexual abuse history that should alert therapists to the possibility that their client has been sexually victimized in the past. Examples include self-mutilating behavior, the presence of dissociative symptoms (see also Vanderlinden, Vandereycken, van Dyck, & Vertommen, 1993), alcohol and drug use at an early age, a history of suicide attempts at an early age, sexual acting out, placing self in dangerous situations, a history of estrangement from mother, and having an intrusive, possessive father.

Developing the Client's Capacity for Self-Soothing

Before introducing techniques to help the client remember and work through abusive memories, it is important that the therapist assist her in developing the capacity for self-soothing. The use of transitional objects, and of behavioral and cognitive techniques, helps the survivor to tolerate the affect and to relieve the tension during the phase of working through the abuse.

Internalization of Therapist as Soothing Object. Van der Kolk and Kadish (1987) refer to the "therapist as a soothing object." The therapist's empathetic responses to the client's victimization experiences permit the internalization of soothing and tension-reducing mechanisms. Helping clients to feel a sense of calm and control, both within themselves and in the therapeutic process, is critical if healing is to occur. The first step in this regard is to educate the client about the physical and psychological aftereffects of trauma and to help her identify these as they occur in the client's own situation. Often the symptoms of PTSD increase temporarily during the working-through process of therapy. The client needs to know that difficulties in falling asleep, hypervigilance, distressing dreams about the event, and psychological distress at exposure to events that symbolize or resemble an aspect of the event, are all symptoms of PTSD. The client must be reassured that experiencing these phenomena does not mean she is "going crazy."

Therapists must also introduce, develop, and strengthen inner soothing techniques of survivors. They must model the soothing, for example, by pacing the work. For clients in the numbed, dissociated phase of PTSD, techniques that encourage expression (journal writing, guided imagery, psychodrama) should be used. If memory has returned in flooding flashbacks, techniques that offer support and slow down the process enable the therapist to work carefully and slowly with memory segments (Courtois, 1988). For many trauma victims, initially the methods of soothing may have to be quite concrete. The therapist should ensure that the office is physically comfortable and that the session is calm and free from distraction. It is important that the therapist display a sense of control (e.g., maintaining time limits on the session) and exhibit the ability to remain emotionally in touch with the client even in the face of intense affect or resistance.

Development of Affect Tolerance. It is important to encourage clients to develop strategies to deal with uncomfortable feeling states resulting from the working through of sexual abuse. Our clients have discovered certain soothing techniques for themselves; these include rereading favorite children's books, meditation, relaxation tapes, or gardening. Exercise seems to be helpful in dealing with constriction and with high levels of anxiety and tension. It is also useful to encourage clients to keep a special box for storing memories that they bring to sessions. They can open the box in the safety of the psychotherapy session, and can work through the memories with the therapist. When they close the box, they will be closing off the memories until the next session. This technique becomes a way of placing a boundary of memories outside the session.

Evenings and nighttime hours can be particularly difficult for many clients. During these times, the client may find assurance in form of a transitional object such as a letter or a relaxation tape from the therapist, a card with affirming messages from therapy group members or significant others, or a list of people the victim can call to feel less alone. The goal is to interrupt the client's sense of being alone with her terror and to replace it with healing connections with others. It is also useful to encourage clients to distract themselves in a positive way from the work on sexual abuse. Clients must learn that they are permitted at times to not work on abuse and to distract themselves, as by viewing comedy tapes, completing crossword puzzles, or playing tennis. In the course of therapy, so much feeling is stirred up in the internal world that external diversions are a healthy break. The overriding concern is to help the client develop wholesome ways to tolerate feelings rather than turn to inanimate objects such as food and alcohol in order to handle difficult flashbacks and memories.

Techniques for Assisting in Memory Recall

In a safe therapeutic relationship, repression often lifts during the course of therapy; memories return and must be worked through. At times, however, techniques are needed to facilitate the retrieval of memories. Recovery from sexual abuse is aided by rendering memories available for recall, by making these memories "concrete," by developing an object that symbolizes the abuse, and by reenacting the abusive event. Each of the techniques described below serves to empower the client by allowing her to gain control over what once was an uncontrollable event.

Evoking Abusive Memories. Guided imagery, a fantasy-inducing process that combines deep muscle relaxation with suggestions of images, is especially useful in recovering repressed memories and reconstructing disconnected memory traces. A theme-centered guided imagery has been developed (Kearney-Cooke, 1988) to assist clients in understanding the role of past sexual experiences in their current feelings about body and eating. After a short relaxation exercise, clients are encouraged to remember the following scenes: early sex play with peers, early sexual experiences with adults (including incest and pedophilia), masturbation experiences during adolescence, and recent sexual experiences. Clients visualize the actual settings where sexual experiences occurred and recall their feelings about their body and their eating habits at that time. When the imagery is concluded, clients use clay to sculpt the most salient images from the sequence.

Guided imagery can also be used to help a client complete a memory fragment. This memory is demonstrated in the following example.

A 26-year-old woman suffering from anorexia nervosa (we will call her Kirstin) described waking up at 2:30 a.m. and being unable to fall asleep again. She had experienced a disturbing dream; she did not recall the entire dream, but remembered only that her mother and father were fighting and that she felt responsible for their fight. She blushed as she described the dream fragment. The therapist commented on the blushing; Kirstin reported feeling embarrassed but did not know why.

We worked with the dream in the following way. The therapist asked Kirstin to close her eyes, to go back to the dream, and to use her five senses to describe the room she was in.

Kirstin: I am in my bedroom. It is about 6:30 p.m. I can smell dinner cooking—it's hot in the room. It's summertime, and there is no air conditioning. I hear Dad, who is drunk, arguing with Mother who has just returned from work.

Therapist: What are they arguing about?

Kirstin: Can't hear them.

Therapist: What do you imagine they are arguing about?

Kirstin: Don't know. Money maybe . . . can't hear.

Therapist: How are you feeling as you hear them fighting?

Kirstin: Bad, embarrassed, guilty. Like I've done something wrong.

Therapist: Hold onto that feeling. Imagine we have a magic rope in here that can safely take you back into time. Imagine putting your right hand on a rope, then left hand behind right, right behind left as you move back through time. You are getting younger, beginning to see people from your childhood, your school, house, etc. You are moving back through time until you end up in a scene where you have a feeling similar to the one you had in the dream. Don't censor. Trust whatever scene comes. Describe it as if it is happening in the here and now.

Kirstin: I am in a bar. I am seven years old. My dad takes me to this bar sometimes and always buys me beer nuts and Coke. Because I am the only kid in the bar, a lot of men are nice to me and give me a lot of attention. (Silence)

Therapist: What happens next?

Kirstin: My father is getting drunk. The bartender asks my dad who he is going out with now, who he's dating. My father looks at me and says "My little lady." The bartender says "You don't mean Kirstin." Father says "I do." The bartender says "That's sick," and walks away from us and goes to the other end of the bar.

[Kirstin begins to cry in session and says] I'm shattered. What did he mean, it was sick? My daddy meets me at the corner after school because my mommy works, and he does special things to me. He told me he was teaching me special things and they were our secrets. That bartender said it's sick.

Therapist: You feel betrayed, sad, dirty?

Kirstin: Yes. My dad leaves the bar, takes me to another bar. I want to go home—maybe Mom is home now. He gets more drunk. When we get home I sit down and open the window and look out. Mom comes home and Dad immediately starts criticizing her. They are fighting. They are fighting about me. I know it's my fault. Does she know, or does she think I am sick too? He told me I was special, his little lady. He lied to me.

Therapist: You were betrayed and wounded by your father. This is a disturbing memory and we will spend time working with this. Experiences like this often teach us something about ourselves or myths about what life will be like. What did you learn about yourself or life?

Kirstin: That I am bad, dirty. I would have to hide this from others forever. That I could never let anyone get too close or they will see how sick I am.

When the traumatic state is reactivated in the present, it is characterized by a subjective sense of loss of control similar to what occurred in the original traumatization. Emotions connected to the trauma state are primitive, intense, and overpowering, leading to a sense of helplessness and a feeling of inability to function (Krystal, 1978). When the client relives a traumatic event, the strong affect activated by the therapeutic intervention may lead to fragmentation. Therefore, to help the client return to the real world, therapists need to allow 10 to 15 minutes at the end of the session to assist the client in making the shift back into day-to-day life. To aid this shift, several interventions are useful. The therapist should make an empathetic connection, for example, by saying "You've shared a lot today. We will spend time in the next few sessions working with this memory." The therapist may explicitly refer to the present situation:

"There are five minutes left in the session, and you will be returning to work soon." Moreover, the therapist may offer a chance for cognitive mastery: "Let's stop and see if we can understand what it means." These interventions communicate that the client has control, that she can move from an affective state to a cognitive understanding of the event.

Childhood abuse often occurs in the context of extreme familial disruption and chaos (Chu, 1991). In the absence of adequate interpersonal support, the trauma results in overwhelming dysphoric affects, which are repressed and dissociated. When the trauma is reexperienced in the session, it is overwhelming again—but the sharing of the experience with a safe person makes it bearable. A new anchor is provided for the victim: An empathetic therapist or group members listen, acknowledge the reality of the abuse, and are there for the client. The intense aloneness of being abused without help from another person is alleviated. One of the results, according to Chu, is that the trauma is retained and integrated into memory as past experience rather than remaining a dissociated time bomb that is waiting to explode into consciousness.

Creating Concrete Representations of the Abuse. After a client has retrieved memories of abuse, it is useful to ask her to sculpt these memories in clay or to draw them. These methods are effective for helping victims to organize chaotic feelings and memories in the external environment, where they can be examined. This process helps to structure and integrate the memories and feelings by providing a concrete representation of the affective experience. For example, an incest victim sculpted a female body with a major piece missing in the genital region. She wrote "My father took a part of me that I can never get back." Another client, a bulimic woman, sculpted a torso and head with no arms or legs, and poked holes in it with pencil. She said "My body must be punished and mutilated." She had been raped repeatedly by her older next-door neighbor when she was eight years old.

Reenactment of the Abusive Experience. After retrieving the memory through guided imagery and making a concrete representation through sculpting, the client must describe the trauma to the therapist. The therapist should reassure the client and help clarify the details of the abusive experience. The therapist should encourage the client to be specific and not to speak in generalities. The client should be encouraged to talk about the age at which the abuse occurred, the frequency, the duration, the relationship to the molester, exactly what was done, why the molester did it, and why it ended. The therapist must believe the client's story and must appreciate the complexity of the victim's feelings towards the perpetrator. The client may feel confused, concerned, affectionate, angry, or betrayed.

The therapist must be willing to listen to the client's positive feelings toward the perpetrator or toward aspects of the abuse. For example, the client may have felt sexually aroused and, as a result, may assume responsibility for the abuse. Clients often feel reassured when being told that it is not unusual to experience sexual pleasure or excitement during abuse because the perpetrator often touches parts of the body that are easily excitable. The victim may view the perpetrator as the only source of affection and caring in her life. Therapists who do not accept these positive feelings will be reinforcing the client's belief that her feelings are shameful or bad.

Reenactment of the abusive experience is the next step in the treatment process. This is best accomplished in group therapy. The therapist helps the client to explore the meaning of her images by proposing structured activities to assist her in reexperiencing the abuse. This experience is organized to facilitate catharsis, insight, and eventual mastery of the original trauma. Psychodrama, role playing, and gestalt therapy techniques seem most effective in reaching these goals and are best implemented in group psychotherapy. These methods seem to break through the intellectualizing and denial that many eating-disordered clients use as a defense against their feelings.

Susan, a 23-year-old bulimic woman who had been sexually abused by her father, described how he had taken her body and her power. The therapist suggested that a black cloth represent the power he took and proposed that Susan attempt to grab this power (the cloth) from her father (played by one of the therapists). On a movement level, this act gave her an opportunity to be creatively aggressive and to take back what belonged to her. Susan started out weak, but eventually grounded her body and used her body and words to take back the power. She said "Give it back, it belongs to me. You shouldn't have taken it in the first place. You can't come in me like that anymore. It's mine. I'm taking it back."

Both the client and the therapist gain much during a reenactment. The therapist and the group members experience the event as if it is occurring in the present, and feel it in intense detail. The feelings of the victim, as well as of other members of the group, then become available for joint exploration and support. This process often dramatizes the victim's fears and intense anger toward the perpetrator. In playing roles and observing, members of the group learn about themselves and make connections to their own lives. As other members of the group remember their own sexually intrusive experiences, these become available for immediate feedback and therapeutic intervention. Sharing her experience with the group in such an intense way offers the victim the chance to feel that she belongs and breaks down her feeling of isolation.

Often the client is terrified by her own anger. The therapist must help her to see that the group can tolerate the rage and will provide a context in which to develop healthy ways of expressing it. The victim needs to see that she will not lose or destroy this group when she expresses her rage.

This form of treatment encourages victims to reexperience very intense feeling states. Therefore it is important to make the reenactment a structured experience in which the therapist provides rules and safeguards that protect the victim at a time when she may feel out of control and when her defenses are weakened. The victim is offered time after the session, if needed. During the actual reenactment, other members support her physically and emotionally by playing roles and protecting her from physical injury.

Dealing with Shame

Feelings of shame and guilt do not dissolve after the sexually abusive relationship ends, but persist into adult life. Shame is a powerful emotion involved in the development of psychiatric symptoms in general (Lewis, 1987) and eating disorders in particular (Rodin, 1992; Silberstein, Striegel-Moore, & Rodin, 1987). A primitive, imaginative emotion, shame presents itself in various, often very subtle ways. Seldom do clients speak explicitly of shame; instead they may speak of feeling foolish, ridiculous, pathetic, damaged, insignificant, invisible, or worthless. This is exemplified by a quote from a sexually abused woman: "I couldn't figure out why that person had done this to me. Did he think I was pretty enough to desire in an unhealthy way? (After all, everyone else was saying how homely I was at that time.) Or did he abuse me only to make fun of my physical plainness and humiliate me? . . . I think of my body as a toy for someone to play with. I feel humiliated and dirty most of the time."

The therapist must become familiar with the language of shame in order to recognize and probe for underlying shame feelings and experiences. It is important to label shame and to point out areas in which the client seems most shame-bound. Clients need to be encouraged to examine self-talk about shame and to replace it with positive affirmations. It may be helpful to compare the brain to a computer: Our brain will believe what we tell it, that is, how we program it. For example, "I am bad" can be replaced with "Something bad happened to me." The adult self is strengthened by confronting irrational beliefs about the self and linking them to their sources in traumatization. Gestalt exercises such as the "empty chair" in which the client talks to the shamed child, also can be helpful.

A shame ritual to help resolve the feelings of shame and guilt resulting from sexual abuse has been developed. This shame ritual is most effectively performed in group psychotherapy. Our work with shame rituals draws upon the extensive history of acknowledging ritual as an important aspect of healing. Rituals speak on multiple levels, metaphorically and directly, physiologically and cognitively, consciously and unconsciously (Van der Hart, 1983). The shame ritual is a ritual of transition, which facilitates the passage from a state of shame to one of shamelessness. The following account describes the sequence of steps in our ritual.

Participants are asked to cover themselves with black cloths and to remember the times when they have felt ashamed of their bodies. Then each client is instructed to find a partner who will be her listener for the first half of the ritual and for whom she will serve as listener during the second half. The client in the listening role covers her partner with the cloth, places her hands on her partner's shoulders, and leads her backwards, as a symbol of receding into the past. Slowly she repeats the statement, "Tell me about the times you felt ashamed of your body." She listens and accepts the other woman's response by not asking questions or making comments. She simply repeats "Tell me about the times you have felt ashamed of your body." These are some examples of responses: "The time my father gave me a back rub and casually slid his hands down the side of my body, touching the sides of my breasts." "The time I had an abortion." Next, still leading her partner backwards, the listener slowly repeats the statement, "Tell them about the masks you wore to hide the shame." Examples of responses include the following: "I lost weight and tried to make myself less noticeable." "I acted like I was hard. No one could ever affect me or get to me." Then, continuing to lead her partner backwards, the listener slowly repeats the statement, "Tell me about the ways you punished your body because of the shame." "I tried to make myself disappear by starving myself." "I pinched the flabby/fat parts of my arms and thighs to try to make the fat disappear." The listener then repeats the question, "Which names would you be called if you no longer felt ashamed of your body?" Repeating the names spoken by her partner, she now moves her partner forward and slowly removes the cloth. Clients have spoken these names, among others: "shameless," "honest," "feminine," "Joan of Arc," "Margaret Mead," "white dove." The participants thank each other and exchange roles. The dyads then return and form a circle to process the ritual as a group. The following responses are among others that have been given during the processing phase of the ritual. "I feel like I've been carrying around this load—feel like it's been unloaded and I have been accepted for who I really am.'' ''Shame let me sink into my dark lonely world of depression, void of caring, love, trust, pleasure, and enjoyment. The shame restricted me from telling anyone what happened, but I see today that by keeping it to myself I felt worse. By talking about it I feel relieved and at peace with myself. Shame will no longer pollute my body, soul, or emotions. It's time to let go of the shame. Most of it belongs to someone else. I no longer need to use my body as a battleground where I hide, but want to take care of it.''

We have found that through this ritual, group members can grant each other absolution as nobody else can. The ritual diminishes the humiliation of the client's role because, in each dyad, each group member gives to the other and in turn becomes the other's source of acceptance and support. Taking the helping role enables all of the participants—but especially those who have been sexually abused and who feel undeserving—to accept attention and care from others.

Ending the Cycle of Repeated Victimization

Research suggests that victims of child sexual abuse are at high risk for revictimization in the form of physical or sexual abuse (Briere & Runtz, 1988; Jackson, Calhoun, Amick, Maddever, & Hasif, 1990; Wyatt & Newcomb, 1990). This indicates that treatment needs to incorporate a component dealing specifically with the pattern of revictimization.

In a recent group session, Mary, a 29-year-old bulimic woman, related the following experience: Her best friend asked her to come to the bar where the friend's boyfriend was playing in the band. Mary was tired, so she told her friend that she would come but would stay only for an hour. When Mary arrived at the bar, her friend's boyfriend was drunk and began to harass her. Between sets of playing music, he called her names and told her how selfish she was. Mary stayed at the bar until 2:00 a.m., and binged and purged as long as she stayed. After listening to her story, a group member asked Mary why she stayed at the bar so long. Why didn't she leave as soon as the boyfriend began to harass her? Mary said she never considered leaving. Once he began to abuse her, her energy went into survival—how could she get through the night?—and she called on ''her old friend bulimia'' to help her. She could take his abuse as long as she was bingeing and purging.

Mary had never learned the skills required to protect herself and assert her rights in a relationship. She had acquired only a very limited or inaccurate sense of what she might reasonably expect from others. Freud's concept of the repetition compulsion is helpful in understanding the role of trauma in continued victimization and ultimately in psychological problems. In his 1920 paper, ''Beyond the Pleasure Principle,'' Freud described the role of repression in the development of the repetition compulsion, which he saw as the emergence of repressed instinctual conflicts that became superimposed on current reality. He described how the client can remember little or none of what is repressed, and stated that he or she tends to repeat the repressed material in present life rather than remembering it as something in the past. Chu (1991) points out that actual trauma that has been repressed is often repeated. Persons who experienced trauma in the past find these experiences intrude into their current reality and they often feel a true compulsion to repeat repressed experiences. Repressed and dissociated events can emerge through dreams and nightmares, or as flashbacks. In addition, the victim unconsciously may find others with whom to act out traumatized relational patterns.

Thus it is crucial to the treatment to explain the concept of repetition compulsion. Clients must be encouraged to examine their present lives by identifying self-destructive patterns and relationships that they wish to change. The effects of repeated victimization must be discussed—how each experience deepens the individual's distrust of other people and increases feelings of aloneness. This pattern can lead to dependence on inanimate objects such as food or drugs to fill the self because the client has no hope that her needs can be met in a relationship.

Survivors' ability to assume control over sexual experiences is central to their healing and sense of control over their lives. Treatment should include strategies aimed at decreasing the likelihood of subsequent sexual abuse. Helpful interventions include teaching clients to identify the early signs of an abusive relationship (e.g., threats by the lover if she does not comply with his demands), examining clients' feelings and attitudes about abuse (e.g., clients may think that sexual abuse by a partner is due to men's inability to control intense sexual feelings and is a necessary aspect of sexual relationships), and facilitating responsible decision making about the potential consequences of sexual relationships such as pregnancy and sexually transmitted diseases (Wyatt, Guthrie, & Notgrass, 1992). As Wyatt et al. (1992) describe, sexually abused women need to learn to perceive themselves as sexual beings and not as sexual objects, to communicate their sexual needs, to anticipate when contraceptive use is needed, and to negotiate with partners about the type and frequency of behaviors in which to engage. This may be crucial to efforts to prevent revictimization. It is important not to limit questions on the client's ability to identify and communicate her own needs and her skills regarding sexual relationships. Rather, therapists should be careful to include an exploration of the client's partner's ability or willingness to relate to the client in a nonabusive way.

CONCLUSIONS

We possess a rich literature on behavioral and cognitive approaches to important issues in the treatment of eating disorders such as dietary restraint and cognitive distortions. Little has been written, however, on the treatment of sexual abuse. In this chapter we discussed how sexual abuse can become the pathway for the development of an eating disorder and we described an approach to the treatment of abuse from a feminist psychodynamic perspective.

We have learned that through the development of self-soothing techniques, the client can tolerate the affect that is generated by working through the abuse and can achieve a sense of calm and control both in and outside of therapy. Through the appropriate pacing of memory retrieval techniques, the client can reconstruct the traumatized memory traces and can regain a sense of continuity and safety in her life. By experiencing and describing the effects of abuse in words, visual arts, and movement, she receives an opportunity to give a voice to the frightened, abused child and to say what could not be said in the original abusive scene. Through acceptance and care by the therapist, and at times by other group members, the survivor can let go of the shame, which in fact belongs to the perpetrator.

Recovery from abuse involves learning the details of the abuse and discovering how it has affected the victim's life. Understanding the past enables the client to move to the next step, that of writing a new story for her life and body. This is no longer a tale of repeated victimization, but instead is an account of listening carefully to internal feelings and reactions, taking them seriously, and insisting that others take them seriously as well. It involves claiming the whole self in the world, reintegrating all parts of the self—past and present, anger and joy, sensuality and sexuality—a process that leads to more vitality and energy with which to meet the demands of adult life. Through a safe therapeutic connection, in which victims can be close to the therapist without risking betrayal or loss of self, survivors develop a renewed hope that their needs will be met with people rather than with food or other inanimate objects. Their focus switches from the arena of food, appetite, and weight to the world of relationships.

REFERENCES

Briere, J., & Runtz, M. (1988). Symptomatology associated with childhood sexual victimization in a nonclinical adult sample. *Child Abuse and Neglect, 12,* 51–59.

Bruch, H. (1978). *The golden cage: The enigma of anorexia nervosa.* Cambridge, MA: Harvard University Press.

Burnham, M. A., Stein, J. A., Golding, J. M., Siegel, J. M., Sorenson, S. B., Forsythe, A. B., & Telles, C. A. (1988). Sexual assault and mental disorders in a community population. *Journal of Consulting and Clinical Psychology, 56,* 843–850.

Chu, J. A. (1991). The repetition compulsion revisited: Relieving dissociated trauma. *Psychotherapy, 28,* 327–332.

Cole, C. L. (1985). A group design for adult female survivors of childhood incest. *Women and Therapy, 4,* 71–82.

Cole, P. M., & Putnam, F. W. (1992). Effects of incest on self and social functioning: A developmental psychopathology perspective. *Journal of Consulting and Clinical Psychology, 60,* 174–184.

Connors, M. E., & Morse, W. (1993). Sexual abuse and eating disorders: A review. *International Journal of Eating Disorders, 13,* 1–12.

Courtois, C. A. (1988). *Healing the incest wound.* New York: Norton.

Crisp, A. H. (1980). *Anoerxia nervosa: Let me be.* London: Academic Press.

Fairburn, C. (1993, January). *The epidemiology of bulimia nervosa.* Paper presented at Yale University, Hartford, CT.

Freud, S. (1955). Beyond the pleasure principle. In J. Strachey (Ed. and Trans.), *The standard edition of the complete psychological works of Sigmund Freud* (Vol. 18, pp. 7–64). London: Hogarth Press. (original work published 1920)

Garber, J., & Hollon, S. D. (1991). What can specificity designs say about causality in psychopathology research? *Psychological Bulletin, 100,* 129–136.

Hasif, V. L. (1990). Young adult women who repeat childhood intrafamilial sexual abuse: Subsequent adjustment. *Archives of Sexual Behavior, 19,* 211–221.

Herman, J. L. (1981). *Father-daughter incest.* Cambridge, MA: Harvard University Press.

Herman, J. L. (1992). *Trauma and recovery.* New York: Basic Books.

Herzog, D. B., Staley, J. E., Carmody, S., Robbins, W. M., & Van der Kolk, B. A. (in press). Childhood sexual abuse in anorexia nervosa and bulimia nervosa: A pilot study. *Journal of the American Academy of Child and Adolescent Psychiatry.*

Jackson, J. L., Calhoun, K. S., Amick, A. E., Maddever, H. M., & Hasif, V. L. (1990). Young adult women who report childhood intrafamilial sexual abuse: Subsequent adjustment. *Archives of Sexual Behavior, 19,* 211–221.

Johnson, C., & Connors, M. E. (1987). *The etiology and treat of bulimia nervosa: A biopsychological perspective.* New York: Basic Books.

Kearney-Cooke, A. M. (1988). Group treatment of sexual abuse among women with eating disorders. *Women and Therapy, 7,* 5–21.

Krystal, H. (1978). Trauma and effects. *The Psychoanalytic Study of the Child, 33,* 81–116.

Lewis, H. B. (1987). *The role of shame in symptom formation.* Hillsdale, NJ: Erlbaum.

Miller, A. (1984). *Thou shalt not be aware: Society's betrayal of the child.* New York: Farrar, Straus, & Giroux.

Polivy, J., Herman, C., Jazwinski, L., & Olmstead, M. (1984). Restraint and binge eating. In R. Hawkins, W. Fremoun, & P. Clement (Eds.), *Binge eating: Theory, research, and treatment.* New York: Springer.

Pope, H. G., & Hudson, J. I. (1992). Is childhood sexual abuse a risk factor for bulimia nervosa? *American Journal of Psychiatry, 149,* 455–463.

Pribor, E. F., & Dinwiddie, S. H. (1992). Psychiatric correlates of incest in childhood. *American Journal of Psychiatry, 149,* 52–56.

Rodin, J. (1992). *Body traps.* New York: Morrow.

Root, M. P. (1991). Persistent, disordered eating as a gender-specific, post-traumatic stress response to sexual assault. *Psychotherapy: Theory, Practice, and Research, 28,* 96–102.

Root, M. P. & Fallon, P. (1988). The incidence of victimization experiences in a bulimic sample. *Journal of Interpersonal Violence, 3,* 161–173.

Root, M. P., & Fallon, P. (1989). Treating the victimized bulimic. *Journal of Interpersonal Violence, 4,* 90–100.

Silberstein, L. R., Striegel-Moore, R. H., & Rodin, J. (1987). Feeling fat: A woman's shame. In H. B. Lewis (Ed.), *The role of shame in symptom formation* (pp. 89–108). Hillsdale, NJ: Erlbaum.

Striegel-Moore, R. H., Silberstein, L., & Rodin, J. (1986). Toward an understanding of risk factors for bulimia. *American Psychologist, 41,* 246–263.

Surrey, J. (1985). *Self in relation: A theory of women's development* (work in progress, No. 14). Wellesley, MA: Wellesley College, Stone Center.

van der Hart, O. (1983). *Rituals in psychotherapy: Transition and continuity.* New York: Guilford Press.

van der Kolk, B. A., & Kadish, W. (1987). Amnesia, dissociation, and the return of the repressed. In B. Van der Kolk (Ed.), *Psychological trauma.* Washington, DC: American Psychiatric Press.

Vanderlinden, J., Vandereycken, W., vanDyck, R., & Vertommen, H. (1993). Dissociative experience and trauma in eating disorders. *International Journal of Eating Disorders, 13,* 187–194.

Waller, G. (1992). Sexual abuse and the severity of bulimic symptoms. *British Journal of Psychiatry, 161,* 90–93.

Wonderlich, S. (1993, May). *Eating disorders and sexual abuse.* Paper presented at the meeting of American Psychiatric Association.

Wyatt, G. E., Guthrie, D., & Notgrass, C. (1992). Differential effects of women's child sexual abuse and subsequent sexual revictimization. *Journal of Consulting and Clinical Psychology, 60,* 167–173.

Wyatt, G. E., & Newcomb, M. (1990). Internal and external mediators of women's sexual abuse in childhood. *Journal of Consulting and Clinical Psychology, 58,* 758–767.

PART III

Dialogue

12

Sexual Revictimization: A Cautionary Note*

MARY CHEWNING-KORPACH**

This chapter addresses the process of some instances of revictimization, through the lens of the repetition-compulsion phenomenon. The repeat victim's reenactment of sexual and other abuse both within and beyond the therapeutic environment is addressed. Nonverbal behaviors, in particular, are discussed as the overt manifestation of unconscious transference reactions which may contribute to trauma being repeated or reenacted. Some repeat victim "types" are discussed within this context, although more specific descriptions are most appropriately left to the individual case. Finally, some issues regarding treatment are noted.

---

*In this chapter, observations refer to the process of revictimization, rather than the original victimization. Revictimization is defined as repeated victimization that occurs with different perpetrators, or with the original perpetrator, when the victim has the realistic option of making herself unavailable to the perpetrator. Both incest and extrafamilial assaults are included. The case of continuous, ongoing victimization with the original perpetrator is not. Rather, this situation is considered to be part of the critical, original violation, which has likely contributed to shaping the victim's interpersonal behaviors and unconscious drives.

**The author wishes to acknowledge the helpful comments of Craig Johnson on an earlier version of this chapter, and Roy J. O'Shaughnessy on the final draft. The chapter is intended to address issues with women only. No statements or conclusions will be generalized to the male population. For this reason, the feminine pronoun is used throughout.

Prevalence of sexual abuse is well documented (e.g., Cole & Putnam, 1992; Koss & Burkhart, 1989; Wyatt, 1985). Authors estimate that between 28% (Bagley & Ramsey, 1986) and 62% (Wyatt, 1985) of the female population has been sexually abused by the age of 18. Sexual assault during childhood, in particular, is common and associated with high rates of psychological morbidity, including sexual dysfunction, personality alteration, and impairment in capacity to trust and to be intimate (e.g., Cole & Putnam, 1992; Pynoos, 1993). The literature regarding sexual abuse in childhood and incidence of sexual abuse includes studies on subsequent revictimization in adulthood. For example, Root and Fallon (1988) found that of 46% of women who had been sexually abused as children, 33% were also victimized as adults. In studies examining sexual revictimization as a distinct phenomenon, Wyatt, Guthrie, and Notgrass (1992) found that among a sample of adult women abused as children, 44% experienced sexual revictimization as adults. These authors determined that women who were abused as children were 2.4 times more likely than those not abused to be revictimized as adults. To summarize, approximately one-third to one-half of victims who have been assaulted sexually in their childhood will be revictimized in their adult lives.

Empirical observation that childhood victims of sexual assaults have a higher rate of subsequent revictimization in adulthood presents not only a fascinating observation, but also a clinical challenge. Understanding this complicated process often involves the implicit assumption that the victim in some way plays a role in further revictimization. For example, it has long been recognized by therapists that some survivors tend to be revictimized both sexually and physically, and often appear to choose inappropriate men with a history of abusing others or controlling and dominating women. It is clear in both the literature and clinical observations that revictimization is not only a significant trauma, but also may contribute to exacerbating the psychopathology and perpetuating ongoing dysfunction and symptoms. Preventing revictimization is an obvious goal of psychotherapy. The psychological literature is conflicted over not only how to understand the process of revictimization, but what type of treatment would be best suited to prevent it.

What is considered to be the "appropriate" treatment stance with these patients has taken a dramatic turn since Freud's (1896) original "seduction hypothesis." This position essentially assigned full responsibility for the victimization. Blaming victims is obviously unhealthy as well as incorrect from a moral perspective. In reaction, our society has seized an opposite stance, and many therapists have insisted that survivors are victims of circumstances completely beyond their control. Their approach is to focus on how the abuse has affected the person. Therapy focuses on assisting the victim to resolve issues of self-blame, guilt, and shame by externalizing the blame for victimization onto the offender, toward the ultimate goal of self-esteem reparation.

While it is imperative to focus on the effects of assault on victims, and in particular to dispense with inappropriate self-blame or guilt, I am also concerned that the extremes within this approach may lead to overidentification with the victim, coupled with a sense of advocacy and protection that, for some patients, may be counterproductive. Few other authors have questioned this stance. Of these, van der Kolk's (1989) observations are noteworthy. Commenting on Reiker and Carmen's (1986) work on victim's internal processing, he asserts,

> Assuming responsibility for the abuse allows feelings of helplessness and vulnerability to be replaced with an illusion of control. Ironically, victims of rape who blame themselves have a better prognosis than those who do not assume this false responsibility; it allows the locus of control to remain internal and prevents helplessness.

It is obvious that no single psychological explanation will account for revictimization; rather, this is a complex process. In formulating a comprehensive treatment for repeat victims it is essential to consider both interpersonal and intrapersonal motivations and behaviors. Using methods found particularly in the countertransference literature, this chapter seeks to describe how interpersonal reactions to these patients may be useful in diagnosis and treatment. Countertransference reactions are treated as diagnostic and useful data, characterized as the totality of the therapist's feelings, attitudes, and action tendencies toward the patient (Kiesler, 1979; Tanzey & Burke, 1989). The assumption is that the therapist is more human than otherwise (Sullivan, 1953), and countertransference reactions are natural, role-responsive ways of responding to the patient's style of relatedness or transference (Epstein & Feiner, 1979).

Operating from these assumptions, the specific hypothesis is that women who have found themselves revictimized sexually and otherwise are likely to make some unconscious interpersonal contribution to the repetition of this cycle. Furthermore, through heightened awareness or insight into this contribution and reparative experiences, the victim in some circumstances may take a proactive, more empowered role in the cessation of the repetition-compulsion cycle. I now turn to explore the process of revictimization and some potential countertransference reactions.

PROCESS OF REVICTIMIZATION

The repetition-compulsion of repeat sexual trauma victims may be manifest through self-destructive behavior, identification with the aggressor, or reenactment (van der Kolk, 1989). While all of these would be considered important treatment issues, reenactment, both within and beyond the therapeutic setting, will be specifically addressed here.

Intratherapeutic Reenactment

Among the pitfalls of working with patients presenting with a history of revictimization and comorbid diagnoses of Axis II disorders is the strong role reciprocity provoked by the transference/countertransference relationship. This has been addressed by numerous authors and assigned such labels as "projective identification" (Horowitz, 1983; Ogden, 1979), "role suctioning" (Redl, 1963), "complementary response" (Kiesler, 1986), and "participant observation" (Sullivan, 1953). In essence, it is a moment-by-moment interpersonal process in which the patient reenacts the transference from the original (parental or guardian) relationship within the therapeutic environment, thereby eliciting a covert or overt response from the therapist. With victims of incest or similar betrayal by an adult significant other, implications for the therapeutic setting are particularly noteworthy.

Therapists may notice themselves responding in a manner inconsistent with and atypical of their usual responses. Response patterns can generally be categorized in complementary roles reminiscent of the patient's chaotic childhood. Among others, patients and therapists may find themselves recreating reciprocal roles such as omnipotent parent/helpless child, helpless parent/angry child, ineffective parent/adultified child-spouse, and rejected spouse/victorious spouse-substitute. Initially, therapists cannot help but be pulled into these natural role-responsive stances, as it is the "dance" of therapy (Kiesler, 1986). Remaining "hooked" in these roles, however, may contribute to a number of countertherapeutic clinical phenomena, the most obvious being unwittingly perpetrating against the patient/victim. For example, through nonverbal behavior that typifies passive-dependent, passive-aggressive, or overtly aggressive behavior, the patient may provoke the therapist into an uncharacteristically dominant or directive stance. In addition, female therapists may find these patients subtly competing through remarks about external appearance; the therapist's interpretations, position, or boundaries; or devaluating treatment. These behaviors, with their concomitant nonverbal presentation, may provoke direct defensiveness, judgment, criticism, helplessness, or withholding from the therapist. At this point in the relationship, the patient has made an unconscious contribution to her own revictimization by eliciting a perpetratorlike or failure-to-protect motherlike response from the trusted therapist. Thus, the repetition-compulsion is perpetuated through this reenactment.

An equally insidious response pattern may occur when patients become "special." The special patient syndrome has been aptly described by Main (1957), and generally implies a patient who has established a structure in the therapeutic relationship that is significantly different from that between the therapist and other patients. Means of achieving special status may be overt, as in the "V.I.P." case or covert and less conscious, as through relational idiosyncrasies. In either case, a sense of entitlement is implied on the part of the patient, and she is not likely to directly protest her special status.

When patients present their sense of entitlement in a covert fashion, a rather pernicious process may ensue. These are typically likable patients who provoke strong overidentification countertransference reactions from therapists. Their manner may be apologetic, kind, self-effacing, respectful, deferent, and forgiving. They may appear physically frail. Their concomitant dissociative defense, while adaptive from an intrapsychic perspective, may perpetuate an image of helplessness and emotional fragility on an interpersonal level. These repeat victims are often replete with praise toward the therapist and process. Statements that begin with, "This is the first time I've ever . . ." are not uncommon. The therapist who is unaware of such transference-countertransference reactions may unconsciously or consciously be gratified by the implicit sense of being special to the patient, in turn. This reaction may have the unwanted effect of perpetuating the patient's childlike helplessness and dependency on the therapist.

An even greater risk of failure to recognize this countertransference is the possibility it may lead to boundary violations. The patient covertly or overtly may seek greater involvement from the therapist in other areas of life, such as finances or dealing with family members outside the therapeutic relationship. Therapists may find themselves treating the patient as special by, for example, waiving fees, contacting others on the patient's behalf, or meeting at odd hours to suit the patient's schedule. An expansion of boundary violations occurs when the therapist starts disclosing personal information to this special patient. These situations set the stage for possible further boundary violations, even to being physically or sexually intimate with the patient. In effect, the unwitting therapist has recapitulated the same type of boundary violation found in the original incest situation.

In female patient/therapist dyads, this may take a different form. Relational boundary transgressions may occur in the form of, for example, calling to check on the patient, spending personal time with a patient, or inviting a patient into the home. Therapists who find themselves in these situations with patients firmly believe they are acting in the patient's best interest. Instead, the therapist may be gratifying the patient's every narcissistic impulse, without regard to the reality base of this arrangement. At some point in the future, the therapist will inevitably be unable to gratify the patient's many demands. The patient may then regard the therapist's nonomnipotent qualities as frustrating and burdening, as the once-idealized therapist now implicitly seeks gratification of his or her own needs through the relationship. When this occurs, it is not uncommon for repeat victims, particularly those with comorbid Axis II disorders, to regress temporarily. The overidentified therapist may accompany them through the process of projective identification, experiencing similar emotional despair, anguish, and even rage. This countertransference reaction obviously prolongs and intensifies the patient's deterioration.

In summary, overt and covert presentations and elicitations by repeat victim patients are often fueled by unconscious and interpersonal repetition-compulsion patterns. Presented as interpersonal bids, they may provoke a host of negative, uncomfortable covert and overt countertransference responses from therapists, which could potentially serve to revictimize the patient. Revictimization is also likely when the therapist overidentifies with the patient and actively participates in allowing her to be a "special" patient. It is important to note that these dynamics are general categorizations of a host of more specific counter-transference and transference reactions. However, this approach was selected in order to focus specifically on the process of some fairly common instances in which the repeat victim/patient reenacts the repetition-compulsion within the context of therapy.

Extratherapeutic Reenactment

The recreation of this pattern is unfortunately not limited to the therapeutic situation. It is generally agreed that patients will also reenact these roles and elicitations with significant others in their environment (e.g., Kiesler, 1986; Tanzey & Burke, 1989). This process is very similar to that within the therapeutic environment (or vice versa!). The specifics of this process were detailed above, and will only be addressed here briefly.

The repetition-compulsion pattern may be reenacted by cycling through various roles or becoming locked into specific behaviors and roles with particular significant others. For example, one woman may find herself being abusive, victimized, and rescuing with an alcoholic mate at different instances within a short period of time. Another may become paralyzed and dissociative during a sexual assault by an older, otherwise respected relative. Still another may find herself behaving helplessly or provocatively with most men, and with hostility, criticism, or competition when in the company of women. How the revictimization process is activated with significant others is relatively understandable, given the combination of an attempt at intimacy and the victim's likely deficits in self-image. What is far more difficult to explain, however, is how the revictimization process may be reenacted with mere acquaintances or virtual strangers.

Within the context of social situations, some repeat victims may emit and elicit a host of nonverbal behaviors that could play a part in the unconscious repetition-compulsion. Researchers in the area of nonverbal communication have developed a generally accepted, comprehensive system for understanding nonverbal behaviors and the concurrent messages they send (e.g., LaFrance & Mayo, 1978; Mehrabian, 1972). Accordingly, within an interpersonal exchange, the "receiver" will consciously or unconsciously respond to a "sender's" overt nonverbal behaviors, without regard to the sender's conscious or unconscious intentions. Considering that nonverbal behavior may be received through all of the five senses, the repeat victim may unwittingly send a host of messages to a would-be perpetrator. Repeat or potential perpetrators have likely developed a complementary response, a "radar" of sorts, for victimlike behavior. In addition, the repeat victim has, in some instances, developed a complementary "radar" for nonverbal behavior of perpetration-prone others. Although she may feel no conscious attraction to abusive men, their perpetratorlike interpersonal styles are quite familiar and therefore "comfortable" or complementary. It is in this fashion that in a group of people, a repeat victim may scan the crowd and somehow connect with a historical or potential perpetrator. This pattern is also evidenced by women who, relationship after relationship, continue to select men who are in some way abusive.

In addition to the interpersonal process, repeat victims reenacting the repetition-compulsion may have a tendency to place themselves in situations where victimization is more likely than others. An example is the woman who takes her garbage to the apartment dumpster late at night, when several recent rapes have been reported in the complex. I would not for a moment support that she would like to be sexually violated or is intentionally endangering herself. I would, however, wonder about the influence of some less-than-conscious drives inciting reenactment.

Accepting the validity of the repetition-compulsion cycle and concomitant subtle interpersonal behaviors, some patterns of revictimization with even acquaintances and strangers can be explained. My concerns for the women who may be victims of this insidious process prompts me to turn to some notes regarding treatment.

TREATMENT CONSIDERATIONS

"Culturally correct" treatment for victims of sexual assault has recommended that therapists take a supportive, somewhat directive stance. Authors generally agree that victims must go through various stages of recovery. Sgroi (1989) notes five: 1) acknowledging the reality of the abuse; 2) overcoming secondary responses to the abuse; 3) forgiving oneself (ending self-punishment); 4) adopting positive behaviors; and 5) relinquishing survivor identity. It is the therapist's task to guide and support the patient through these stages toward the goal of extricating self-blame and any part of the self embedded in the sexual trauma, while reinforcing exploration of more healthy options for self-description.

I generally agree with this approach, especially for first-time victims of sexual assault. However, this model may be less successful with repeat victims who present with comorbid diagnoses, particularly Axis II, multiple personality, dissociative, or posttraumatic stress disorders. The clinical picture and therapeutic relationship and treatment are even more complex in these cases. With these patients, treatment initially focuses on stabilizing the patient within the therapeutic relationship. For some repeat victims, this may simply require logging time and establishing rapport. For others, stabilization may be complicated by a thought disorder, psychotic episodes, and/or severe depression. Particularly with a family history of chemical dependency or psychiatric illness, a medication trial may be helpful to allow the patient to actually enter or tolerate the therapeutic relationship.

With all repeat victims, therapy must strive to accept and understand the patient in her entirety. A responsive, boundaried therapeutic relationship is one reparative factor in and of itself, without which other aspects of treatment are not likely to be effective. As the therapeutic bond begins to strengthen, the patient is encouraged to work through stages one through four, outlined by Sgroi. This work may include memory retrieval, writing and presenting in detail the circumstances of the assaults (in the spirit of mastery), experiential work, and confrontation of self-destructive behavior and its effect on current relationships. From a clinical perspective, repeat victims appear to cycle through these stages numerous times.

This cyclical process is similar to the repetition-compulsion, and occurs in several ways. For example, repeat victims with repressed memories may cycle through these stages with the emergence of each new, previously unavailable memory. Also, repeat victims often rework these stages with each new instance of abuse, sexual or otherwise. Finally, patients with severe character disorders are likely to cycle through these stages for no overtly obvious reason. They courageously struggle to finally develop more positive coping skills, only to quickly regress to denying the impact of the trauma. There are at least two explanations for this regression.

First, with positive changes, some patients become terrified of the unfamiliar, and experience an ominous dread, as though something terrible is soon to happen. Consciously, the patient may acknowledge growth as being positive. Unconsciously, however, she is far from her psychological "home," and is convinced that she does not deserve and cannot live comfortably in this new place. Many of these patients experience extreme guilt following what others would label positive behavior or events, and are therefore unconsciously driven to preserving the status quo through reenacting some form of abuse. Self-destructive behavior, defensive dissociation, or regression often follows.

A second explanation is observable through the therapeutic process of helping the patient to integrate split-off intrapsychic aspects of the self, so eloquently detailed by Davies and Frawley (1991). Briefly, these authors note that initial presentation of the adult self is common with victims of incest. As therapy progresses, the injured, helpless child emerges. During this process, patients may exhibit a number of infantile and childlike mannerisms, such as an attraction to drawing/coloring, a change in external appearance, and a decrease in responsibility level. These authors note the complexity involved with assisting the patient to integrate these aspects of self. During this process, they describe the emergence of an angry, acting-out adolescent, who may influence the self-system toward self-destructive behaviors, including pulling away from the adult therapist, who, like others, will inevitably prove to be disappointing.

Therapy with repeat victims through this cyclical process can be extremely challenging for even the most skilled therapist. A variety of countertransference reactions, elicited through the patient's overt and covert behaviors, typically occur. It is important that therapists remain actively aware of their numerous covert and overt responses. When therapists deny, discount, or simply are unaware of countertransference reactions, they are in a dangerously vulnerable position for boundary transgressions. For example, a common countertransference reaction to cyclical regression is that of helplessness and despair. This is sometimes provoked by the repeat victim's overt cries for help, while consciously or unconsciously sabotaging treatment strategies. Scanning the therapist's nonverbal signals of helplessness, the patient may directly or indirectly offer the therapist a variety of suggestions, most of which are avenues toward boundary violations. Any eager, well-intended therapist is especially vulnerable at this point. With repeat victims presenting comorbid Axis II traits, it is an especially thorny task to provide an appropriate "holding" environment during these elicitations.

Once the transference/countertransference reactions have somewhat stabilized, the therapist must determine a way to address the victim's unconscious contributions to her own revictimization, without revictimizing her. Understanding and sharing covert countertransference reactions by the therapist is useful in some situations. Only after thorough internal processing and consideration of appropriate timing should reactions be shared. These reactions should be presented as directly related to the patient's specific behaviors and patterns. They must be offered with the clear intention and goal of providing the patient with feedback to promote change, rather than gratifying the therapist's own countertransference responses and needs. With particularly complex and fragile patients, it may be helpful to first seek feedback from treatment team members or colleagues.

There are additional considerations for sharing countertransference feedback, given the gender of the therapist. For example, male therapists may more quickly provoke a sense of revictimization within the female repeat victim, particularly if sexual perpetrators have been male. Therapist concern with revictimization, coupled with a sense of "gender shame" (Johnson, 1993), may contribute to the male therapist's difficulty in addressing the repeat victim's unconscious contribution. For female therapists, there is less access to direct observation of patient's interpersonal behaviors with males, and information must be gleaned largely from patient self-report. Also, when countertransference reactions are shared with repeat victims, patients may react defensively as though feeling blamed, or by discounting the therapist as jealous and competitive. Defensive behavior may be provoked as the female therapist's feedback symbolizes "too little, too late" protection not available from the original maternal caregiver.

After details particular to previous victimizations have been addressed, the focus of treatment turns almost exclusively to here-and-now process issues. It is essential to carefully target specific behaviors that have been observed and specific patterns that the patient details. Feedback is offered, noting concern for the patient's future well-being. That is, it is important to acknowledge that many sexual assaults occur randomly. In addition, it may be useful to point out to the patient that she appears to have been assaulted by "more than her share" of perpetrators and to wonder aloud about the possibility that she may unconsciously emit some victimlike behaviors to which perpetrators may be drawn. A joint venture to investigate this possibility is then begun. The patient is encouraged to role-play new behaviors and to rehearse these roles in vivo. She is encouraged to seek feedback from respected others, and to rehearse alternative behaviors in front of a mirror. The particular interpersonal impact of the patient's nonverbal behaviors is immediately shared with the patient. It is crucial that the patient acquire the experience that she is, in fact, capable of having a relatively predictable effect on healthy others through her verbal and nonverbal behavior. Furthermore, she learns that she is capable of and responsible for controlling her own behavior and is not merely helpless and ineffective, at least with regard to her own behavior.

Finally, it is important for treatment to identify and curtail signs of the repetition-compulsion. Patients may be taught to identify their idiosyncratic vulnerable situations, and to respond accordingly. The techniques and traditions of the 12-step model of treatment and support may be extremely useful at this point. The simplicity and structure of this resource is reassuring to repeat victims struggling with the seeming chaos of Axis II disorders and repetition-compulsion issues. Integrating this approach into a traditional psychotherapy model can be complicated, and is aptly described by Johnson and Sansone (1993).

In summary, treatment strategies with repeat victims may employ techniques from psychodynamic, interpersonal, gestalt, behavioral, cognitive, biological, and 12-step models. "More human than otherwise" (Sullivan, 1953) countertransference reactions elicited by patients' unique manifestations of their own transference issues are inevitable and critical to the treatment venture. They essentially provide the therapist, and eventually the patient/repeat victim, with insight into repetition-compulsion patterns and entrances into reparative, therapeutic experiences.

REFERENCES

Bagley, C., & Ramsay, R. (1986). Sexual abuse in childhood: Psychosocial outcomes and implications for social work practice. *Journal of Social Work and Human Sexuality, 4*, 33–47.

Cole, P. M., & Putnam, F. W. (1992). Effect of incest on self and social functioning: A developmental psychopathology perspective. *Journal of Consulting and Clinical Psychology, 60*, 174–184.

Davies, J. M., & Frawley, M. G. (1991). Dissociative processes and transference paradigms in the psychoanalytically oriented treatment of adult survivors of childhood sexual abuse. *Psychoanalytic Dialogues, 2,* 5–36.

Epstein, L., & Feiner, A. H. (1979). Countertransference: The therapist's contribution to treatment. *Contemporary Psychoanalysis, 16,* 489–513.

Freud, S. (1962). The aetiology of hysteria. In J. Strachey (Ed. and Trans.), The standard edition of the complete psychological works of Sigmund Freud (Vol. 3, pp. 189–221). London: Hogarth Press. (original work published 1896)

Horwitz, L. (1983). Projective identification in dyads and groups. *International Journal of Group Psychotherapy, 33,* 259–279.

Johnson, C. J. (1993, March). Personal communication, Tulsa, OK.

Johnson, C. J., & Sansone, R. A. (1993). Integration of the twelve step approach with traditional psychotherapy for the treatment of eating disorders. *International Journal of Group Psychotherapy, 14.*

Kiesler, D. J. (1979). An interpersonal communication analysis of relationship psychotherapy. *Psychiatry, 42,* 299–311.

Kiesler, D. J. (1986). The 1982 interpersonal circle: An analysis of DSM-III personality disorders. In T. Millon & G. L. Kleerman (Eds.), *Contemporary directions in psychopathology: Toward DSM-IV* (pp. 571–597). New York: Guilford Press.

Koss, M., & Burkhart, B. (1989). A conceptual analysis of rape victimization. *Psychology of Women Quarterly, 13,* 27–40.

Lafrance, M., & Mayo, C. (1978). *Moving bodies: Nonverbal communication in social relationships.* Monterey, CA: Brooks/Cole.

Main, T. F. (1957). The ailment. *British Journal of Medical Psychology, 30,* 129–145.

Mehrabian, A. (1972). Nonverbal communication. Chicago: Aldine.

Pynoos, R. S. (1993). Traumatic stress and developmental psychopathology in children and adolescents. *Review of Psychiatry, 12,* 205–239.

Redl, F. (1963). Psychoanalysis and group psychotherapy: A developmental point of view. *American Journal of Orthopsychiatry, 33,* 135–147.

Reiker, P. P., & Carmen, E. H. (1986). The victim-to-patient process: The disconformation and transformation of abuse. *American Journal of Orthopsychiatry, 56,* 360–370.

Root, M. P. P., & Fallon, P. (1988). The incidence of victimization experiences in a bulimic sample. *Journal of Interpersonal Violence, 3,* 161–173.

Sgroi, S. M. (1989). Vulnerable populations (vol. 2). Lexington, MA: Lexington Books.

Sullivan, H. S. (1953). *The interpersonal theory of psychiatry.* New York: Norton.

Tanvey, M. J., & Burke, W. F. (1989). *Understanding countertransference from projective identification to empathy.* Hillsdale, NJ: Erlbaum.

van der Kolk, B. (1989). The compulsion to repeat the trauma: Re-enactment, revictimization, and masochism. *Psychiatric Clinics of North America, 12,* 389–411.

Wyatt, G. E. (1985). The sexual abuse of Afro-American and White-American women in childhood. *Child Abuse and Neglect, 9,* 507–519.

Wyatt, G. E., Guthrie, D., & Notgrass, C. M. (1992). Differential effects of women's child sexual abuse and subsequent sexual revictimization. *Journal of Consulting and Clinical Psychology, 60,* 167–173.

13

Recognition of Sexual Abuse: Progress and Backlash

SUSAN C. WOOLEY

The discovery of high rates of sexual abuse in the histories of eating-disordered women is different from other clinical discoveries. Unlike other causes of psychological distress, sexual abuse is a crime, and its identification in individual cases can have far-reaching consequences. More than other historical events, sexual abuse is difficult to detect and more difficult still to verify because secrecy is its most essential feature, creating a psychic pressure "not to know" that can lead to partial or complete repression by both victim and perpetrator. Finally, the unmasking of sexual abuse is a cultural event that is potentially transformative of gender relations.

If sexual abuse is not, in the end, the most damaging symptom of gender inequality, it is certainly among the most dramatic, richly symbolic of much that has been problematic between men and women throughout the history of most known cultures: the abuse of physical, social, and economic power by males, coupled with the historical treatment of the female body as male property. For all these reasons and more, the assimilation of knowledge about sexual abuse within the helping professions and in the larger culture has been and remains a highly charged process, deserving of ongoing scrutiny.

Despite numerous reports of high rates of sexual abuse in eating-disordered women, our field has been slow to accept this knowledge or to
emphasize abuse in diagnosis and treatment. Elsewhere (Wooley, 1994a)
I have examined the information on sexual abuse within the field and
described what I believed to be a covert rift between many male and
female researchers and clinicians that, like a family secret, draws its
power from silence. Key issues in this largely submerged debate have
included a scientific double standard, which has held abuse reports to a
higher standard of proof than that historically demanded for other clinical
findings, and the misinterpretation of prevalence studies through the application of a faulty logic of causality. Beneath these scientific arguments
appears to be a mutual distrust expressed in male skepticism about reports
of abuse and female skepticism about men's objectivity. Findings on
abuse both challenge traditional formulations of psychological disorders
and raise troubling questions about male socialization in a society in
which sexual abuse appears to be endemic.

The struggle of our field to embrace the forbidden knowledge of sexual
abuse has taken place within a culture-wide convulsion of discovery,
acceptance, and denial. As the problem of sexual abuse has been disclosed
in patient narratives, self-help books, investigative journalism, highly
publicized court cases, and television talk shows, Americans have reacted
with predictable extremes of feelings, leading to charges of hysteria and
countercharges of backlash. Public discussion continues unabated, lend-
ing everchanging meanings to scientific debate and coloring our emotional and intellectual interpretations of patients' reports. We ignore these
influences at our peril; since we cannot escape them we must work to
name and understand them.

The contributions to this collection, along with many other discussions
of sexual abuse that have appeared within the past year, represent an
apparent turning point in which sexual abuse is finally receiving wider
attention within the eating disorders field. The perseveration of prevalence
studies appears to be yielding to a more sophisticated examination of
diverse questions and to a real dialogue on issues of diagnosis and treatment. Yet Chewning-Korpach's reference to "culturally correct" views
in the preceding chapter signals the political charge attaching to even
professional discourse and suggests the need to anchor our discussions
to the surrounding social context. Listening carefully to other voices pro-
tects us from surreptitious influence. It also exposes us to important other
perspectives. A successful assault on the damages of sexual abuse will
surely require all the resources of contemporary culture.

PROGRESS AND BACKLASH IN THE CULTURE

In 1984, Jeffrey Masson published his now famous work, *The Assault on Truth,* in which he reported that his studies in the Freudian archives had revealed Freud's deliberate suppression of the discovery of sexual abuse. Although preceded by Florence Rush's (1980) text, *The Best Kept Secret,* setting forth similar arguments and exploring the history of childhood sexual abuse, *The Assault on Truth* captured the public imagination, in part, perhaps, because of the heated reaction. Denounced as a traitor by Freud's heirs and as an arrogant boor by *New Yorker* writer Janet Malcolm, Masson mounted a vigorous defense, including a lawsuit against Malcolm.

It is difficult, now, to remember the silence shrouding abuse in preceding decades. Before the 1970s, none of the now-familiar social institutions designed to assist female victims of sexual and physical violence existed. Childhood sexual abuse was regarded by most clinicians as rare and had been characterized in the well-known Kinsey report as essentially harmless (Kinsey et al., 1953). Masson's book became part of an explosion of knowledge in which high prevalence rates of abuse, and the consequent psychological damage, became widely known. As Diana Russell (1986) has noted, the unmasking of sexual abuse in contemporary society was largely an accomplishment of feminists, given momentum by victim accounts as well as the writings of feminist clinicians.

Brought out of the shadows, sexual abuse soon found its way into the public spotlight. Each day brought new allegations of sexual harassment or abuse, many leading to highly publicized proceedings such as the McMartin preschool trial, the Thomas–Hill hearings, and the William Kennedy Smith and Mike Tyson rape trials. Celebrities such as Oprah Winfrey and Rosanne came forward to disclose histories of childhood sexual abuse. Reports of abuse by priests and other clergy became increasingly common. Dozens of personal accounts and self-help books appeared, describing the sequelae of abuse and educating the public on posttraumatic stress symptoms and the mechanisms of repression and recall. ''Take Back the Night'' demonstrations in communities across the nation called attention to abuse and its victims, giving further momentum to a feminist movement which sought to influence laws, public policies, and funding of victim assistance programs.

It was, of course, inevitable that there would emerge a counterreaction or backlash to these events, and several forms of this are now visible. Among the first were challenges to the credibility of abuse charges, leading eventually to the formation of a political action group representing the "falsely accused," under the name FMSF for False Memory Syndrome Foundation (Wylie, 1993). Among the first popular critiques of the validity of "recovered memories"—and still among the most chilling—was Rabinowitz's (1990) article describing teacher Margaret Kelly Michaels' arrest and conviction for sexual abuse of children in a New Jersey daycare center. Rabinowitz described a process in which, following a single questionable complaint, dozens of children were interviewed and their denials of abuse systematically ignored until, with the help of outside "experts," they were coached into descriptions of an improbable, if not impossible, scenario of bizarre acts. Five years later, Michaels was released when an appeals court overturned her conviction. As with all such accounts, it is difficult to know with certainty what actually occurred, but perhaps as a cautionary tale it is necessary to know only that such a miscarriage of justice *could* occur, a caution supported by research on the effects of interviewer suggestion on children.

The credibility of sexual abuse reports—so problematic in the case of young children— has increasingly been raised with adult informants. In a startling polemic, "Beware the Incest Survivor Machine," feminist psychologist Carol Tavris (1993) charged the self-help movement with encouraging patients and therapists to interpret virtually all symptoms as evidence of abuse and creating a flood of unfounded accusations—an assertion unsupported by abuse verification studies (Herman & Schatzow, 1987) and stretched well beyond its probable grain of truth.

The debate is fast becoming a staple of popular culture. Within two weeks' time a *Philadelphia Daily News* syndicated cartoon depicted a receptionist for "Dr. Vic Timm," asking a new patient, "How much abuse can you afford to remember?"; a poster listed itemized charges ($10,000 for memory of abuse by a parent; $20,000 for memory of abuse by a teacher, and $30,000 for a priest); a *Time* magazine (McDowell, 1993) story entitled "Lies of the Mind" and a *Newsweek* story, "Misty, Watercolored Memories" (McDowell, 1993), alleged widespread quackery in the "recovered-memory movement"; a *New York Times* story, "Sex Abuse: The Coil of Truth and Memory" (Chira, 1993), reported on the crossfire; and experts speculated on the plausibility of Steven Cook's allegations of abuse by Cardinal Bernardin in media accounts too numerous to mention.

"You have a combination of two professions that are overpopulated and underregulated," stated Patrick Schlitz, a defense lawyer for 12 religious organizations, quoted by *Newsweek* (Woodward & Springer, 1993): "One is the field of psychology, the other is the field of law." "In essence, therapists create the problem they have to treat," asserted psychologist Michael Yapko in the same article. In a comment that sounds as much like a threat as a prediction, *Time* (McDowell, 1993) quotes Paul McHugh: As the public begins to recognize that people have been falsely accused by recovered-memory patients, it "opens us up to skepticism and dismay about our capacity to do things. . . . We will have to recreate the trust this country puts in psychotherapy." *Time* added its own ominous warning: "Recovered-memory therapists might do well to heed those guidelines before they cause irreparable damage to their profession" (McDowell, 1993).

Other experts, however, regard the furor as backlash. *Time* reported that authority Christine Courtis regarded the "wholesale degradation of psychotherapy by some critics" as "displaced rage" at therapists for bringing the issue to public attention (McDowell, 1993). "We're back where we were 20 years ago," commented Judith Herman to the *New York Times* (Chira, 1993). "This is a mobilization of accused perpetrators and their defenders to take the spotlight off perpetrators of crimes and put it back on victims and issues of credibility. . . . Some of the outrage about repressed memory, [Janice] Haken suggests, stems from resentment about psychology's intrusion into family," reported the same article.

The timing of this debate, coinciding with crucial government decisions about the funding of psychotherapy, is probably not entirely accidental. In a recent paper (Wooley, 1993), I noted that the institution of psychotherapy had changed radically in the past 20 years; where once it helped the powerless to "adjust" to their condition, now it spawned first one advocacy movement, then another, creating a shift in power relations certain to be passionately opposed by many. The managed care movement, with its concentration of power in the hands of increasingly few entrepreneurs, if not already the instrument of backlash, certainly has the ominous capacity to become one, and perhaps the current debate is the realization of that process. "The battle could not have come at a worse time," suggested *Time* (Chira, 1993), in a statement attributed to psychologist Steven Cici, "It's not a good time for us to be airing our dirty laundry."

Within a span of mere weeks, the existence of "a thriving recovered-memory industry" has seemingly been accepted as fact, dutifully repeated by professional bystanders as well as parties to the debate. No doubt some quackery does exist, but this sudden pronouncement and its even more sudden acceptance in the absence of documentation is reminiscent of the similarly seized-upon report, made infamous by Susan Faludi (1991) in *Backlash,* and repeated endlessly even by professionals: that a single woman beyond the age of 40 had a greater chance of being murdered by a terrorist than marrying. Perhaps before we find ourselves wiping egg off our faces again we should demand some factual investigation of the true extent of the "recovered-memory industry."

As the debate intensifies, many important distinctions are falling victim to the heat. The well-known problems associated with the suggestibility of young children have been conflated with the lesser problems of adults in arguments that freely interchange data obtained from one population with the other. Creating further confusion, "therapist-assisted recall" is being conflated with unassisted recall after a period of repression. In reviewing our series of abuse cases, I found no instance in which a patient had first remembered her abuse within a therapy session, and extremely few patients who had first recalled it while undergoing therapy, though many had remembered abuse they had once forgotten, which often caused them to seek therapy. Therapists can hardly be blamed for influencing a process to which they were not even witness. In addition, skepticism about the credibility of wholly repressed memories has crept over to the far more common and less controversial scenario of partial repression, in which incomplete memories become elaborated within, or outside of, therapy. The epidemic of reported abuse contains a fairly small proportion of patients reporting total repression. And finally, the rarer reports of memories of satanic cults, ritual abuse, and abduction into UFOs is casually interchanged with the everyday business of unraveling abuse histories. Ignoring these distinctions allows critics to cast the shadow created by the most controversial phenomena over the entire field, resulting in the absurd complaint that virtually the entire psychotherapy profession can be found on "the lunatic fringes of science" hysterically described by *Time* (Chira, 1993).

Simultaneous with charges of improper "therapist-assisted recall," there has been an attention-grabbing attack on feminist views of sexual abuse by such strident voices as Camille Paglia (1992) and, more recently, Katie Roiphe (1993a). Paglia argues—incompatibly it would seem—that sexual assault is frequently the fault of victims, that risk of sexual assault is the price of freedom and one that women should stop whining about, and that much alleged assault is not assault at all but consensual sex followed by misgivings. These assertions are illustrated in the following quotes:

> My kind of feminism stresses independence and personal responsibility for women. Blaming the victim makes perfect sense if the victim has behaved stupidly. Theft, rape and murder are facts of life in large societies, except police states. (p. 56)

If you get raped, if you get beat up in a dark alley in a street, it's okay. That was part of the risk of freedom; that's part of what we've demanded as women. . . . What feminists are asking for is for men to be castrated, to make eunuchs out of them. (p. 63)

In dramatizing the pervasiveness of rape, feminists have told young women that before they have sex with a man, they must give consent as explicit as a legal contract. In this way, young women have been convinced that they have been the victims of rape. (p. 47)

That Paglia is herself confused about the meaning of rape is made clear by her statements, made in interviews just two months apart, and appearing only four pages apart in her book: *"I've never been raped,* but I've been very vigilant" (p. 58, emphasis added) and, "In that moment when [a man] decides that the only way he can get what he wants . . . is to rape . . . he is confessing to a weakness that is all-encompassing. . . . *I was raped once* and it helped me to think of it like that" (p. 62, emphasis added).

Described on the cover of her book as an "intellectual provocateur," Paglia might be ignored as an aberration, unrepresentative of even a small minority. But Roiphe's success is harder to dismiss. In a *New Yorker* review of Roiphe's (1993a) book, *The Morning After: Sex, Fear and Feminism on American Campuses,* which challenges the definitions of date rape used to document an "epidemic," Katha Pollit (1993) writes:

Her explosive charges have already made Roiphe a celebrity. The *Times Magazine* ran an excerpt from her book as a cover story: "Rape Hype Betrays Feminism." Four women's glossies ran respectful prepublication interviews . . . Clearly, Katie Roiphe's message is one that many people want to hear: sexual violence is anomalous, not endemic to American society, and appearances to the contrary can be explained away as a kind of mass hysteria, fomented by man-hating fanatics. (p. 220)

Pollitt makes short work of Roiphe's research, citing her unfamiliarity with the literature, her reliance on personal experience and unconfirmed anecdotes, and her misreporting of fact. But her greater contribution is to point out that even the apparent "excesses" of the movement embody welcome social change:

Roiphe is right to point out that cultural attitudes towards rape, harassment, coercion, and consent are slowly shifting. . . . Roiphe

may even be right that it muddies the waters when women colloqui-
ally speak of ''rape'' in referring to sex that is caddish or is obtained
through verbal or emotional pressure or manipulation or when they
label as ''harassment'' the occasional leer or off-color comment.
But if we lay these terms aside we still have to account for the
phenomenon they point to: that women in great numbers . . . feel
angry and exploited by behavior that men assume is within
bounds. . . . Like many of those men, Roiphe would like to short-
circuit this larger discussion, as if everything that doesn't meet the
legal definition of crime were trivial, and objection to it mere para-
noia . . . What's so ''utopian'' about expecting men to act as though
there are two people in bed and two sexes in the classroom and
workplace? (p. 223)

Challenges to definitions of rape have been linked with and buttressed
by recent overarching critiques of ''victim feminism'' in the popular press
(e.g., Kaminer, 1990, 1992; Paglia, 1992; Roiphe, 1993a, 1993b; Wolf,
1993). Separately and collectively, these books have charged ''difference
feminism'' with recreating the Victorian image of the ''angel in the
house'' and have complained that an emphasis on female victimization
saps women's self-confidence.

The most recent of these books, Naomi Wolf's *Fire with Fire* (1993),
has received the greatest amount of media attention. In it, Wolf argues
that Anita Hill set off a ''genderquake'' that has made ''ideological feminism'' obsolete and paved the way for a new ''power feminism'' focused
on such broad issues as pay, health, and political representation. To en-
large feminism's appeal, Wolf urges feminists to abandon such traditional
causes as reproductive rights and gay/lesbian rights and instead to project
an image that is inclusive, sexy, and ''fun''—a word she uses often.
Especially relevant to the discussion here is Wolf's abandonment of her
argument in the earlier *Beauty Myth* (1990) and her reassessment of the
meaning and importance of sexual exploitation. In a bizarrely grim carica-
ture of dismal surroundings and relentlessly humorless and self-sacrificing
volunteers in a rape crisis center, Wolf argues that such images operate
as a ''turn-off'' to mainstream women.

The contradictions in Wolf's book are so glaring and the vision so
thin, one might be tempted to dismiss it were it not for the attention it is
attracting. Reviews range from the fawning (''What Susan B. Anthony
was to the first wave of feminism and Betty Friedan and Gloria Steinem
were to the second, Ms. Wolf may be to the third . . . and perhaps final
wave'' [Francke, 1993]) to the frankly contemptuous (''Let's find better

women. . . . And better books'' [Shapiro, 1993]) with far more of the former. Clearly she has hit a nerve. The will to roll back a decade of discovery, reflected in the growing tide of such works, deserves a fuller analysis than can be given here and constitutes a serious threat to the supportive political climate widely agreed to be essential to the successful detection and treatment of sexual abuse.

We have not heard the last of this debate. One may wonder if we've even heard the beginning. As Adrienne Rich (1979) pointed out long ago, successful women are under tremendous pressure to repudiate the opinions and demands of their sex as a condition of continued membership in elite, still largely male, institutions. Female tokenism, especially at the highest echelons, is by no means behind us, and the women who uneasily occupy these niches are certain to feel intensifying pressures to destigmatize behaviors whose regulation by new laws and social policies poses a threat to influential and often well-liked male colleagues.

As professionals, we must appreciate a context in which sexual mores are being redefined and in which such redefinitions, having begun to have their impact, are certain to be attacked. Scientific discourse is by no means removed from these pressures and, in fact, is more closely than ever watched by a public with conflicting but intensely held interests.

REVICTIMIZATION: ANXIOUS DISCOURSE

When I was asked to write a chapter here, the editor admitted to a fear that I might react negatively to inclusion of Chewning-Korpach's chapter, which examines victims' contributions to sexual revictimization. Although his fear was not, in fact, founded, it was understandable. Victim-blaming, with its long and infamous history, is rightly a sore spot among feminists and one newly inflamed by recent events.

In every advocacy movement, majority supporters of minority rights encounter a host of unexpected problems—enough to drive many off the road. White liberals who joined blacks in the civil rights movement were stung to learn that their seemingly sincere efforts were often experienced as condescending, intrusive, and racist. But to lift themselves out of passivity and demoralization, leaders of oppressed groups have to become, remain, and influence others to be very angry. By the time converts from majority groups arrive on the scene, the emerging minority has, of necessity, developed a powerful and encompassing rhetoric that portrays even the unarmed foe as potentially dangerous by virtue of fundamentally conflicting loyalties. Many would-be helpers retreat into denial to lick their wounds. Some return later, disabused of the expectation that they will be warmly welcomed as the saintly exception to their group's rule and prepared instead for hard work with scant rewards—in short, the same burdens endured by the people they aim to help.

It is not possible to fully avoid rough passages in a sea of the magnitude before us. Men and women committed to substantive and original contributions that do not merely parrot existing beliefs will doubtless risk unpredictable and passionate responses. We have apparently progressed from the problem of *whether* we talk about sexual abuse to the problem of *how* we talk about it. It would be unfortunate indeed if women's commitment to helping victims and to bringing the issues surrounding abuse to light should operate to stifle inquiry and debate, demanding an alignment with victims so blind that their full dilemma cannot be seen and denying, for example, that abuse does in fact change people, distorting their relational development in ways that truly effective therapies must address.

Chewning-Korpach's manuscript arrived at a fateful moment and has already enjoyed a turbulent history, which, among other things, required me to rewrite this reply. Between the first and second draft, the second author, a prominent male, withdrew his name. With him went (though not necessarily through a causal link) several pages of anxious caveats reassuring readers that the authors did not condone abuse: "We believe that any type of sexual abuse is a cruel and heinous act. . . . We believe that it is always the perpetrator who should bear the responsibility, blame, shame, and consequences of the victimization. . . . Even in the case of masochism, sadomasochism or re-enactment, we believe unconscious, repressed material is the force acting on the 'will' of the victim."

More important, the second draft contained a number of substantive changes reflecting retrenchment. Chewning-Korpach explained to me that she had felt compelled to "soft-pedal" certain issues in response to reviewers' comments and that her changes were based on political rather than scientific considerations. I offer no judgment of the reviewers' responses, which I did not see. Whether the revision is better or worse than the original is a matter of opinion; some of both, in my view, but there is clearly room for debate. What is at issue is whether such debates are better conducted publicly or in private.

At a time when scientific debate can be seized and misused by an overaroused public, the impulse to caution is perhaps inevitable. But a strong argument exists for preserving scientific inquiry. We cannot long make meaningful contributions if we submit to a censorship of ideas, however subtly enforced. The questions now undergoing public debate might have been better addressed had there existed a more vigorous and sustained scientific one. The charge surrounding this chapter suggests that we, too, may be conflating issues, equating unconscious behavioral contributions to revictimization with the now popular, and extremely dissimilar, notions discussed earlier: that abuse victims are merely relabeling consensual, but regretted, sexual acts; that the expectation of moving freely in the world in itself constitutes responsibility for rape; or that most abuse reports are fraudulent anyway.

Chewning-Korpach's is hardly the first discussion of the dynamics of revictimization, but, until now, none has raised any hackles. It is primarily the timing of this presentation that accounts for the intense reactions to it. Although I question some of Chewning-Korpach's conclusions, I am concerned that we not cause theorists to become tongue-tied by the threat of politicized responses that decide truth before the fact of inquiry. For it is surely the social climate, more than the scientific one, that Chewning-Korpach has in mind when she refers to ''culturally correct treatment'' for victims of sexual assault, apparently a euphemism for ''politically correct,'' avoided in order to escape association with the societal backlash.

RESPONSIBILITY AND REVICTIMIZATION

Early in her chapter, Chewning-Korpach offers her characterization of the current social and professional climate surrounding abuse:

What is considered to be the ''appropriate'' treatment stance with [abuse] patients has taken a dramatic turn since Freud's (1896) original ''seduction hypothesis.'' [O]ur society has reactively seized a polar-opposite stance on believability of, and responsibility for, both victimization and revictimization [as did Freud]. . . . Therapy, in particular, focuses on assisting the victim to resolve issues of self-blame, guilt and shame by in effect externalizing the blame for victimization onto the offender . . . I am . . . concerned that . . . this approach may lead to overidentification with the victim, coupled with a sense of advocacy and protection that, for some patients, may be counterproductive.

Noting the common finding that prior victims of sexual assault are more likely than nonvictims to be abused, Chewning-Korpach asserts her central thesis that, ''Women who have found themselves revictimized sexually and otherwise, are likely to make some unconscious interpersonal contribution to the cycle.'' Although she cites van der Kolk's (1989)

suggestion that self-destructive behavior, identification with the aggressor, and reenactment are all expressions of the "repetition-compulsion,"
Chewning-Korpach limits her focus to reenactment within and outside
the treatment setting.

She first observes that therapists are often drawn into "complementary
identification" (Tansey & Burke, 1989), in which therapist and patient
assume reciprocal roles that replicate past relationships, for example,
"omnipotent parent/helpless child," "helpless parent/angry child," and
"ineffective parent/adultified child-spouse." She omits from discussion
one of the more common variants in which the therapist reacts to the
patient's victimlike interpersonal stance with anger and even contempt,
experienced as frustration that the patient does not experience the feelings
toward the perpetrator that the therapist believes to be appropriate.

At this point the presentation takes a somewhat puzzling turn, focusing
on the patient who, by virtue of her "special status (as in the well-known
case or person)" or "relational idiosyncracies," positions herself as a
"special patient," exhibiting overt or covert entitlement and evoking
intense countertransference responses, which include overprotectiveness,
despair, rage, and boundary violations. Discussion of the problems encountered in treating "special patients" dominates the section on reenactment in treatment, although it is never made clear why sexually abused
and "special" have been equated. In referral centers where 60% or more
of patients are abuse victims, they can hardly all be "special." I would
suggest that some abused patients who elicit extra care may in fact have
special needs calling for flexibility and accommodation, a point to be
elaborated later. Some of Chewning-Korpach's discussion seems really
to be aimed at certain types of character disorders, and other parts of it
to describe countertransference problems that have less to do with the
patient's abuse history than the therapist's fears of judgment by colleagues or "very important people."

The second half of the paper deals with revictimization outside the
therapy, in the patient's real life. Revictimization is said to arise from a
repetition-compulsion in which the patient cycles through various roles,
for example, "being abusive, victimized and rescuing with an alcoholic
mate" or becoming "locked into roles or behaviors" such as becoming
"paralyzed and dissociative during sexual assault by an older, otherwise
respected relative" or "behaving helplessly or provocatively with most
men." Abuse by strangers is explained by the would-be-perpetrator's
"radar" for victimlike behavior, and vice versa, so that the assumption
of roles is telescoped in time. Finally, the author notes that repeat victims
may place themselves in dangerous situations. Of this she says, "I would

not for a moment support that she would like to be sexually violated, or is intentionally endangering herself. I would, however, wonder about the influence of some less than conscious drives, including reenactment.''

Perhaps it is inescapable that discussions of conscious and unconscious motivations sound like doublespeak, or perhaps Chewning-Korpach is being so careful to avoid criticism that she never really gets to the core of reenactment: the internal logic of repetition that lies at the heart of the debate. Not all her examples of reenactment appear to involve motivated behavior, conscious or otherwise. Nor does she clearly address what the unconscious motivator is, a point on which few experts agree. Herman (1992) and van der Kolk (1989), both eminent authorities and long-time colleagues, offer differing explanations. Herman describes reenactment as an attempt at mastery, while van der Kolk argues that mastery is a Freudian myth, and that exposure to trauma is sought because of its power to numb feelings, a result primarily of opponent process conditioning and/or influences on brain biochemistry.

In a final section, Chewning-Korpach describes the formation of a therapeutic relationship and a therapeutic process—familiar to all who treat abuse—in which patients rework the trauma in steps, interspersed with periods of stasis or regression in which they repudiate earlier insights and gains. Such regressions are attributed to fear of the unfamiliar, guilt, and the emergence of split-off aspects of self, creating stressful courses of treatment in which therapists may become helpless, discouraged, and subject to boundary transgressions. Once these transference/countertransference reactions are stabilized, the author advises the judicious sharing of countertransference feelings in order to help the patient recognize how she provokes or invites victimization in other relationships.

REVICTIMIZATION: A REPLY

For the most part, Chewning-Korpach offers useful observations, applicable to at least some patients, some of the time. On the other hand, one chapter cannot do everything, and there are significant omissions in the discussion, especially from the perspective of feminist analysis. ''Victim contribution'' is a slippery slope women have been cascading down for centuries. Perhaps we will be forgiven for taking a closer look before we leap at the central argument here: that since past victims are more likely than others to be future victims, they must be doing something to make this happen and that the ''something'' is motivated behavior.

Revictimization might be explained by situational factors and personal attributes that have little or nothing to do with behavior. For example, previous victims may be at elevated risk because they are members of a family with an intergenerational pattern of child abuse and sexual assault, because they live in an impoverished or dangerous neighborhood, or because they are members of an ethnic or ideological subculture that has historically tolerated abuse. Victims may have contributory characteristics that do not involve interpersonal behavior. For example, they may be endowed with bodies that attract sexual interest, possess a temperament that predisposes them to be docile and compliant or explosive and provocative, or be limited in their physical capacity for self-defense. It is important to remember in any discussion of revictimization that studies of violence have consistently shown that the characteristics of perpetrators are far stronger predictors of abuse than the characteristics of victims (Hotaling & Sugarman, 1986).

Even if we accept the assumption that abuse changes its victims so as to make them more susceptible to future abuse, we need not conclude that the change involves motivated behavior, either conscious or unconscious. A victim blinded in a physical assault becomes, as a result of blindness, more vulnerable to further assault, but not by intention. Researchers and clinicians have described many psychological sequelae of abuse that could explain increased vulnerability without invoking the repetition-compulsion. Abuse victims appear to be more suggestible than others and more prone to involuntary dissociation. They have elevated rates of drug and alcohol abuse and, as a result, may suffer from impaired judgment and capacity for self-defense. Like other PTSD sufferers, they may experience such chronically high levels of agitation and nervous activation that they are relatively insensitive to signals of danger in their interpersonal or physical environment. A diminished sense of efficacy, along with a susceptibility to shock and confusion, may erode victims' instinct for self-protection, already compromised by failures of protection in childhood. If, as a child, the victim witnessed others' acquiescence to assault, this may constitute yet another lesson that resistance is impossible or hopeless. Her trust impaired by the initial betrayal, the abuse victim may be socially isolated and starved for human attention. Finally, sexual abuse victims are sensitized to sexual communications, whether or not they want to be.

As many have cautioned, concern with individual psychopathology diverts attention from cultural pathology. Being victimized is not the only way that women are trained to behave like victims. Indeed, almost everything in female socialization prepares a woman for this role: fear that assertiveness will cause her to be labeled "bitchy"; a habit of attention and accommodation to others', especially men's, overt and covert needs; a distortion of physicality that encourages self-objectification over physical instrumentality; and the repeated experience of defeat in social, intellectual, and physical contests skewed to favor men. Bereft of many sources of self-esteem and affirming human contact that men take for granted, women often overvalue affectional/sexual experiences; for many, interactions that lead up to or include sex provide the only opportunity for sustained male attention.

The risk in pathologizing "victimlike" behaviors is that they become decontextualized from a gender politics in which, for many women, the apparent choice to act differently is more illusory than real. I was never raped, but as a young woman I sometimes had sex I didn't really want because it seemed the price of what I did want. I don't blame the men involved, although in retrospect I have a clearer picture of their selfishness. I remember the date who, when I refused sex, berated me for "leading him on" and expelled me unceremoniously into the winter night, several miles from the nearest phone. And the group of male acquaintances who called me over to their table in the college cafeteria the day advanced placement test results were announced and, greeting me with "friendly" sexual innuendos, demanded to see my scores. For whatever reason—compliance, the hope of proving myself in a situation in which I really could not win, or simply the failure to think fast—I mutely handed them the envelope. I had done well; better, probably, than any of them. The laughter stopped, but so did the interest. None ever spoke to me again.

By decontextualizing victim behavior, Chewning-Korpach points us away from the victim's relationship to her social context. Discussing only individual therapy, she ignores the importance of involving family, confronting past abusers, and helping other family members to offer the protection they failed to give during the victim's childhood—protection the victim may be too damaged to provide for herself without such a healing experience. Nor does the author address the importance of groups that allow abuse survivors to grasp the psychological consequences of abuse, separating posttraumatic symptoms from innate personal deficiencies, and working together in a social structure that, because of its resemblances to a family, can symbolically reconstruct such vital functions of family as belonging, emotional safety, intimacy, and a secure relational network in which to practice emotional expression and conflict resolution. The crucial importance of a supportive community in recovering from abuse is a point on which many experts agree (e.g., Herman, 1992; Koss & Harvey, 1991; van der Kolk, 1987).

Finally, there is the matter of the broader cultural context. Early in her discussion Chewning-Korpach quotes a passage by van der Kolk (1989) meant to support her argument that it is therapeutic for victims to recognize their responsibility in revictimization: "Assuming responsibility for the abuse allows feelings of helplessness and vulnerability to be replaced with an illusion of control." But an *illusion* of control is not good enough. Collectively women must aspire to more than the illusion of control on the part of victims. Sexual abuse must be controlled in actuality, and this is not a job that can be accomplished by individual women, however successful their therapy.

It has been found that patients who prosecute their abusers have a slower recovery (Sales et al., 1984), raising a very difficult question: whether to encourage women to endure additional distress in order to help create, for all women, a safer world. Miller (1993) notes that of the 131 sexual abuse perpetrators described by the 60 abuse victims in her study, only nine had been reported to the criminal justice system, only three were prosecuted, and only two penalized. Prosecution is not the only, and probably not even the best, weapon against sexual abuse, but it *is* one weapon that remains tragically underused. These are not issues that women can adequately explore except in dialogue with one another, and one function of therapy is to provide the setting for such discussion.

"SPECIAL PATIENTS" OR SPECIAL NEEDS?

The pull of the "special" patient deserves a fuller analysis than Chewning-Korpach has offered. Some sexually victimized patients do exert a special pull on us as therapists, and it is a very complicated phenomenon. Sometimes it represents a reenactment of the specialness that was the sole compensation of the abuse. Sometimes it is an aspect of character pathology in which the patient tests our ability to be congruous in thought and deed, unlike the important figures of her childhood. A bid for special status is a quick way to learn if a therapist can be corrupted: if she or he can refuse invitations that set off a small inner alarm. Inability to do so shows the patient that the therapist is as afraid of confrontation as she, and is unlikely, as a result, to be of real help. Nonetheless, the patient may remain in treatment, punishing the therapist for the failure to be what she needs.

But there is more. Abuse patients *are* special. Their unremitting anguish can require us to be flexible, tolerating cries for help at inopportune times, running sessions past the time limit, assisting them in things adults "ought" to be able to do for themselves. To accomplish the leap of faith involved in trusting another human being, abused patients may require a level of intense and unbroken concentration not normally demanded by therapy. Many years ago I treated a young woman who, I eventually learned, was a victim of maternal sexual abuse. I remember feeling constrained from glancing at my clock, sensing that even this subtle gesture would disrupt our precarious connection. I learned to schedule her at the end of the day so that runovers would not create a problem and waited many months before I discussed this with her. The conventional wisdom is that patients need the safety of an ending as well as a starting time. But not *all* patients need that; some need us to make their rhythm more important than the clock's—at least for a while. These are difficult judgments, and therapists sometimes compensate for early excesses by unnecessary rigidity.

The issue of touch is perhaps the most complex of all. Touch by a therapist, especially a therapist of the same gender as the offender, is obviously fraught with peril because of its isomorphism with the initial injury. But this fact cuts both ways. Sexual violation *is* a bodily experience and it is often carried bodily—in body memories, distorted postures, and overconditioned anxiety or erotic responses to even benign touch. A case can be made that therapies should address the body, for example, through the use of reenactments, which recreate the dissociation and physical paralysis that accompanied the original abuse but which progress to physical as well as emotional activation and response.

An inescapable question for therapists who work with abuse is how to respond to the states of astonishing fear and overwhelming grief that so often accompany the retelling and reliving of the abuse. Each therapist must find a solution that is personally authentic and that does not evoke a sense of threat or self-compromise, for these emotional states are easily sensed by the patient. For some therapists, especially those of the same gender as the patient, consoling touch proves comforting and healing, reflecting not a boundary violation but a boundary exception, or perhaps a differently situated boundary (see Wooley, 1994b). A benefit of groups is that they offer opportunities for such touch with lesser risk than incurred in individual therapy. We need to talk about this, to struggle with the complexities of touch—historically a part of countless healing rites—rather trying to fit all patients in the Procrustean bed left to us by Freud. One simple principle—simple to enunciate, but harder to live by—is never to ignore an inner prohibition.

We must learn to live with ambiguity, while we are taught about a form of human experience long hidden from us. Sexual abuse *is* different, and it calls upon us to be willing to change, as therapists and perhaps as people. Like the society around us, we must struggle to assimilate the forbidden knowledge of sexual abuse and outlast the individual and collective will to distort, deny, or contain it. We can progress best by attending to the process as well as the content of our debate, and making room for everyone to speak.

REFERENCES

Chira, S. (1993, Dec. 5). Sex abuse: The coil of truth and memory. *New York Times,* E-3.

Faludi, S. (1991). *Backlash.* New York: Crown.

Franke, L. B. (1993, Nov. 28). Woman the conqueror. *New York Times Book Review,* 9–10.

Herman, J. L. (1992). *Trauma and recovery: The aftermath of violence.* New York: Basic Books.

Herman, J. L., & Shatzow, E. (1987). Recovery and verification of memories of childhood sexual trauma. *Psychoanalytic Psychology, 4,* 1–14.

Hotaling, G. T., & Sugarman, D. B. (1986). An analysis of risk markers in husband to wife violence: The current state of knowledge. *Violence and Victims, 1,* 101–124.

Kaminer, W. (1990). *A fearful freedom: Women's flight from equality.* Reading, MA: Addison-Wesley.

Kaminer, W. (1992). *I'm dysfunctional; you're dysfunctional: The recovery movement and other self-help fashions.* Reading, MA: Addison-Wesley.

Kinsey, A. C., Pomeroy, W. B., Martin, C. E., & Gebhard, P.H. (1953). *Sexual behavior in the human female.* Philadelphia: W. B. Saunders.

Koss, M. P., & Harvey, M. R. (1991). *The rape victim: Clinical and community interventions.* Newburg Park, CA: Sage.

Masson, J. M. (1984). *The assault on truth: Freud's suppression of the seduction theory.* New York: Farrar, Straus & Giroux.

McDowell, J. (1993, Nov. 19). Lies of the mind. *Time,* 52–59.

Miller, K. J. (1993). Prevalence and process of disclosure of childhood sexual abuse among eating disordered women. *Eating Disorders, 1,* 211–225.

Paglia, C. (1992). *Sex, art and American culture.* New York: Vintage.

Pollitt, K. (1993, Oct. 4). Not just bad sex. *The New Yorker,* 220–224.

Rabinowitz, D. (1990, May). From the mouths of babes to a jail cell. Child abuse and the abuse of justice: A case study. *Harper's Magazine,* 52–63.

Rich, A. (1979). *On lies, secrets, and silence.* New York: W. W. Norton.

Roiphe, K. (1993a). *The morning after: Sex, fear and feminism on American campuses.* Boston: Little, Brown.

Roiphe, K. (1993b, June 13). Rape hype betrays feminism. *New York Times Magazine,* 26–30, 40, 68.

Rush, F. (1980). *The best kept secret. Sexual abuse of children.* New York: McGraw-Hill.

Russell, D. E. H. (1986). *The secret trauma: Incest in the lives of girls and women.* New York: Basic Books.

Shapiro, L. (1993, Nov. 15). She enjoys being a girl. *Newsweek,* 82.

Tansey, M. J., & Burke, W. F. (1989). *Understanding countertransference.* Hillsdale, NJ: Analytic Press.

Tavris, C. (1993, Jan. 3). Beware the incest survivor machine. *New York Times Book Review,* 27.

van der Kolk, B. (1987). The role of the group in the origin and resolution of the trauma response. In B. van der Kolk (Ed.), *Psychological trauma.* Washington, DC: American Psychiatric Press.

van der Kolk, B. (1989). The compulsion to repeat the trauma. *Psychiatric Clinics of North America, 12,* 369–411

Wolf, N. (1990). *The beauty myth.* London: Chatto & Windus.

Wolf, N. (1993). *Fire with fire.* New York: Random House.

Woodward, K. L., & Springer, K. (1993, Dec. 13). Misty, watercolored memories. *Newsweek,* 68–69.

Wooley, S. C. (1993). Managed care and mental health: The silencing of a profession. *International Journal of Eating Disorders, 14,* 387–401.

Wooley, S. C. (1994a). Sexual abuse and eating disorders: The concealed debate. In P. Fallon, M. Katzman, & S. Wooley (Eds.), *Feminist perspectives on eating disorders.* New York: Guilford.

Wooley, S. C. (1994b). The female therapist as outlaw. In P. Fallon, M. Katzman, & S. Wooley (Eds.), *Feminist perspectives on eating disorders.* New York: Guilford.

Wylie, M. S. (1993, Sept.–Oct.). The shadow of a doubt. *Family Therapy Networker,* 18–30.

14

Reenactment and Trauma

MARK F. SCHWARTZ

LORI D. GALPERIN

Reenactment is a confusing concept in a rational society that prefers binary conceptualizations of right-wrong, good-bad, fault-blame-responsibility, know-don't know. When things get tough, the tough get tougher, don't cry over spilt milk, we have all had tough childhoods, just toughen up and take control, get over it. In this world of self-made individuals, people should just forget the past and create their future. These concepts are pernicious and leave individuals feeling to "blame" for not being able to "get over it" and "get on with their lives." Even in treatment settings the messages may echo society at large, implying that individuals should be able to stop being depressed, quit repeating self-destructive behavior, and need to take responsibility for not getting in control of addictive behavior. The message of self-responsibility is an essential one, but taken to an extreme, it is revictimizing. It leaves individuals feeling they are failures or weak. Then they are further victimized by being labeled "treatment failures" in mental health systems. Some subset of the estimated 13–15 million individuals taking antidepressant medication in this country are unable to benefit from cognitive-behavioral or 12-step approaches to psychotherapy. They upset therapists, who then may label them as recalcitrant, borderline, hysterical, sociopathic, or some other characterological diagnosis, and, therefore, untreatable.

An enlightened approach is simply stated by Claudia Black (1976): "One must finish the past in order to go on with the future" (p. 52). The premise of a trauma-based approach is that it is *what was done to you and what you did as a result*, rather than what's wrong with you. There is no reason to expect that a person who lived in a rageful, destructive, sadistic, cruel family for 18 years should suddenly have the capacity and tools to feel and be competent, capable, and responsible.

If one studied combat victims and documented, as has been published recently (Weiss et al., 1992), that 35% have been homeless, 70% have been divorced one time, 30% have been divorced two times, 50% reported significant marital or parenting difficulties, and 25% felt very isolated and were five times more likely to be unemployed, the conclusion would be that combat was so devastating a trauma that many or most individuals were permanently injured and psychotherapy has been only selectively useful. But to then blame those who didn't respond, recover, or were unable to take self-responsibility would indeed be revictimizing.

Survivors of trauma are the last people on earth who want to think of themselves as victims. The entire coping response of the average survivor of trauma is to do whatever it takes to maintain some semblance of power and control. When a woman is raped, she does not think, "I am a victim." She thinks, "What did I do to make that happen? Perhaps I should have fought harder. Perhaps I should not have been where I was. Perhaps I asked for it in some way." When a man in war sees his best friend blown to bits in front of him he does not think, "I have been ravaged by an insane process." He thinks, "It should have been me. Perhaps if I'd done something different, my friend would still be alive." A child whose parent beats her and tells her she is evil does not think, "My parent is hurting me." She thinks, "I'm evil. I must try to be better."

The self-blame, guilt, profound worthlessness, and self-hatred that evolve out of these cognitive distortions and misattributions feel to the survivor a smaller price to pay than the cost of truly embracing the reality of his or her utter helplessness in the face of such cruelty, exploitation, and dehumanization. In short, feeling like the most evil, worthless, undeserving, subhuman being that ever walked the earth is preferable to feeling like a victim.

And the inherent philosophy of society at large is collusive. It is, after all, very unpleasant to think of these things—to imagine they can happen on our block or to people like us. So you say, "Well, okay, perhaps it did happen, *but* that's all in the past. People need to put these things behind them and get on with life. No use dwelling on what can't be changed." And, of course, this would be great advice—if only it worked. This is, in fact, the exact advice survivors of trauma give themselves, and they try desperately to make it a reality.

Childhood trauma seems especially pernicious in comparison to adult trauma in that to feel "in control" and that there is someone to care for them, children always believe that they are the bad ones who make bad things happen. Discovery that their parents' parenting was imperfect and sometimes destructive frees them from feeling innately damaged, defective, and bad. Recognizing their victimization is a necessary and essential early step in recovery. In childhood trauma, the internal experience of the child is often that a part of self splits off to contend with the myriad double-binds implicit in the abuse situation or environment—at other times to permit the child to endure the magnitude of physical and psychological pain. This part of self embodies the injury or multiple injuries—the more abuse, the more separate it must become to allow the child to continue functioning or at least going through the motions of functioning. This injured part of self then continues to exist as an encapsulated frozen ego-state, easily accessed in hypnosis, frozen in time and in trauma. Working with the ego-state and facilitating integration with the adult can be another useful step in recovery. The adult part of self has typically developed over the core injured self, hidden from others' vision, except in destructive transactions.

Reenactment is both a cognitive-behavioral and learned process, as well as a more complex unconscious repetition process. Certainly individuals are willing to accept and expect the familiar, and if one is accustomed to violence, chaos, and deceit, bonding with a kind individual would be unpredictable and terrifying. Also, if one has not learned how to communicate, solve problems, and negotiate effectively, destructive transactions transpire. If one is compulsive, generates crises, and creates urgency with every disagreement, intimacy difficulties abound. Eating disorder symptoms sometimes arise as a direct result of repetitive trauma at the dinner table and parents' need for a perfect narcissistic reflection of self by the child such that no deviation from a perfect body weight is acceptable. Thus, there are multiple learned and modeled aspects to reenactment.

The unconscious factors are less obvious. The brain seems to get stuck developmentally in a traumatic "cycle" attempting to master the puzzle with insufficient and incorrect data. Why do "nice, respectable" fathers rape one daughter and not another? Teams of researchers are unable to explain sufficiently such irrational behavior with rational explanation, much less the child who is the victim. The eating disorder may be a solution to the five-year-old's desperate need to control what goes into the body, which makes little sense in the postabuse environment unless understood in terms of the originating context. So the unconscious reenactment may be a re-creation of unresolved early conflicts in order to discover the solution. If I marry a man like dad, maybe this time I can have sufficient control to change the outcome (see Schwartz & Gay, this issue). The result is trauma-generating systems where two individuals repeat and re-create; the result is complex, self-destructive behaviors, which include addictive numbing and intrusions similar to the chaos of their childhood.

Mental health professionals who step into such systems and give the individual tools for behavioral change can improve aspects of the system. However, it is the premise of trauma-based therapies that, similar to grief therapy, one must go back and finish or complete the trauma cycle, and reintegrate the split-off parts of self, in order to break the trauma bond. Cognitive-behavioral, 12-step, and other skill-building and insight-oriented approaches can then be more effective following trauma resolution.

The goal in trauma resolution is, in essence, to make the person more aware. As a result of dissociation, the individual is numbed out and unaware of associations, for example, the cues for danger do not elicit fear. Krystal (1989) has termed this *alexithymia*—the inability to use feelings to guide actions. There are physiologic correlates suggesting that the neurohormones that signal fear are severely altered, though there is no evidence that trauma resolution therapy changes this physiologic state (see van der Kolk, 1989). There is also physiologic evidence that following trauma, the individual experiences chronic release of stress hormones, so that situations that are not emergencies feel as if they are; therefore, the result is crisis generation. Because individuals feel numb, dissociated, and adhedonic following chronic trauma, they utilize acting-in and acting-out behavior to escape the inner emptiness. When they begin to think, feel, and experience intrusive memories, they use acting-in or acting-out behaviors to numb-out.

Richard Berendzen, former president of American University, in his recent autobiographical work (1993), *Come Here*, details his determined efforts, following incest with his mother, to leave the past behind, to throw himself into the work he loved, to accomplish and achieve on behalf of worthy goals. He had tremendous success in doing so, until the past would at last be denied no longer. He began to make bizarre, obscene telephone calls from his office compulsively and eventually was arrested. He writes,

Like under a thundering mountainside of snow, I was smothered by feelings I thought had ended forty years before. Panic, fear, confusion, helplessness, anguish and desperation jackknifed inside me. This time, I could not escape. Every emotion I had ever buried, every thought I had ever suppressed, came back with unimaginable force and intensity. I leaned against the wall and gasped for breath.

My legs buckled. I thought I would vomit. . . . My bones felt hollow, incapable of supporting weight. My heart raced. I held my chest. Never before had I felt such throbbing, thundering pain. My face flushed. The room spun. As images sped around me and through me, I choked on silent screams. I wasn't remembering, I was reliving the abuse by my mother. Over the years I had trained myself to handle memories. But this was different. This was cataclysmic. Like entering a warp in space and time, I catapulted back more than four decades. Trapped between the shadow of a boy and the shell of a man, I relived every sordid afternoon all at once. (p. 26)

Richard Berendzen had always been a logical man, an academic, a tremendously hard worker. His philosophy was, ''That was then. This is now.'' He states, ''I coped, as I always had, by working hard. I returned to the survival strategy I had relied on since childhood—leave no time to think about anything else.'' Berendzen was part of a ''scientific culture [which] at that time rejected and even ridiculed therapy a priori.''

I never considered therapy for myself . . . I found therapy dubious; leaders in my profession found it absurd. As time blunted the immediacy of my anguish, I resumed working intensively.

But for Berendzen, as for so many determined survivors of traumatic abuse, all the hard work, achievement, accomplishment, and determination to put the past behind him still could not blot out the damage of the past or keep it inevitably from intruding into the present and threatening to obliterate all he had so diligently, so unstintingly worked to achieve. If only, when we attempt to ''put things in the past,'' they would cooperate and stay there, but alas, this is not the way of trauma.

The psychiatric symptoms that are manifested are forms of communication. For Berendzen, the phone calls were a message that something was buried very deep, the incest with his mother and early trauma were not resolved, only covered over. The more successes he experienced, the more his adult self became divergent from the damaged inner self. The greater the discrepancy, the greater the dissonance, and the greater the need to stabilize. The symptom is a cry for help. To attempt to remove the symptom or punish it, simply sets an individual up for subsequent relapse.

The authors have treated hundreds of patients over the past 10 years who have recovered from alcohol, drug, and eating disorders in the previous decade. Although their symptoms have been controlled, they have remained miserable, with chronic depression, suicidality, and in many cases, other forms of addictive behavior such as sexual compulsivity. Following trauma resolution therapies, they seem to find dramatic relief of their depressive, anxiety, somatic, dissociative, relational-sexual, and compulsive symptomatology (Schwartz et al., 1993).

The goal of the new trauma therapies is not to create a society of victims. It is, instead, to acknowledge the endemic levels of severe child abuse, neglect, and violence that our youth have experienced and to give them hope for a decent life despite their early trauma. The new backlash that is gaining momentum that suggests that somehow therapists create victims to keep busy is not only absurd, but is part of the same blind machinery that has enabled the horrors pervasive in contemporary society.

Treatment of both victims and victimizers with respect and compassion is a prerequisite of an enlightened society. The current trend to blame and punish in order to control the behavior is absurd and ineffective. Blame, fault-finding, revenge, and punishment are part of the same ideology that allows the current endemic levels of violence in this society. This is a true example of reenactment—the society of victims become victimizers.

REFERENCES

Berendzen, R. (1993). *Come here*. New York: Villard Books.

Black, C. (1976). *It will never happen to me*. Denver: Medical Administration Co.

Krystal, A. (1989). *Psychic traumatization*. Boston: Little, Brown.

Schwartz, M., Roe, C., & Hemphill, P. (1993). Sexual trauma, sexual compulsivity, and post-traumatic stress disorder and dissociation. Presentation at Association for the Treatment of Sexual Abusers Meeting, Boston, MA.

van der Kolk, B. (1989). The compulsion to repeat the trauma: Reenactment, revictimization, and masochism. *Psychiatric Clinics of North America, 12,* 389–411.

Weiss, D., Marmar, C., Schlenger, W., Fairbank, J., Jordan, K., Hough, R., & Kulka, R. (1992). The prevalence of lifetime and partial post-traumatic stress disorder in Vietnam theater veterans. *Journal of Traumatic Stress, 5,* 365–376.

15

In Response to Wooley and to Schwartz and Galperin

MARY CHEWNING-KORPACH
ROY J. O'SHAUGHNESSY

"Sexual Revictimization: A Cautionary Note" was written by the first author, from an individual psychotherapy point of view. It essentially maintains that at least one facet of the treatment of some repeat victims might involve examining the possibility that the repetition-compulsion might be operative. It particularly supports the use of countertransference reactions in diagnosis and treatment formulation, and refers especially to the repeat victim manifesting character disorders. In addressing the possibility of victim reenactment, it strays from the "no responsibility to the victim" herd, and presents an aspect of case conceptualization whose sociopolitical ramifications could be tremendous. One concern in presenting such a politically unpopular thesis is that it engenders rightly passionate responses from those who fear the misuse and abuse of scientific ambiguity. Used irresponsibly, naively, or outside of context, such information can even be used to perpetuate victimization on a sociolegal level.

In their reaction, Schwartz and Galperin imply that the article blames victims and is based on the erroneous notion that victims feel like victims, rather than "the most evil, worthless, undeserving subhuman being that ever walked the earth." Briefly, we share these authors' moral outrage with such assumptions and strongly support what they refer to as Claudia Black's enlightened trauma-based approach to treatment. In addition, as both individual therapists and feminists, we support the process of empowerment, especially with women who have been victimized repeatedly, under any type of circumstance.

In a thoughtful sociopolitically driven paper, Wooley presents an eloquent feminist political comment, with which we largely agree. Her concern that focusing on individual psychotherapy diverts attention from cultural pathology is noteworthy. In addition, she notes that pathologizing "victimlike" behaviors has the effect of decontextualizing them from the gender politics to which they often belong. Again, we agree with these assertions. "Sexual Revictimization" was written from a purely individual psychotherapy perspective, and sought to contribute to, or at least provoke thought within, this arena. As Wooley is highlighting, this perspective can be conflictual with that of a sociocultural or systemic point of view. Developing and implementing treatment integrating these two perspectives can be difficult, indeed.

Wooley has made an important contribution to putting the issue of revictimization and reenactment into perspective, while raising another provocative issue. Toward the end of her article, she addresses one issue pertaining to the "special" patient, by discussing the special needs patient. In doing so, she provides a foyer into empirical and clinical dialogue pertaining to such sticky issues as therapist touch, therapeutic boundaries, and, less directly, therapist role in patient/victim advocacy. This latter issue is particularly complicated, given her reference to the finding that patients who prosecute their abusers take longer to get better. Implicitly, we as therapists and feminists must wonder where our roles as individual therapists begin and end in working with victims of sexual assault. For example, when we are hired to provide individual therapy, are we venturing into dangerous moral and ethical waters by either implicitly or explicitly serving the role of victim advocate? Where does therapy with the victim end and political activism begin? Within the individual psychotherapy relationship, when is physical touch appropriate? Finally, by accommodating the special needs patient, do we serve to perpetuate psychopathology, reinforce maintenance of the victim/survivor role, or perhaps even provide for the possibility of dual relationships?

Many important questions have been raised by the contributors to this book. Having a forum within which to discuss aspects of these issues, across all levels, is critical to scientific and clinical development, and to providing for the best interest of our patients.

Epilogue:

Delayed Memory Syndrome*

LEIGH COHN

MARK F. SCHWARTZ

As editors of this volume, we cannot ignore the "false memory syndrome" controversy, a topic that has polarized the mental health community, the legal community, and society at large. We, and most of our colleagues, sympathize with the troubled individuals who have unlocked deeply embedded memories of sexual abuse, but we cannot ignore the devastating consequences of false accusation. Everyone seems to have strong convictions about "delayed memory." Here are ours.

There are four logical possibilities regarding the memory of sexual abuse: an actual event may be remembered, the occurrence may be forgotten, there may be an accurate memory that there was no abuse, or there may be the memory of abuse when it did not actually happen (Andersen, 1995). It is this last scenerio that is commonly referred to as "false memory," and it is within this context that problems arise.

Everyone agrees that memory is fallible. Amnesia is pathognomonic of trauma. Children's perceptions are developmentally coded according to their chronological age. It is likely that traumatic memory is somatosensorily coded also, since most survivors begin to remember in their early 20s. Such memories generally take the form of fragmented images, which follow a sensory stimulus or flashback (Roe, Schwartz, & Peterson,

---

*Excerpts from Sandra Bloom's article "When Good People Do Bad Things: Meditations on the 'Backlash.'" in the *Journal of Psychohistory*, throughout this chapter, have been reprinted with permission.

1994; van der Kolk, 1994). Although retrieval of memory can be biased and is subject to distortion, to not believe a patient's memories of early abuse is illogical and very likely harmful.

With that said, it is useful to understand that survivors of abuse are actively attempting to create a narrative in order to "know" why they feel so bad. Such narrative construction may contain factual errors, and dates or events may be transposed, while themes are remarkably accurate. One way to determine the accuracy of memory and to validate the memory is to question the perpetrator or other effected family members. In the hands of skilled clinicians a variety of interview techniques can be used to break down the minimization and denial of perpetrators and to affirm verification of memories. Confirmed by other family members, the memory—of physical abuse, emotional abuse, or neglect—often is accurate. Such abuse would sufficiently account for symptoms regardless of sexual abuse issues.

It is important to examine the false memory issue at its most basic level. In all instances, the patient is emotionally troubled and is seeking the help of a therapist. Except, perhaps, in the most blatantly malicious cases, therapists have no vested interest in fabricating a history of sexual abuse. Rather, they are appropriately serving as trained professionals concerned simply with guiding clients to emotional well-being.

> Whatever the case, the patients who went to a therapist in the first place went because they were suffering from symptoms, so we know something was definitely *wrong*, and a definition of mental health does not extend to someone who is able to be easily persuaded to betray the trust of a beloved family member on the suggestion of a therapist. Common sense would dictate that there is something most definitely wrong here *before* they get to a therapist, regardless of what a therapist is or is not doing. This would seem to be routine logic, but not if you read or watch the media presentations which have given instant and uncritical credibility to the reality of the "false memory syndrome" without any research validation, without even asking the simple question, 'What is *wrong* with these people in the first place?' " (Bloom, 1995)

The fact is that child abuse hot lines receive reports of three million children each year being victimized by severe abuse and neglect. The minimal incidence of endemic child abuse in the population is well established. Also, there is no question that trauma has emotional consequences. Mardi Horowitz (1993), one of the leaders in the study of traumatic stress, recently stated:

It is the intensification, prolongation, or irrational elaboration of memories and emotions that leads to a diagnosis of disorder rather than normal distress. Pathological grief has components of (1) overwhelming, intense, intrusive emotions and memories, (2) persistent, unending experiences without a sense of progression, or resolution, and (3) avoidance of grief.

Clearly, prolongation and irrational elaboration of memory are at the heart of posttraumatic stress disorder. Memory is not made of facts; it consists of developmentally perceived and construed precepts. This is not to say that the child's memory is not accurate; a wealth of clinical data from children demonstrates that, even at a very young age, children can provide remarkable detail and accuracy (Terr, 1990).

Eating disorders and other forms of self-injury are and can serve as somatic memory, revealing that certain past experiences require processing and metabolizing. If there is an effect, there is a cause. Sandra Bloom writes:

Overwhelming, excessive, repetitive stress—as experienced through the eyes, mind, and spirit of the child—can lead to chronic and permanent damage to key brain structures. Although medical and psychological treatment can bring later relief to adult symptoms, the underlying causes cannot necessarily be reversed since they amount to developmental insults. Additionally, we have long maintained the delusion that we can do anything we want to children because "they won't remember." Research studies continue to support that traumatic memory is processed entirely differently from normal memory and that traumatic memory may be stored in different ways as well, as non-verbal images, memories of the body that are not forgotten but are also not articulated in linguistic form. There are strong indications that such memories can, and do, influence behavior, even when the individual has no ready recall of the early experiences (van der Kolk, 1994).

Most clinicians reasonably practice with an understanding of these basic precepts about memory; however, there are voices, currently being heard loud and clear in the media, that represent a rather reactionary position. Using as ammunition the fact that two recent lawsuits have been decided against therapists who have "uncovered" memories of past abuse that were later recanted by the individuals involved or found not to have objective validation (Andersen, 1995), they condemn the entire mental health profession. Tabloid journalism and television talk shows provide a perfect outlet for the most sensational aspects of this controversy. Consequently, fallacious and deceptive sentiments have been expressed that place responsible therapists on the defensive. Fair, responsible discussion seems to have no place in commercial media.

Individuals who actually believe that memories are created by therapists are, for their own reasons, motivated to *not* know and *not* see the extent to which abuse actually exists in our culture. Bloom points to a culture so horrified by the reality of rampant sexual abuse that it cannot tolerate the truth. If the statistics are accurate, then our friends and neighbors are having incestuous relationships with their daughters and sons, and by ignoring it, so are we. The victims are not nameless outcasts on daytime TV, but are our wives and children. This reality is too terrible for anyone to claim responsibility in the face of it. Instead, perpetrators deny the truth of their deeds, and society denies the memories that embody that truth. But the facts are incontestable:

One of the charges repeatedly lodged by false memory advocates is that the increase in child abuse reports is socially induced, a form of mass hysteria. If anything, child abuse experts bemoan the conservative nature of the institutional response. A large percentage of reports—up to 60% in some states—are declared unsubstantiated, which certainly does not indicate a naive credulity on the part of investigators. In fact, one study showed that investigators dismiss 82% of all day care operator accusations. One study of the criminal justice system found that only about 42% of serious and substantiated sexual abuse allegations are actually forwarded for prosecution. Although 75% of the prosecutions result in convictions, 90% of these result from guilty pleas or plea bargains. Only 19% of convicted child abusers serve longer than one year in jail and 32–46% of convicted child sexual abusers serve no jail time (Finkelhor, 1994).

These figures do not bespeak a hysteria that is sweeping the nation and undermining our social system. (Bloom, 1995).

In the battle for public opinion, the deniers present an old formula for casting doubt. Let us say, a young woman who has discovered sexual abuse in her past makes accusations against the relative who committed incest against her. Normally one would think of the woman as a "victim," the therapist as a positive force for having assisted her in the search for inner peace, and the assaulter as the target of blame. But, in the arenas of civil liability and popular media, when the accused is a clean-cut man who says all of the right things, which include contradicting the testimony of a "mental patient," he is perceived as the victim, she as misguided, and the therapist as the villain, who for financial gain and personal power has placed suggestions of abuse into the compliant woman's head.

The stakes are high. One who is convicted of sexual abuse stands to lose everything dear: family, friends, dignity, and freedom. A therapist convicted of inducing false memories can lose livelihood, reputation, professional accreditation, and huge sums of money awarded in damages. As Bloom points out, "This is not an intellectual war, but a war that is being fought in the media, in the courtrooms, and in legislative chambers. Even now, moves are afoot to propose legislation at the state and federal level that, if passed, would effectively eliminate the practice of psychotherapy entirely under the auspices of aiming to legislate out of existence something called 'memory retrieval therapy.' " (Bloom, 1995; Quirk & DePrince, 1995)

Mental health professionals cannot properly serve their patients while constantly looking over their shoulders; they must be willing to probe deeper with clients, especially those who are ready to unlock doors to the past. In an unpublished article, Arnold Andersen (1995) observes, "Where such abuse has occurred, it may be a source of lifelong misery, of troubling flashbacks, of distressed interpersonal relationships, of lowered self-esteem, and it sometimes may have a major role in the production of eating disorders."

Certainly, eating disorders therapists have every reason to suspect the presence of sexual trauma in their patients; and so they are particularly vulnerable to the constraints of an environment that gives unquestioned credence to the false memory perspective. The greatest potential for trouble occurs when a subject becomes "hot." For example, amid reports of a high incidence of sexual abuse among eating-disordered women, there might be a tendency to think that every bulimic asking for guidance has been abused. There may even exist a temptation to lead a client toward memories of abuse without substantiated reason coming directly from that client.

> The clinician therefore, has to be aware that error may exist in both directions: failing to diagnose past actual sexual abuse, and inducing false memory of abuse that never occurred. It is clear on a legal, moral, and practical clinical basis, that some degree of corroboration of reports of sexual abuse needs to be attempted. The clinician must be aware of which methods of inquiry have a high degree of yielding accurate information and which ones play upon the vulnerability of

individuals. The legal system is clear that some methods of psychological inquiry are largely discounted as valid. In fact, the Amytal interview may invalidate or undermine obtaining legal remedies for actual past sexual abuse which is later demonstrated to have occurred. The same caution goes for hypnosis. Information obtained by these means will generally be considered contaminated from a legal basis. (Andersen, 1995)

The so-called false memory syndrome represents a backlash. The mental health field should not, and cannot, be intimidated away from practicing sound psychotherapy. Clinicians must treat every patient individually, following the natural course of discovery appropriate for that person. The patients are who they are; it is the therapist's job to help them remember, if there is something to remember, at their own speed. When the memory of actual abuse is uncovered, it is the therapist's responsibility to be an advocate for the client. It is our responsibility as a society to support the truth.

REFERENCES

Andersen, A. E. (1995). *False memory syndrome and the eating disorders therapist: A dilemma.* Unpublished article.

Bloom, S. L. (1995). When good people do bad things: Meditations on the "backlash." *Journal of Psychohistory, 22*(3) Winter, 273–304.

Finkelhor, D. (1994). Current information on the scope and nature of child sexual abuse. *Sexual abuse of children.* The future of Children, the David and Lucille Packard Foundation, (*4*), (2) Summer/Fall.

Horowitz, M. & Reidbord, S. (1993). Memory, emotion and response to trauma. In S. Christianson (Ed.), *Handbook of emotion and memory.* Stockholm: Lawrence Erlbaum.

Quirk, S. A., & DePrince, A. (1995). Backlash legislation targeting psychotherapists. *Journal of Psychohistory, 22*(3) Winter.

Roe, C. M., Schwartz, M. F., & Peterson, Jr., F. L. (1994). Forgotten memories of childhood sexual abuse: A descriptive study. Paper presented at the meeting of the International Society of Traumatic Stress Studies, Chicago.

Terr, L. (1990). *Too scared to cry: Psychic trauma in childhood.* New York: Harper & Row.

van der Kolk, B. (1993). *DESNOS and DSM-IV.* Paper presented at the meeting of the International Society for Traumatic Stress Studies, San Antonio, TX.

van der Kolk, B. (1994). The body keeps the score: Memory and the evolving psychobiology of posttraumatic stress. *Harvard Review of Psychiatry, 1*(3).

Index